'Teacher education programmes throughout the world are grappling with one of the most expansive transformations in teacher preparation in a century: updating archaic programmes to address the ever-increasing diversity in our 21st-century schools. Parents, accrediting bodies, policy-makers, and students themselves, are demanding that teachers be inclusive, culturally-competent educators. Walton and Osman's book takes on this challenge in conceptual, empirical and practical ways. With an international focus and a cadre of scholars, each chapter demonstrates how to transform teacher education into an enterprise that truly prepares teachers for the vibrant, diverse world that is at the doorstep of schoolhouses throughout the world. This is a book that universities and teacher education programmes need now—in fact, it is overdue.'

**Professor Ronnie Casella**, State University of New York–Cortland, USA

'The global Sustainable Development Goals (SDGs) place equitable, inclusive and quality lifelong learning at the heart of its education vision. Achieving this requires motivated and dedicated teachers who are committed to the learning of all, particularly the marginalized. Yet this global framework pays scant attention to those who produce the next generation of teachers, the teacher educators, and the extent to which future teachers are learning to work with diversity within and outside the classroom. Ignoring diversity imperils the extent to which we can create just, peaceful and inclusive societies.

This book edited by Walton and Osman brings together a collection of teacher education research which collectively speaks to the need for (re)thinking what we value and what counts in producing the kinds of teachers required for the world we want. It is a must-read for everyone committed to invigorating a vision for social justice and quality education, which has at its core a critical and reflexive account of, and approach to, diversity in and through education. I commend the editors and authors for providing a timely and much needed resource for teacher education in these troubling and uncertain times.'

**Professor Yusuf Sayed**, University of Sussex, UK

'This book attends to debates that link teacher education and the recognition of, and working pedagogically with, complex human diversities in institutions such as schools and university faculties of education. The authors, drawn from different contexts, variously argue that teacher education must involve engaging with diversity in an inclusive and responsive manner, including how students learn under conditions of exclusion related to class, race, geography, gender, sexuality and disability. The book presents a cogent set of arguments, informed by rigorous empirical research and theoretical application, about the way in which inclusion and recognition are able to proceed in educational sites, where normative assumptions are challenged, and rigorous dialogue enacted in pursuit of our common humanity. This book is a much needed addition to the study of teacher education in complex times.'

**Professor Aslam Fataar**, Stellenbosch University, South Africa

# TEACHER EDUCATION FOR DIVERSITY

Foregrounding the diversity that characterises various educational settings, this book discusses how histories and geographies of oppression, exclusion and marginalisation have impacted on teacher education. Contributors draw on first-hand experiences of living and working in countries including Brazil, China, South Africa, New Zealand and Malawi.

Positioned in a geographical and metaphorical 'Global South', the book draws critical attention to debates which have been otherwise marginalised in relation to those conducted in the 'Global North'. Chapters address difference and diversity on both a conceptual and empirical level, acknowledging the significance of various global trends including increased migration and urbanisation; and broadening understandings of race, religion, gender, sexuality and (dis)ability. Taken together, these chapters reveal the extent of the work which still remains to be done in the field of teacher education for diversity.

The issues discussed are of global significance, making this text key reading for teachers, teacher educators, and those concerned with the advancement of social justice and reduction of inequality through education.

**Elizabeth Walton** is an Associate Professor in Inclusive Education at the University of the Witwatersrand, South Africa.

**Ruksana Osman** is Professor of Education and Dean of the Faculty of Humanities at the University of the Witwatersrand, South Africa.

# TEACHER EDUCATION FOR DIVERSITY

Conversations from the Global South

Edited by Elizabeth Walton and Ruksana Osman

LONDON AND NEW YORK

First published 2018
by Routledge
2 Park Square, Milton Park, Abingdon, Oxon OX14 4RN

and by Routledge
711 Third Avenue, New York, NY 10017

*Routledge is an imprint of the Taylor & Francis Group, an informa business*

© 2018 selection and editorial matter, Elizabeth Walton and Ruksana Osman, individual chapters, the contributors

The right of Elizabeth Walton and Ruksana Osman to be identified as the authors of the editorial material, and of the authors for their individual chapters, has been asserted in accordance with sections 77 and 78 of the Copyright, Designs and Patents Act 1988.

All rights reserved. No part of this book may be reprinted or reproduced or utilised in any form or by any electronic, mechanical, or other means, now known or hereafter invented, including photocopying and recording, or in any information storage or retrieval system, without permission in writing from the publishers.

*Trademark notice*: Product or corporate names may be trademarks or registered trademarks, and are used only for identification and explanation without intent to infringe.

*British Library Cataloguing in Publication Data*
A catalogue record for this book is available from the British Library

*Library of Congress Cataloging in Publication Data*
Names: Walton, Elizabeth Florence, editor. | Osman, Ruksana, editor.
Title: Teacher education for diversity / Elizabeth Walton and Ruksana Osman, editors.
Description: Abingdon, Oxon ; New York, NY : Routledge is an imprint of the Taylor & Francis Group, an Informa Business, [2018]
Identifiers: LCCN 2017043818 (print) | LCCN 2017061544 (ebook) | ISBN 9781315209418 (ebook) | ISBN 9781138630406 (hbk) | ISBN 9781138630413 (pbk) | ISBN 9781315209418 (ebk)
Subjects: LCSH: Teachers--Training of--Developing countries. | Culturally relevant pedagogy–Study and teaching (Higher)--Developing countries.
Classification: LCC LB1707 (ebook) | LCC LB1707 .T3975 2018 (print) | DDC 370.71/1091724--dc23
LC record available at https://lccn.loc.gov/2017043818

ISBN: 978-1-138-63040-6 (hbk)
ISBN: 978-1-138-63041-3 (pbk)
ISBN: 978-1-315-20941-8 (ebk)

Typeset in Bembo
by Taylor & Francis Books

# CONTENTS

*List of illustrations* ix
*Introduction: (Re)considering teacher education and/for diversity* x
Elizabeth Walton and Ruksana Osman

1 Assimilation and celebration?: Discourses of difference and the application of Critical Diversity Literacy in education 1
  *Finn Reygan, Elizabeth Walton and Ruksana Osman*

2 Engaging forced introspection: Teaching social justice in Critical Diversity Literacy 21
  *Peace Kiguwa*

3 Deconstructing heteronormativity and hegemonic gender orders through critical literacy and materials design: A case in a South African school of education 36
  *Navan N. Govender*

4 The role of developing pre-service teachers' pedagogical reasoning to support contextually responsive teaching 53
  *Lee Rusznyak and Alfred Masinire*

5 Diversity of teacher autonomy in response to curriculum reform: Towards a humanistic focus on teacher education 69
  *Jing Xiao and Ora Kwo*

6 Educating in diverse worlds: The immigrant Somali parent as a strategic partner of South African education 87
  *Doria Daniels*

| | |
|---|---|
| 7 Equity through individualised and interconnected teacher education<br>*Mandia Mentis and Alison Kearney* | 103 |
| 8 Teacher education and notions of diversity in Malawi<br>*Myriam Hummel and Petra Engelbrecht* | 121 |
| 9 Teacher education for diversity in Brazil: Perspectives from the National Observatory on Special Education<br>*Enicéia Gonçalves Mendes and Leonardo Santos Amâncio Cabral* | 139 |
| 10 Difference in current postapartheid education<br>*Nazir Carrim* | 153 |
| *About the contributors* | 168 |
| *Index* | 172 |

# ILLUSTRATIONS

**Figures**

| | | |
|---|---|---|
| 1.1 | Heritage Day article from *The Randburg Sun*, 22 September, 2016 | 6 |
| 3.1 | Processes of producing the workbook | 41 |
| 3.2 | Phase 1 extract: Family | 43 |
| 3.3 | The universal man | 45 |
| 3.4 | Sex/gender model | 46 |
| 3.5 | The interactions between Foucault's (1984) *Social Relations and Sexual Relations* being enacted through Butler's (2006) *Gender Performance* (Reproduced) | 46 |
| 3.6 | The identity gem – mapping sex, gender and sexual identities | 47 |
| 7.1 | The personal, professional, and interprofessional dimensions of the T-shaped learning in the programme | 109 |

**Tables**

| | | |
|---|---|---|
| 1.1 | CDL in pre-service teacher education and classroom practice | 13 |
| 3.1 | Applying a critical pedagogical structure | 49 |
| 5.1 | Summary of teachers' responses to perceived institutional pressures | 81 |
| 6.1 | Demographic information on the participants | 92 |
| 8.1 | Overview of data collection | 126 |

# INTRODUCTION

(Re)considering teacher education and/for diversity

*Elizabeth Walton and Ruksana Osman*

Foregrounding the diversity that characterises classrooms, staffrooms and teacher education institutions of the 21st century is not new. The perceived homogeneity of the past has been countered by global trends that include migration, urbanisation and the inclusion of people with disabilities. Recognition of the multi-dimensionality of identity has required acknowledgement of and pedagogic responsiveness to people's individuality. This responsiveness includes engaging with the reality that many identity markers are not valorised in societies, nor in schools, and that many people therefore teach and learn under the oppression of their class, race, ethnicity, gender, sexuality and/or dis/ability. Teacher education has had to take cognisance of these forms of difference and cannot work with assumptions of normativity in any context. This book offers the reader a collection of conceptual and empirical work done by teacher educators who are concerned with aspects of difference and diversity. It focuses on the complexity of 'diversity work' at different sites, showing how histories and geographies of oppression, exclusion and marginalisation in different contexts impact the ways in which teacher development is conceptualised and enacted.

Teacher education is burdened by overwhelming responsibility in developing contexts, given that it is often seen as a possible site for the disruption of the cycle of poor educational outcomes and the poverty associated with them. Diversity necessarily features strongly in teacher education, as pedagogical responsiveness to different learner and learning needs is crucial to ensure equitable educational opportunities for all learners. Importantly, notions of difference stem from valorised normative positions, which means that diversity is not a neutral construct. The recognition of multi-dimensionality is vital to the conceptualisation of diversity, and so too is an acknowledgement that intersecting axes of identity differentially construct privilege and oppression. Therefore, as is suggested in this book, there is a need for Critical Diversity Literacy (Steyn, 2015) to be embedded in teacher education.

This book emerges from the work done by the convener and forum members of the UNESCO Chair in Teacher Education for Diversity and Development. It engages with scholarship on aspects of teacher education for diversity, with a particular focus on the 'South'. We understand the South to be both geographical and metaphorical, and therefore present the work of scholars from countries which are often marginalised when academic debates take place in meetings and journals which privilege the experiences, scholarship and proximity of countries in the Global North. The editors solicited chapters from teacher educators who are living and/or working in diverse countries and are concerned with issues of difference and diversity in relation to teacher development. The resulting collection comprises work done by scholars in Brazil, China, South Africa, New Zealand and Malawi.

Diversity is conceptualised broadly and critically in the chapters which have been selected for inclusion, and there are contributions containing both conceptual and empirical work. The first chapter, by Finn Reygan, Elizabeth Walton and Ruksana Osman, engages with two discourses of diversity or difference – those of assimilation and celebration. The authors show how these discourses do not trouble power and oppression and argue that, as a result, they should be disrupted. The possibility for a critical distance from these discourses is offered through the framework of Critical Diversity Literacy. With reference to recent events in South Africa, the authors suggest ways in which Critical Diversity Literacy might be used in teacher education. In the second chapter, Peace Kiguwa reflects on teaching a course in Critical Diversity Literacy in which she employs a process of 'forced introspection' related to the question 'what does diversity mean to me?'. The author discusses her students' and her own re-imaginings of diversity as concept, identity and experience that are simultaneously personal and political. In so doing, she highlights the affective mobilisations of particular identities as part of everyday struggle. She concludes by reflecting on the function of such an affective orientation to enhancing student learning. Like Kiguwa, Navan Govender, the author of the third chapter, assumes a deeply personal stance in relation to his work. Govender conducts a critical reflection of the processes of production he employed when designing a workbook for an undergraduate critical literacy course. He argues that critical self-reflection enables an understanding of how pedagogical choices might have a real social impact on learners, education and the socio-cultural context. The author shows how his design choices affect engagement with controversial topics in the classroom, particularly those related to issues of diversity in gender and sexuality. Across these three chapters, it emerges strongly that critical diversity work is not just done to or for others. But, to paraphrase Allan (2005), it is work that we, as teacher educators, must do on ourselves.

The fourth chapter in this book is the first of a cluster of empirical studies. Lee Rusznyak and Alfred Masinire identify a challenge that faces South African teacher educators, namely how they can best structure pre-service teacher education programmes to enable prospective teachers to develop teaching practices that effectively respond to the constraints and possibilities of contextually diverse schools. Their study demonstrates that pre-service teachers who have a better conceptual knowledge of teaching, as well as greater levels of content and pedagogical knowledge, are able to respond pedagogically to the different demands of rural classrooms in ways that move beyond a technical approach. The fifth chapter in this book moves from South Africa to China, another country in the BRICS (Brazil, Russia, India, China, South Africa) block. The study, which was conducted by authors Jing Xiao and Ora Kwo, was situated in a College in China in which reform was being effected in the English curriculum. A major aim of the reform initiative was learner autonomy. Querying the presumption of ready-made teacher autonomy, the study addressed the gap between teachers' recognition of their responsibility to facilitate learner autonomy and their own diverse states of autonomy. The authors discuss teacher diversity not in terms of identity markers like gender, sexuality dis/ability etc., but in terms of the ways in which they engage with the competing discourses that challenge their autonomy. The sixth chapter returns to South Africa, and Doria Daniels reports on her ongoing research of immigrant parents' role in their children's educational success. She focuses on the educational investment of a community of Somali immigrant parents, whose children attend a community school. The author argues for teachers to be critically reflective about the many permutations of parent support, and for them to value the potential of the home as an educational site.

The authors of the next cluster of chapters are concerned with issues around teacher education that prepares practitioners to teach children and young people with disabilities and 'special needs'. The seventh chapter, by Mandia Mentis and Alison Kearney, describes a teacher education programme for teachers working in New Zealand to support learners with a variety of educational needs associated with learning, behaviour and sensory or physical impairments. The programme is designed to be individualised and promote teacher interconnectedness on personal, professional and interprofessional levels. The authors argue that both individualisation and interconnectedness prepare resource teachers to better understand themselves, their role, and context, and that this understanding in turn helps them to provide learners at the margins with a more equitable and inclusive educational experience. Myriam Hummel and Petra Engelbrecht turn our attention to Malawi in the eighth chapter. They draw on the broad cultural historical context of Malawi in order to examine how the country's historical legacies of diversity within teacher education shape the teaching and learning support strategies of primary school teachers. The authors argue that – based on the content of their initial teacher education programmes – teachers frame diversity within a narrow deficit individualised approach. Diversity is therefore conceptualised as 'special educational needs caused by disabilities'. The final chapter in this cluster, the ninth chapter, takes us to Brazil, another of the BRICS countries. Enicéia Gonçalves Mendes and Leonardo Santos Amâncio Cabral comment on a policy to develop 'Multifunctional Resource Rooms' for learners with special educational needs within mainstream schools. The research that they carried out suggests that the working conditions and training programmes for specialised teachers in Brazil need attention, and a research-based, collaborative approach is needed.

The final chapter in this book returns to South Africa and offers a conceptual argument. Nazir Carrim contends that notions of diversity and inclusion tend to reify and essentialise people in terms of social categories, and that this defeats the aims of social justice. Carrim argues instead for the conceptual possibility of notions of difference being more appropriate to the challenges of postmodernity.

Taken together, these ten chapters reveal the breadth both of the work that needs to be done and that which is being done in teacher education for diversity. First, there is critical conceptual work, as scholars grapple with what difference and diversity mean in the context of education broadly, and teacher education specifically. In particular, there is consensus that outmoded conceptualisations of difference and diversity do not serve the imperative for social justice in and through teacher education. We suggest that the postcolonial[1] space of the Global South offers the "critical distance" (Janks, 2010, p.71) from dominant discourses that is necessary to develop new discourses of difference and diversity. As scholars of the Global South challenge the "coloniality of knowledge" (Ndlovu-Gatsheni, 2013, p.11), which assumes the primacy of knowledge and thinking of the Global North, they are well positioned to engage with difference and diversity in ways that do not privilege or invisibilise the centre.

Second, this volume highlights a range of identity markers that constitute difference. These include race (Reygan et al.), religion (Kiguwa), gender and sexuality (Govender), geography (Rusznyak and Masinire), ethnicity (Daniels; and Mentis and Kearney) and dis/ability (Reygan et al.; Mentis and Kearney; Hummel and Engelbrecht; and Mendes and Cabral). There is also the reminder that difference might not be related to specific identity markers, but to personal responses and dispositions in the face of institutional pressures (Xiao and Kwo). Woven through these chapters is a recognition of the limitations of unidimensional conceptions of diversity that essentialise identities and standardise expectations. There is also a call for teacher educators and teachers to examine the ways in which power and privilege work in the construction of diverse identities, and to consider what it means to make deep and nuanced pedagogical judgements related to difference.

The reader of these chapters will also be made aware of the bricolage of actors and actions in teacher education for diversity. This volume considers the role of policy makers at various levels, teacher educators, pre-service and in-service teachers, specialised teachers, learners, and parents. Difference and diversity are constructed in social spaces through the interactions of people. The workings of power are not absent in these interactions, and various chapters have shown how the interests of power tend to marginalise the Other. But power is also shown in resistance and the exercise of agency – at least two chapters (Reygan et al. and Carrim) refer to learner and student activism that challenges the institutional status quo. Parents (in Daniels' chapter), teacher educators (in Xiao and Kwo's chapter) and teachers (in Mendes and Cabral's chapter) all find ways to resist structures and practices which do not recognise their presence and voice. These actors also create, enact and resist various pedagogical 'artefacts', which include workbooks (Govender), teacher education programmes (Rusznyak and Masinire; Hummel and Engelbrecht; and

Mendes and Cabral), curricula (Kiguwa; Xiao and Kwo; and Mentis and Kearney), and policies (Reygan et al.; and Mendes and Cabral). The imbrications of people and these artefacts make teacher education for diversity a complex project.

Finally, we signal our awareness of the diversity of scholars represented in this volume. While each contributor is concerned with a particular aspect of teacher education for diversity, and each is concerned in some way with educational justice, there is no singular conception of diversity itself. We can see that there may be significant disagreement among the authors about ideas, methodologies and conclusions. Despite this, all the scholars represented are working within the realities of their particular contexts, each of which bear the legacies of colonialism, oppression and underdevelopment. We are also aware of the inevitable lacunae in a collection like this. There are differences that make a pedagogical difference (see Reygan et al.), which are invisible in this volume. Social class, for instance, is said by Bernstein (2000, p.xxv) to be 'a major regulator of the distribution of students to privileging discourses and institutions', and yet none of our authors explicitly engage with social class in relation to education. Importantly, there are many voices from the Global South not represented here, and there are issues vital to the project of teacher education for diversity that have not been taken up by the authors in this volume.

The reader will find that many of the issues foregrounded by chapters in this book reflect the reality of the colonial legacy. We see value in the idea of:

> ... shifting the geography of reason from the West as the epistemic locale ... to the ex-colonised epistemic sites as legitimate points of departure in describing the construction of the modern world order.
> 
> *(Ndlovu-Gatsheni, 2013, p.13)*

As we shift the epistemic site from the North, which has dominated the scholarship of teacher education, we signal the potential of conversations among countries of the Global South. This will encourage collaborations in finding "appropriate solutions to common challenges" (Chataika, 2012, p.262). Also, we hope that this volume will give rise to conversations with scholars in the Global North. Too often, as Chataika (2012) notes, scholars in the Global South are inevitably the junior partners in any North-South collaborations, with social hierarchies of the world order reflected in academic interactions. We propose that teacher education for diversity in the 21st century in the North and South requires scholars who are willing to be prompted to question the 'way we do things' through engaging in critical conversations with others. It is often the 'outsider' who enables non-intuitive insights by asking difficult questions and presenting previously unthought-of alternatives.

## Note

1 We concur with Chataika (2012) that 'postcolonialism' should not be hyphenated, because so doing suggests that the effects of colonialism disappear once rulership transfers from the colonial power to indigenous people.

## References

Allan, J. (2005). Inclusion as an ethical project. In S. Tremain (Ed.). *Foucault and the government of disability* (pp. 281–297). Ann Arbor: University of Michigan Press.

Bernstein, B. (2000). *Pedagogy, symbolic control and identity: Theory, research and critique* (revised edition). Lanham, MD: Rowman and Littlefield.

Chataika, T. (2012). Disability, development and postcolonialism. In D. Goodley, B. Hughes and L. Davis (Eds.). *Disability and social theory: New developments and directions* (pp. 252–269). Basingstoke: Palgrave Macmillan.

Janks, H. (2010). *Literacy and power*. London: Routledge.

Ndlovu-Gatsheni, S. (2013). Why decoloniality in the 21st century? *The Thinker*, 48, 10–15.

Steyn, M. (2015). Critical diversity literacy: Essentials for the twenty-first century. In S. Vertovec (Ed.), *Routledge international handbook of diversity studies* (pp. 379–390). London: Routledge.

# 1

# ASSIMILATION AND CELEBRATION?

Discourses of difference and the application of Critical Diversity Literacy in education

*Finn Reygan, Elizabeth Walton and Ruksana Osman*

## Introduction

Globally, classrooms have become more complex and more demanding spaces for teaching and learning in recent years. This is the result of the interplay of numerous factors, which include the demands of late capitalism and the impact of social media.[1] In addition, diversity in terms of race, class, gender, sexuality, religion, dis/ability, age, ethnicity, and language, among other identity markers, has become a defining feature of schools. As a result, teachers need to be increasingly 'diversity literate' to negotiate the demands of the classroom. The challenge teacher educators now face is to determine how best to educate a generation of teachers with a sophisticated understanding of the diverse identities of their learners, as well as how these identities intersect. This is important because not all identities are equally valorised in schools and society, and oppression is experienced by those whose identities are not valued. Indeed, multiple axes of oppression converge to determine the scholastic outcomes – and life courses – of particular groups of learners. Grant and Zwier (2011, p. 182) contend that there is a "need for theory and practice that would consider the intersection of multiple identities and how these [produce] lived experiences of oppression and privilege". This leads us to ask: What are the determining discourses around difference that pervade school settings and what is both foregrounded and repressed in these discourses? And: How can teachers be equipped to move beyond outmoded ways of thinking about difference and diversity[2] so as to create genuinely inclusive school spaces?

Despite the need to complexify education spaces, given that issues of diversity and inclusion have come to the fore in recent years as evidenced by a range of frameworks and approaches to education, discourses of diversity in education seem to remain largely uninterrogated in classrooms. The frameworks and approaches include the impetus towards Education for All and inclusive education, which foreground the necessity to enable teachers to engage with issues of diversity. Our experience in schools and universities suggests that responses to diversity have been somewhat limited, and are often characterised by discourses of 'assimilation' and 'celebration'. These discourses work to elide, dehistoricise and decontextualise difference, and largely obscure the deeper workings of power. This chapter offers a critical engagement with these discourses, specifically as they manifest in education, and the discussion draws on some recent South African events. We then propose the development of a Critical Diversity Literacy (CDL; Steyn, 2015) among pre-service teachers to enable them to trouble these prevailing discourses, and ultimately to foster more nuanced understandings of power, privilege and difference within school communities.

## Discourses of power, privilege and difference

We recognise two common discourses of diversity – assimilation and celebration. These discourses can be found in South Africa and elsewhere, both societally and in education. We understand assimilation to refer to a process whereby people from diverse backgrounds and identities come to participate in the life of a broader community. Complete assimilation hypothetically creates a situation in which there are no separate social structures based on differences such as those related to class, race, gender, dis/ability or sexual orientation. There are various forms of assimilation, including limited desegregation, pluralism, purported integration, and assimilation that can be partial, individual or group based. Assimilation aims to negate difference and co-opt it into the norm, thereby eliding the salience of difference and perpetuating hegemonic norms. The celebration approach to diversity – what Banks, Cochran-Smith, Moll, Richert, Zeichner, LePage and McDonald (2005) call the 'Heroes and Holidays' approach – is one in which minority content is limited to special days, weeks, months and related celebrations. In this approach, learners coming from cultures other than the historically dominant group are accommodated by the tokenistic inclusion of some aspect of their culture. As Vandeyar (2006) points out, the notion of the 'culture day', with an array of attire, food and dance, is little more than an add-on to an unchanged school culture and curriculum. There is therefore little space for critical engagement on equality of access to knowledge, on whose voice and perspective are being privileged, and whose cultural values and histories are being acknowledged. The discourse of celebration tokenistically recognises difference, but only in a superficial way, thereby denuding difference of its substance. We will present examples of the ways in which these two discourses might shape the educational space and show some of the ways in which these discourses are being resisted by students.

### *Discourse 1: Assimilation and limited notions of hospitality*

The presumption of the assimilation of the other has a lot in common with the view that inclusion hinges on hospitality. Hospitality is usually based on the assumption of a prior claim to or ownership of a space into which the gracious host 'welcomes' the outsider. But this welcome is usually conditional on the guest's compliance with the host's wishes and conventions, and is intended to "preserve the world of the host" (Dass, 2015, p. 104). Dass describes the workings of such limited and conditional notions of hospitality as designating:

> ... a kind of violence because they all work by prescribing, determining and knowing the guest in terms of the host. What is established in the process is a diminished form of the guest, a limiting of the other, which allows for disregard, abuse and harm.
>
> *(Dass, 2015, p. 105)*

Educational institutions at various levels have adopted the language of hospitality as they have sought to 'include' those previously excluded. Hospitality metaphors abound in inclusive education discourses (Walton, 2016), as schools 'welcome' learners with disabilities, strive to 'accommodate' them and 'cater' for their needs. This hospitality is, however, premised on the convenience and capacity of the host school, which typically reserves the right to set "clauses of conditionality" (Slee, 1996, p. 107) that regulate the limits of inclusion. Byrne (2013), in an article that explores the contradictions and conditionalities of the inclusion of people with disabilities, notes that "practices of 'inclusion' are grounded in the taken for granted rules of a non-disabled arbitrary for whom the phrase 'Welcome into *my* world' is intransigent" (emphasis in the original) (p. 234). In higher education institutions, staff (Dass, 2015) and students (Njovane, 2015) have also experienced the expectation to assimilate to an environment governed by limited notions of hospitality, as they have been 'included' into what have remained essentially untransformed institutional spaces, replete with many reminders of the elitism, whiteness, patriarchy and heteronormativity on which these institutions were established. Njovane (2015, p. 128), for example, explains how the success of a student's academic endeavour "depends on whether or not she is willing to part with who she is in order to pander to what she is expected to be". Donaldson (2015, p. 144) contends that universities have an obligation to go beyond making queer students and staff feel "included and comfortable", and to challenge and disrupt heteronormativity. The elitism of university spaces is perpetuated by entrenched notions of 'academic excellence'.

Notions of 'support' tend to be evoked in the assimilation/hospitality discourses of difference, as the 'other' is offered assistance to meet the requirements and expectations of the dominant order. Support is usually predicated on an assumption of deficit, and is framed as a compensatory measure. Often, the personal, cultural and additional resources the 'other' brings are negated, or simply disregarded. Consider, for example, the 'refugee' learners who were 'included' in a school in Durban, South Africa. Here, "learners of war and flight" (Sookraj, Gopal & Maharaj, 2005, p. 1) were 'included' and 'supported' through measures like the provision of food parcels and extra English lessons. These gestures were seen by the learners as paternalistic, and a response to an exotic perception of them amidst a "miraculous synergy of violent battle and escapade imagery" (Sookraj et al., 2005, p. 11). The curriculum remained unresponsive to these learners and did not include them in any substantive way. There was little recognition of their linguistic aptitude, their positive attributes and the potential contribution of their stories. This led the authors to speak of a form of inclusion "that alienates in a context where the persons that symbolically exclude do so without the specific intention of excluding" (p. 11). In other schools, learners who experience learning difficulties or disabilities may be provided with modifications to the curriculum or assessment, or with personal learning facilitators (Walton, Nel, Hugo & Muller, 2009) to 'support' them and to compensate for their 'deficiencies'. While we do not deny the importance of assistive devices and other arrangements that secure access, we maintain that there is a danger that certain measures become assimilationist – if not in intention, then in effect. This may occur if such measures are constructed on restricted, ableist assumptions of normality, when they limit learner participation in the learning activities of their peers, and when they prevent conventional, exclusionary curricula, and ways of teaching, from being challenged (Booth & Ainscow, 1998).

Resistance to an assimilationist approach to diversity is well illustrated by the student protests at South African universities in 2015 and 2016. The movement started at the University of Cape Town with the #RhodesMustFall protests, and was followed by the #FeesMustFall protests across higher education in South Africa. The discourse emerging from the movement has been a rejection of the assimilation of black students into the relatively unreconstructed white space of the academy. In short, the movement is pushing back against an education system that prioritises the assimilation of black students while remaining ideologically, philosophically and pedagogically unchanged. The #FeesMustFall movement is articulating a politics of presence, which is the political importance of having marginalised voices and bodies present in a space so as to stake a claim on that space. The movement is also naming racist, sexist and – at least in 2015 – cisnormative ideologies[3] that continue to find expression in curricula, as well as exclusionary pedagogies, and what remains a largely untransformed academic body. The alienation and sense of dislocation experienced by many black students in institutions of higher learning has been the catalyst to push back against a model of assimilation that in many ways leaves white privilege unchallenged.

## *Discourse 2: Celebration, understanding and sympathy*

An approach to diversity that purports to 'celebrate' difference can be found in various discourses that promote inclusivity in education and society at large. Engelbrecht (2006, p. 254) suggests that democracy in South Africa is premised on "acknowledging the rights of all previously marginalized communities and individuals as full members of society, and requires the recognition and *celebration of diversity*" (italics ours). Prerequisites for inclusive schools comprise having institutional cultures that celebrate difference (Corbett, 2001). These celebratory discourses can be seen as a response to the pathologisation of difference and views of the other as abnormal and an aberration, which consign such individuals to segregated spaces

(Baglieri, Bejoian, Broderick, Connor & Valle, 2011). Efforts to establish superficial understandings of difference and empathy towards the other are often embedded in celebratory approaches to diversity. We critically explore this phenomenon, employing two reference points. The first is the 'celebration' of the heritage of South Africans as presented in a local newspaper, and the second is disability 'awareness', which is attempted through the media, literature and textbooks.

'Heritage Day', which is celebrated on 24 September in South Africa, ostensibly encourages South Africans to celebrate their cultures and their diversity in terms of beliefs and traditions, in the broader context of nation building. However, iterations of this public holiday have the potential to perpetuate outmoded and simplistic understandings of difference among South Africa's peoples, thereby preserving hierarchies of privilege and marginalisation. A Heritage Day article from a local 'free-to-read' newspaper (*The Randburg Sun*, 22 September, 2016) exemplifies the celebration approach to Heritage Day, enjoining readers to "celebrate their culture and the diversity of their beliefs and traditions". Permission to reproduce the article was refused, so a brief description is given in Figure 1.1 below, along with limited extracts from the article.

In the article, ethnic groups are reduced to clichéd monikers that perpetuate the trope of the simplicity of Africa as opposed to the sophistication of Europe. For example, the Swazi people are 'traditional', the Venda are 'spiritual leaders', the Xhosa are 'extremely proud', the Pedi are all about 'dance and song', whereas the English 'brought civilization'.[4] The normative whiteness of this construction of South African diversity is apparent in the invisibility of whiteness in the article. The semiotics of the article foreground the ways in which privilege (in this case whiteness) does not need to name or show itself. As a result, while there are visual representations of black African ethnic diversity, with photographs of people in traditional attire, there is no apparent need to display whiteness (in this case Englishness). This romanticisation and simplification of black African identity is juxtaposed with the cohering and organising impetus of whiteness, which 'brought civilisation' to underdeveloped peoples.

Casual Day is not an official public holiday in South Africa. It is, however, a day when South Africans are encouraged to 'dress down', donate to disability charities, and become more aware of people with disabilities (www.casualday.co.za). The South African government also marks an annual National Disability Rights Awareness Month. The awareness generated through these initiatives may be valuable, but it also risks slipping into the celebratory discourses in which ableism is invisible, and people with disabilities become the objects of 'understanding' and are characterised as the exotic other. McRuer (2010, p. 386) maintains that in response to the disability rights movement:

> the dutiful (or docile) able-bodied subject now recognizes that some groups of people have chosen to adjust to or even take pride in their "condition", but that recognition, and the tolerance that undergirds it, covers over the compulsory nature of the able-bodied subject's own identity.

| | |
|---|---|
| The article is presented as a "feature" in this newspaper, and occupies the top third of the tabloid-size page on two facing pages. The layout combines text and photographs and uses three different coloured backgrounds in combination. The details below attempt to capture some of the detail of the article. The position of photographs and text on the pages has been approximated. ||
| Page 10 ||
| Across the top of the page is a strip of an abstract design. It is made up of various shapes and is multi-coloured. ||
| The title in bold in large font is **"SA's multi-cultural heritage celebrated"** ||

| | | | |
|---|---|---|---|
| Photograph: Medium shot of a woman wearing traditional dress, including elaborate beaded head-dress and beads adorning the neck, shoulders and torso. The position next to the text suggests that this woman depicts Ndebele culture. | An introduction to Heritage Day is given, noting that "South Africans across the spectrum are encouraged to celebrate their culture and the diversity of their beliefs and traditions in the wider context of a nation that belongs to all its people". | Photograph: Head and shoulders shot of a woman among others. Colourful beads and fabric worn on the neck and shoulders. | Photograph: Medium shot of a man with a colourful blanket around him. He is wearing a beaded head-dress. |
| | | ❖ Swazi are "Traditional". The text notes that many Swazi traditions have remained intact since the days of their founding monarch, and that ceremonies, including the reed dance, are important. | ❖ Venda are "Spiritual leaders". The Venda culture is said in the text to be "closely associated with the spirit world". Mention is made of the sangoma who is a "traditional healer" and ancestors who must be appeased. |
| | ❖ Ndebele are "Most distinctive" The culture is said to be renowned for its beadwork and mural art. A description is given of an Ndebele cultural village, including the roles and activities of men and women. | Photograph: Wide-angle shot of men dancing. Five men are foregrounded in silhouette, their faces not clear. Their torsos are bare and they are carrying sticks. Others are in the background, and a fire provides the backlight. ||
| | | ❖ Tsonga are "Cultivators" It is said that Tsonga people are farmers who engage in pastoralism and mixed agriculture. The text notes the prevalence of polygamy. ||

**FIGURE 1.1** Heritage Day article from *The Randburg Sun*, 22 September, 2016

## Page 11

Across the top of the page is a strip of an abstract design, repeated from the previous page. It is made up of various shapes and is multi-coloured.

| | | |
|---|---|---|
| ❖ Tswana are "Hunters, herders and cultivators" The text provides a historical angle, noting the migration of the 'tribe' in the 14th century where they found the "high plains to their liking". The long grass, disease-free area was found suitable for cattle, and the soil easy to cultivate. A list of crops planted is provided | Photograph: A shot of a group of six women with five men standing behind them is offered. The women are wearing beaded garments and head-dresses. The men are bare chested, wearing strings of beads. Their head-dresses are made of animal skin and feathers. The people are smiling broadly. | ❖ English "Brought civilization" According to the text, English culture is a "defining element" that has shaped the "Rainbow nation". Their history in South Africa is mentioned from their arrival in 1820, to the South African War of 1899. Note: No photograph is provided to represent English culture. |
| Photograph: The head and shoulders shot is a stock picture of Nelson Mandela, from the site /www.gettyimages.com/license/170278075. The site says that the photograph, taken in 2002, depicts Mandela wearing traditional Xhosa dress as a member of the Tembu Royal family. | ❖ Xhosa are "Extremely proud" The text emphasises the authority of "ancestral spirits" in Xhosa belief and notes the slaughtering of animals to invoke the ancestors. The language is mentioned as "the click language". | Advertisement for fishing and scuba gear |
| The text asks, "How are you celebrating National Heritage Day?" and invites readers to share their photographs on social media using the hashtag #itsmyheritage | Photograph: A close-up shot of a woman with closed eyes, smiling. She is wearing a red cloth head-dress, and large beads around her neck. | ❖ Pedi are "Dance and song" According to the text, discovering the baPedi culture involves eating mopane worms and dancing. The baPedi are said to have traditionally lived in "round huts of clay and cow dung" and their choice of food is "specially cooked spinach …, samp, milk and maize". |

**FIGURE 1.1** continued

Recognition (or tolerance) of some groups within a celebratory discourse fails to acknowledge what McRuer (2010, p. 385) calls "compulsory able-bodiedness". In the media, this results in the portrayal of people with disabilities in terms of one or more tropes. These include presenting people with disabilities as the objects of pity, tragic victims of misfortune who are dependent on charity, or as superheroes, bravely overcoming impossible odds to achieve unexpected feats (Haller, 2000; McDougall, 2006). Characters with disabilities appear on television or in literature in ways that create a false sense of 'understanding', but actually perpetuate stereotypes and reinforce paternalism (Walton, 2016).

With reference to teacher education, Broderick and Lalvani (2017) have identified what they call "dysconscious ableism", which is evident among North American pre-service teachers. They define "dysconcious ableism" as "an impaired or distorted way of thinking about dis/ability [...] one that tacitly accepts dominant ableist norms and privileges" (p. 2). They found that the majority of pre-service teachers ended their semester course titled "The Sociocultural Contexts of Disability and Inclusive Education" with liberal assumptions about disability that "celebrate diversity in the absence of any apparent awareness of the structural inequities in the social order of schooling" (p. 9). In our terms, these pre-service teachers have embraced a celebration discourse of diversity. This form of dysconscious ableism is seen as particularly problematic by Broderick and Lalvani, because pre-service teachers with this orientation are "unlikely to consider themselves in need of further personal, critically self-reflective work on their own dysconscious ableism, nor to engage in collective action to dismantle institutionalised ableism" (p. 9). Similar concerns are raised by Brantlinger (2006) with reference to textbooks used for teacher education. In a comprehensive survey of North American textbooks on special needs education, she notes that diagnostic categories of disability are presented as neutral, and seldom focus on "structural inequalities in institutional and societal hierarchies" (Brantlinger, 2006, p. 55). A similar trend can be found in some textbooks for teachers in South Africa, particularly where the focus is on inclusive education (see, for example, Bornman & Rose (2010); Landsberg, Kruger & Swart (2011) and Pienaar & Raymond (2013)). These books take a cursory tour through a range of diagnoses, leaving pre- and in-service teachers with superficial 'awareness' or 'understanding' of the difficulties that some children experience with learning. They tend to simplify and essentialise disability from a normative viewpoint, and extract disability from other axes of oppression with which it intersects (Walton, 2016).

## A note about discourses

We use the term 'discourse' in Gee's (2008, p. 154) sense of "saying(writing)-doing-being-valuing-believing combinations". This means that there is an inevitable interconnectedness between words, actions and beliefs. Thus, ways of thinking and talking about diversity reflect deeply held (even unconscious) beliefs, which will in turn influence actions. Two points about discourse are salient for our argument in this regard. First, as Gee (2011, p. 36) observes, "Discourses are not 'units' with clear boundaries". As we have described two discourses of diversity (assimilation and celebration), we have created artificial boundaries for ease of discussion. In reality, discourses are fluid, they do not have discrete margins, and they change (Gee, 2011). We thus acknowledge that our isolation of these discourses and the boundaries that we have identified could be contested. In addition, we inhabit our own discourses and "our naturalized ways of talking about the world seem to us to be true and appropriate" (Janks, 2010, p. 65). This means that it is difficult to establish the "critical distance" (Janks, 2010, p. 71) needed to resist the discourses with which we are comfortable and familiar. As we discuss in the next part of the chapter, CDL (Steyn, 2015) may serve as a productive way to gain this distance, and to challenge discourses of assimilation and celebration.

## The challenge to dominant discourses: Critical Diversity Literacy

The challenges of engaging equitably with diversity in schools, along with the limitations in current approaches to difference, suggest that teacher education programmes need to be conceptually robust and classroom-focused so as to develop competent, diversity-literate teachers. Some core questions guiding this endeavour include:

- How do we prepare pre-service teachers to understand and critically engage with multiple and intersecting forms of oppression?; How can these understandings be grounded in interactive pedagogies?
- How do we assist pre-service teachers to become reflective practitioners in the classroom and in their own lives?
- How do we foster a more nuanced, sophisticated understanding of power, privilege and difference that goes beyond simplistic notions of assimilation/ celebration to create genuinely inclusive classrooms?

In this regard, there is extensive literature in South Africa and globally on social justice, as well as on anti-oppressive pedagogies and classroom practices that challenge racism, sexism, and heterosexism and ableism (for example, see Adams, Bell & Griffin (2007); Francis & Hemson (2007); Goodley (2017) and Kumashiro (2002)). In terms of national policy in South Africa, the *White Paper on Education and Training* (Department of Education, 1995, Chapter 3, Section 16) highlights the need for:

> new education and training policies to address the legacies of under-development and inequitable development and provide learning opportunities for all [which] will be based principally on the constitutional guarantees of equal educational rights for all persons and non-discrimination [...].

The South African Constitution and the National Curriculum Statement (NCS) Grades R-12 (Department of Basic Education, 2012) foregrounds issues of human rights, social justice and inclusion. These policies and documents highlight the importance of diversity, but generally fail to provide specific guidance in this area. It is this lack of prescription that has made it challenging to embed the topic of diversity in teacher education programmes and in classrooms. The Minimum Requirements for Teacher Education Qualifications (MRTEQ) (Department of Higher Education and Training, 2015, p. 62) makes "dealing with diversity" part of situational learning, and one of the competences of newly qualified teachers is that they must "understand diversity in the South African context in order to teach in a manner that includes all learners" (p. 62). This indicates that issues of diversity in teacher education must be addressed, but there is nothing that specifies how, or with what lens, this should be done.

Francis and Hemson (2007) list some of the approaches to diversity in education that have been employed since 1994, including multiculturalism, critical multiculturalism and inclusive education. Moletsane, Hemson and Muthukrishna (2004) critique many of these approaches for their lack of engagement with issues of power and privilege, for the ways in which they essentialise difference and promote assimilation. This lack of engagement with issues of power, privilege and difference perpetuates diversity illiteracy in school communities, which in turn inhibits competent classroom practice in this area. There are clearly complexities involved in engaging with issues of diversity in the classroom, as well as a lack of preparedness of many teachers to teach about diversity (Reygan & Francis, 2015). We also know that teaching and learning can be interrupted when power relations and oppression foster an environment in which individual and group identity, in relation to race, class, gender, disability, sexual orientation and so on, interconnect and function as a barrier to teaching and learning (Msibi, 2012).

## *Critical Diversity Literacy in pre-service teacher education*

The interplay of multiple axes of oppression in terms of material, psychological and developmental consequences constitutes complex terrain which requires sophisticated analysis. CDL (Steyn, 2015) offers the possibility of an 'analytical orientation' that provides learners and educators with the 'diversity literacy' necessary to navigate issues of power, privilege and difference. This analytical orientation must necessarily be historically aware and cognisant of race, class, gender, sexual orientation, religion, ethnicity, language, and (dis)ability, among others. One of the weaknesses of approaches to diversity in education – particularly those premised on the 'celebration' of difference – is a lack of interrogation of power and privilege. As Reygan and Steyn (2017) observe, another of these weaknesses is a reductive focus on only a few forms of diversity to the exclusion of others, and an essentialising view of difference. In this regard, CDL offers a ten-criteria framework that troubles discourses of both assimilation and celebration (presented in the next section) and it therefore has relevance in teacher education for inclusive teaching. The following ten analytical criteria (Steyn, 2015) can be employed in any given social context:

i An understanding of the role of power in constructing differences that make a difference;
ii A recognition of the unequal symbolic and material value of different social locations;
iii Analytical skill in unpacking how these systems of oppression intersect, interlock, co-construct and constitute each other, and how they are reproduced, resisted and reframed;
iv A definition of oppressive systems such as racism as current social problems and not only historical legacy;
v An understanding that social identities are learned and are an outcome of social practices;
vi The possession of a diversity grammar and a vocabulary that facilitates discussion of privilege and oppression;
vii The ability to 'translate' (see through) and interpret coded hegemonic practices;
viii An analysis of the ways that diversity hierarchies and institutionalised oppressions are inflected through specific social contexts and material arrangements;
ix An understanding of the role of emotions, including our own emotional investment, in all of the above; and
x An engagement with issues of the transformation of these oppressive systems to deepen social justice at all levels of social organisation.

These ten criteria, while not exhaustive, offer a complex set of analytical skills with which to recognise, think about and interrupt relations of social oppression, including in schools. Diversity literacy is arguably a core competence of teachers in South Africa, given the requirement in education policy that educators have an orientation to social justice (Francis & Hemson, 2007). Teachers should therefore be able to recognise, name and speak back to discourses of exclusion, and this analytical skill should emerge from the development of a critical consciousness around oppression that propels teachers to take action for change. In short, the positioning of teachers is central to the success of social justice and diversity work in education, and the process of critical self-reflection is an important component of this (Francis & Hemson, 2007; Kumashiro, 2002). Teachers' engagement with their own biases is a central component of this work because educators can and do construct discourses that perpetuate the exclusion and debilitation of the 'other' (Solomon, Portelli, Daniel & Campbell, 2007; Tatum, 1997).

There are a number of possible applications of CDL (Steyn, 2015) in the South African context. Kiguwa (this volume) applies aspects of CDL in a postgraduate course. It may also be applied to processes and programmes in teacher education, as well as to materials development, including textbooks. CDL can also enable the interrogation of the experiences of both teachers and learners in schools (see the discussion of Pretoria High School for Girls later in this chapter). For application in pre-service teacher education, the core concepts of CDL require translation into language that is appropriate for both teacher education and for classroom practice, so that it is easily comprehensible to both teachers and learners. Reygan and Steyn (2017) have identified the key concept in each of the ten CDL criteria and 'translated' these into questions. These authors isolated the core conceptual underpinning for each criterion and attempted to find language to express these concepts that was accessible for school communities and pre-service teachers. This process was guided by an awareness of the following: widely divergent classroom realities in South Africa (including access to resources); differing levels of literacies in schools across the country; grade and age differences in schools; the degree of previous exposure of pre-service educators to social justice and intersectional theory; and the general language necessary to make CDL relevant for the practice of teaching and learning in schools. Table 1.1 presents the ten CDL criteria, as well as the question that these authors extrapolated from each criterion to develop a pedagogically useful tool from CDL.

For example, Criterion Two (see Table 1.1) of the CDL framework reads as follows:

> A recognition of the unequal symbolic and material value of different social locations. This includes acknowledging hegemonic positionalities and concomitant identities, such as whiteness, heterosexuality, masculinity, cisgender, ablebodiedness, middleclassness etc. and how these dominant orders position those in non-hegemonic spaces.
>
> *(Steyn, 2015, p. 382)*

Reygan and Steyn (2017) then translated this question into the following question for pre-service teacher education and classroom practice: "What are the 'rules' for different groups of people: women, gay people etc.?" The rubric of questions emerging from the CDL matrix is to be gradually layered from Grades 4 through to 12. This layering is expected to support the deepening of teachers' and learners' understanding of the ways in which power, privilege and difference intersect and co-construct in the processes and outcomes of education.

There is the risk with CDL, as with any other approach to diversity in education, that pre-service teachers and educators more broadly may, in the guise of doing CDL anti-oppressive work, continue to perpetuate discourses that marginalise the 'other' (Solomon et al., 2007; Tatum,1997). Also, as Reygan and Steyn (2017) point out, there are challenges when introducing CDL in education. One such challenge may be the foregrounding and privileging of one form of difference over another in the work. For example, pre-service teachers may be much more literate in relation to racialised difference but, given the role of religion, patriarchy and cultural norms, the issue of sexual and gender diversity may be left unexamined. As a result, a black, female, South African pre-service teacher may experience some discomfort while simultaneously highlighting her privilege in terms of heteronormativity and ableism and possible marginalisation in terms of gender or ethnicity. Another challenge, mentioned by Kiguwa (this volume) and alluded to by Walton and Rusznyak (2017), is that doing this critical work can lead to a sense of

**TABLE 1.1** CDL in pre-service teacher education and classroom practice

| Core idea from Critical Diversity Literacy (Steyn, 2015) | 1. Role of power | 2. Values of different social locations | 3. How oppressions intersect | 4. Oppressive systems are current | 5. Identities are socially constructed | 6. Diversity grammar | 7. Interpret hegemony | 8. Context / material relations | 9. Role of emotions | 10. Transformation |
|---|---|---|---|---|---|---|---|---|---|---|
| Questions for teacher educators, teachers and learners | Where is power in society? | What are the 'rules' for different groups of people: women, gay people etc.? | How are we different in different ways? | What are examples now / in the past of how different people were treated? | How do you learn to be who you are? | What are the important words to talk about being different? | Is it true what people say about people who are different? | What is your school / family / neighbourhood like for people who are different? | How do we feel when people are treated badly for being different? | What can you do to make things better? |

frustration and hopelessness, which may be overwhelming for pre-service teachers who must ultimately be able to work productively in the very systems they critique.

While teacher education and the development of diversity literacy are key components of preparing teachers for inclusive teaching, dominant discourses generally determine what occurs in education settings, and teachers need to be aware of these to create genuinely inclusive spaces. It is our contention that teacher education needs to interrogate the discourses of assimilation/celebration in education in South Africa, as well as the ways in which these perpetuate configurations of power, privilege and difference in education. It is also important that teacher educators examine ways in which these discourses are being challenged by diversity-literate students.

## Critical Diversity Literacy in action: The politics of hair

The rhetoric of celebrating difference and 'unity in diversity' is being challenged by a generation of young South Africans who are imbued with the politics of blackness, intersectionality and 'wokeness', as evidenced by the writing of the young generation of black journalists (Bongela, 2016). They defer to a new canon that includes black consciousness philosophers such as Fanon and Biko, and an interrogation of the tokenistic celebration of difference that remains superficial, and which does little to challenge hierarchies related to race, class, gender and sexual orientation. There is a growing awareness of 'differences that make a difference', namely those that continue to privilege whiteness and exclude blackness, as seen in learner protests at Pretoria High School for Girls, which is an 'ex-Model C' school.[5] In August 2016, the school was accused of discriminatory policies and practices that targeted black learners. The school was accused of forcing black learners to straighten their hair. Black learners were allegedly also victimised for standing in groups and speaking in their home languages. Learners claimed that hairstyles such as afros, dreadlocks and braids were not allowed at the school. This led to the emergence of the hashtag #StopRacismAtPretoriaGirlsHigh, and a global media response. In addition, the Minister of Arts and Culture, Nathi Mthethwa, wrote on Twitter (Mail & Guardian, 2016) "Let us continue to assert our Africanness in all spaces so that we can breathe & be truly, fully ourselves."

The Gauteng Education MEC, Panyaza Lesufi, intervened and met with management and the school community to address the issues. Political parties also weighed in, including the Economic Freedom Fighters (EFF), whose acting national spokesperson said:

> It is deeply saddening that 22 years into democracy, there are still institutions of any kind that seek to directly suppress blackness in its aesthetics and culture… This is a direct result of a society still struggling with transformation and failing to address white hegemony.
>
> *(Mail & Guardian, 2016)*

In this case, the material consequence of privileging whiteness appears to be the exclusion of black learners in the school environment. Following Steyn (2015), it is apparent that certain differences make a real difference, which at Pretoria High School for Girls is the symbolic power of hair to reinscribe white hegemony and perpetuate racist norms. As Carrim (2009, p. 375) points out, hair is "a marking on the body which reinforces the logic and practice of discrimination, and provides […] a bio-physical signifier to justify and naturalize discrimination". The CDL (Steyn, 2015) criteria include a useful analytical tool for teacher education in relation to events such as those at Pretoria High School for Girls. For example, in terms of Criterion One of CDL (listed above), protesting learners at Pretoria High School for Girls articulated a clear understanding of the ways in which power constructs differences that make a difference, which in this case was the role of hair in perpetuating race-based exclusion. In terms of Criterion Two, learners revealed their understanding of the ways in which the different social locations within the school of black and white learners were not equally valued, either symbolically or materially, by school management. Reflecting Criterion Four, the issue of racism was also located by protesting learners in a much broader historical arc, and not just as a current social problem. Finally, in terms of Criterion Nine, the role of the emotional investment of school communities in the perpetuation of unequal power relations was foregrounded by protesters as they gave evidence of the slow and resistant response of school management to changing school policies. We are aware that the case of Pretoria High School for Girls is a South African example, but we suggest that the critique of discourses of assimilation and celebration presented previously is useful in analysing policy and practice responses related to issues of immigration in contexts around the world.

We suggest that all schools and teachers tap into issues of power, privilege and oppression in the classroom. We are also aware that there is an unequal degree of engagement with these issues in schools across South Africa. As a result, CDL (Steyn, 2015) would need to be applied in a way that is sensitive to specific school contexts, particularly those in which power is curtailed in discursive and material terms. Nevertheless, analysing the Pretoria High School for Girls situation through the lens of CDL illustrates how teacher educators could use a current event to develop diversity literacy so as to engage more deeply with the life worlds of learners. This has the potential to foster the ability to name and critique barriers to full participation in a transformed education. The alternative discourses of assimilation or celebration would frame the situation differently. Assimilation would reaffirm the school's right to impose (white) hairstyle and language rules on the basis that learners joining the school should comply with the pre-existing rules as a condition of their inclusion. In so doing, an assimilationist view would reaffirm the status quo and prevent critique of the ways in which power operates in the school to perpetuate (white) privilege. Celebration might focus on 'black hair' and 'allow' it in tokenistic deference to the ideal of 'inclusion'. In so doing, celebration entrenches the invisibility of whiteness (or white hair) as the centre, from which difference (and deviance) are judged. In contrast to these, CDL offers a more nuanced articulation of the ways in which systems of power and privilege intersect, interlock and co-construct environments of teaching and learning. It possesses the capacity to facilitate the emergence of school and classroom spaces that are more inclusive and more conducive to teaching and learning.

Teaching for diversity would require teachers, including those at Pretoria High School for Girls, to examine both the reproduction of white hegemony and how systems can be resisted and reframed, as demonstrated by the response of protesting learners. In this regard, the outcome of the process was that the school was ordered to change its code of conduct and other schools quickly followed suit. What was also apparent was that learners possessed a diversity grammar and vocabulary with which they could engage with issues of privilege and oppression. A similar awareness and vocabulary was largely absent among teachers themselves. The learners also displayed an ability to translate and interpret coded hegemonic practices, which in this case took the form of perpetuation of racist hegemony through hair policies. The articulation on the part of learners that the school had come to function as a site of oppression and exclusion demonstrated an awareness of the diversity hierarchies and institutionalised oppressions. Learners were also engaged with the transformation of these oppressive spaces through varied means, including the use of media and social media.

In many ways, the situation at Pretoria High School for Girls constituted a missed opportunity on the part of the teacher body to engage proactively and in a nuanced manner with issues of power, privilege and oppression in education. The reluctance of teachers and management to engage in self-reflexive debate with learners highlighted a degree of diversity illiteracy, and unearthed the ways in which dominant historical hierarchies remain ensconced. In short, we present the Pretoria High School for Girls case here to foreground a number of key questions that warrant robust engagement in the context of pre-service teacher education. These questions could serve as prompts for discussion and debate, and the further refinement of the CDL (Steyn, 2015) project in the context of education:

- What can be done to develop diversity literacy in teacher education, given the competing demands on the time and content of programmes?
- How can existing teachers be expected to examine 'systems of oppression' and act differently, particularly as they are habituated into dominant ways of 'doing school'?
- How exactly can and should teachers teach for diversity?
- What mechanisms might conceivably make teaching for diversity a 'requirement' and how might this be enforced or ensured?
- How can newly qualified teachers, pre-service teachers and teacher educators at universities be assisted or empowered to modify their practices where needed?

While the rhetoric of inclusive education and teaching for diversity is gaining currency globally, the reality of a genuinely inclusive education system remains elusive. In South Africa, the need to develop learning and teaching support materials that do not perpetuate oppression, marginalisation and exclusion is apparent in the work of the Soudien ministerial committee, which is tasked with reviewing school textbooks for their levels of inclusion and positive portrayals of diversity. In terms of learners with disabilities, a multiyear project funded by the European Union is also developing teacher education processes and materials for all pre- and in-service teachers. In short, there is a persistent and growing call for more inclusive education spaces that are informed about multiple issues of difference and power. This means enabling teachers to see through and decode hegemonic practices that impact teaching and learning outcomes negatively. For example, a recent regional study by UNESCO and GALA (UNESCO, 2016) found that high levels of gender-based violence (GBV) and homophobic bullying in schools across the region are directly related to patriarchal and heteronormative societal and school cultures. This in turn makes it all the more necessary to equip teachers to respond to multiple forms of difference in the classroom. This ability to analyse classroom and broader societal spaces from an intersectional perspective is essential because the material consequences of unchecked oppression manifest in terms of violence in schools and early school leaving (UNESCO, 2016). Such analysis also requires an understanding that current problems are, moreover, historical legacies and that the challenges of promoting inclusive and safer school spaces in the South African context are premised on historical and geographical contingencies that require deep, nuanced engagement.

## Conclusion

A key aspect of teacher education for diversity in South Africa is the intersectionality of race, class, gender, ethnicity, language, and ability, among others, in a context of extreme inequality. In such contexts, there is a need for a nuanced and sophisticated approach to power, privilege, difference and oppression that engages multiple, imbricated axes of oppression and the ways in which these play out in school contexts (often in very tangible and material ways). However, in general in South Africa, pre- and in-service teachers receive little or no preparation for deeper engagement with issues of oppression in the classroom and more broadly in society. Often, teachers are not provided with the tools and language to engage in such conversations and to name unequal power relations and their effects, even if this is the lived reality of many and constitutes experiential knowledge that many learners and teachers bring to the classroom. This understanding of power, privilege and difference in education has implications for what could be done in teacher education. While there is already a considerable body of literature on issues of diversity in teacher education (for example see Amin & Ramrathan, 2009; Banks et al., 2005; Sleeter & Grant, 2008), the specificities of the South African context require particular focus. The work that will engage adequately with this context begins with the development of pedagogies of discomfort that engage pre-service teachers regarding their own embodied knowledges, biases and unelaborated beliefs (see also Kiguwa (this volume) on forced introspection). Anti-oppressive pedagogies also require the use of informed, nuanced and social justice materials (the antithesis of the newspaper article presented in this chapter) that teachers can use in class. These learning support materials need to supplement the use of textbooks that avoid the perpetuation of bias and prejudice through the subtle (and sometimes not-so-subtle) hidden curriculum that reinforces whiteness, heteronormativity and ableism. A necessary response to the challenges of inclusion and diversity includes the development of robust diversity education for pre- and in-service teachers in the South African context. Such education must necessarily engage with historical legacies and current realities. In this regard, localised, historically aware and contextualised understandings of power, privilege and difference are necessary components of developing teacher competencies in teaching for diversity.

## Notes

1 Also, see Carrim (this volume) for a discussion of the impact of social media on education.
2 We acknowledge the conceptual contestations in the use of the words 'difference' and 'diversity', also noting that these terms are often used synonymously. Carrim (this volume) makes an argument for the abandonment of 'diversity' as an outmoded term that is laden with the conditions of modernity, and promotes the term 'difference'. We acknowledge that both terms (diversity and difference) may serve to invisibilise the centre, and "demarcate the boundaries of typicality" (Baglieri, Bejoian, Broderick, Connor & Valle, 2011, p. 2129).
3 Cisnormative ideologies pathologise bodies and identities that exist beyond the societally imposed gender binary.
4 Here we acknowledge that the idea of white people 'bringing civilisation' is highly problematic, when, as Frank (1978) argues, these Western actors were furthering a colonial process of concerted underdevelopment.
5 Within South Africa's school system, so-called 'ex-Model C' schools were previously reserved for white learners. Since 1994 and the end of the apartheid regime, black South Africans have increasingly been sending their children to these schools, which include Pretoria High School for Girls.

## References

Adams, M., Bell, L. A., & Griffin, P. (2007). *Teaching for diversity and social justice*. New York: Routledge.
Amin, N., & Ramrathan, P. (2009). Preparing students to teach in and for diverse contexts: A learning to teach approach. *Perspectives in Education*, 27(1), 69–77.
Baglieri, S., Bejoian, L. M., Broderick, A. A., Connor, D. J., & Valle, J. (2011). [Re]claiming "inclusive education" toward cohesion in educational reform: Disability studies unravels the myth of the normal child. *Teachers College Record*, 113(10), 2122–2154.
Banks, J., Cochran-Smith, M., Moll, L., Richert, A., Zeichner, K., LePage, P., & McDonald, M. (2005). Teaching diverse learners. In L. Darling-Hammond & J. Bransford (Eds.), *Preparing teachers for a changing world: What teachers should learn and be able to do* (pp. 232–274). San Francisco, CA: Jossey-Bass.
Bongela, M. (2016) The politics of the queen's English. *Mail & Guardian*, 18 March 2016. Accessed 20 December 2016 at: http://mg.co.za/article/2016-03-18-the-politics-of-the-queens-english.

Booth, T., & Ainscow, M. (1998). *From them to us*. London: Routledge.
Bornman, J., & Rose, R. (2010). *Believe that all can achieve*. Pretoria: Van Schaik.
Brantlinger, E. (2006). The big glossies: How textbooks structure (special) education. In E. Brantlinger (Ed.), *Who benefits from special education? Remediating (fixing) other people's children* (pp. 45–76). Mahwah, NJ: Lawrence Erlbaum Associates Inc.
Broderick, A., & Lalvani, P. (2017). Dysconscious ableism: Toward a liberatory praxis in teacher education. *International Journal of Inclusive Education*, 21(9), 1–12. doi:10.1080/13603116.2017.1296034
Byrne, B. (2013). Hidden contradictions and conditionality: conceptualisations of inclusive education in international human rights law. *Disability & Society*, 28(2), 232–244.
Carrim, N. (2009). Hair: Markings on the body and the logic of discrimination. *Perspectives in Education*, 27(4), 375–384.
Corbett, J. (2001). Teaching approaches which support inclusive education: A connective pedagogy. *British Journal of Special Education*, 28(2), 55–59.
Dass, M. (2015). Making room for the unexpected: The university and the ethical imperative of unconditional hospitality. In P. Tabensky & S. Matthews (Eds.), *Being at home* (pp. 99–115). Pietermaritzburg: UKZN Press.
Donaldson, N. (2015). What about the queers? The institutional culture of heteronormativity and its implications for queer staff and students. In P. Tabensky & S. Matthews (Eds.), *Being at home* (pp. 130–146). Pietermaritzburg: UKZN Press.
Engelbrecht, P. (2006). The implementation of inclusive education in South Africa after ten years of democracy. *European Journal of Psychology of Education*, 21(3), 253–264.
Department of Basic Education (2012). *Revised National Curriculum Statement (NCS) Grades R-12*. Pretoria: Department of Basic Education.
Department of Education (February, 1995) *White paper on education and training in a democratic South Africa: First steps to develop a new system* (Chapter 3: Section 16). Pretoria: Government Printer.
Department of Education (2001). *White Paper Six*. Pretoria: Government Printers.
Department of Higher Education and Training (2015). *Minimum Requirements for Teacher Education Qualifications (Revised) (MRTEQ)*. Pretoria: Department of Higher Education and Training.
Francis, D. & Hemson, C. (2007). Rainbow's end: Consciousness and enactment in social justice education. *Perspectives in Education*, 25, 99–112.
Frank, G. (1978). *World accumulation*. New York: Monthly Review Press.
Gee, J. P. (2008). *Social linguistics and literacies: Ideology in discourses* (3rd edition). Abingdon: Routledge.
Gee, J. P. (2011). *An introduction to discourse analysis* (3rd edition). New York: Routledge.
Goodley, D. (2017). *Disability studies: An interdisciplinary introduction* (3rd edition). Los Angeles: Sage.
Grant, C. A., & Zwier, E. (2011). Intersectionality and student outcomes: Sharpening the struggle against racism, sexism, classism, ableism, heterosexism, nationalism, and linguistic, religious, and geographical discrimination in teaching and learning. *Multicultural Perspectives*, 13(4), 181–188. doi:10.1080/15210960.2011.616813
Haller, B. (2000). If they limp they lead: News representation and the hierarchy of disability images. In D. Braithwaite & T. Thompson (Eds.), *Handbook of communication and people with disabilities* (pp. 273–288). Mahwah, NJ: Lawrence Erlbaum Associates.
Janks, H. (2010). *Literacy and power*. New York: Routledge.
Kumashiro, K. (2002). *Troubling education: Queer activism and anti-oppressive pedagogy*. New York and London: RoutledgeFalmer.
Landsberg, E., Kruger, D., & Swart, E. (Eds.). (2011). *Addressing barriers to learning: A South African perspective* (2nd edition). Pretoria: Van Schaik.

*Mail & Guardian*. (2016). EFF's Fana Mokoena calls out Pretoria Girls High for 'suppressing blackness'. Accessed 15 January, 2017 at: http://mg.co.za/article/2016-08-29-effs-fana-mokoena-calls-out-pretoria-girls-high-for-suppressing-blackness

McDougall, K. (2006). 'Ag shame' and superheroes: Stereotypes and the signification of disability. In B. Watermeyer, L. Swartz, T. Lorenzo, M. Schneider & M. Priestley (Eds.), *Disability and society* (pp. 387–400). Pretoria: HSRC Press.

McRuer, R. (2010). Compulsory able-bodiedness and queer/disabled existance. In L. Davis (Ed.), *The disability studies reader* (3rd edition; pp.383–392). New York: Routledge.

Moletsane, R., Hemson, C., & Muthukrishna, A. (2004) Educating South African teachers for the challenge of school integration: Towards a teaching and research agenda. In M. Nkomo, C. McKinney & L. Chisholm (Eds.), *Reflections on school integration: Colloquium proceedings* (pp. 61–77). Cape Town: Human Sciences Research Council.

Msibi, T. (2012). 'I'm used to it now': Experiences of homophobia among queer youth in South African township schools. *Gender and Education*, 24(5), 515–533.

Njovane, T. (2015). The violence beneath the veil of politeness: Reflections on race and power in the academy. In P. Tabensky & S. Matthews (Eds.), *Being at home* (pp. 116–129). Pietermaritzburg: UKZN Press.

Pienaar, C., & Raymond, E. (Eds.). (2013). *Making inclusive education work in classrooms*. Cape Town: Pearson.

Reygan, F., & Francis, D. (2015) Emotions and pedagogies of discomfort: Teachers' responses to sexual and gender diversity in the Free State, South Africa. *Education as Change*, 19(1), 101–119.

Reygan, F., & Steyn, M. (2017). Diversity in basic education in South Africa: Intersectionality and Critical Diversity Literacy (CDL). *Africa Education Review*, 14(2), 68–81.

Slee, R. (1996). Clauses of conditionality. In L. Barton (Ed.), *Disability and society: Emerging issues and insights* (pp. 107–122). London: Longman.

Sleeter, C. E., & Grant, C. A. (2008). *Making choices for multicultural education: Five approaches to race, class, and gender*. Hoboken, NJ: John Wiley & Sons Inc.

Sookraj, R., Gopal, N., & Maharaj, B. (2005). Interrogating inclusionary and exclusionary practices: Learners of war and flight. *Perspectives in Education*, 23(1), 1–13.

Solomon, R. P., Portelli, J. P., Daniel, B. J., & Campbell, A. (2007). The discourse of denial: How white teacher candidates construct race, racism and 'white privilege'. *Race Ethnicity and Education*, 8, 147–169.

Steyn, M. (2015). Critical diversity literacy: Essentials for the twenty-first century. In S. Vertovec (Ed.), *Routledge international handbook of diversity studies* (pp. 379–389). Routledge: New York.

Tatum, B. D. (1997). *Why are all the black kids sitting in the cafeteria?* New York: Basic Books.

*The Randburg Sun* (2016). SA's multicultural heritage celebrated. *The Randburg Sun*, 22 September, pp. 10–11. Johannesburg: Caxton.

UNESCO (2016). *Out in the open: Education sector responses to violence based on sexual orientation and gender identity/expression*. Paris: UNESCO.

Vandeyar, S. (2006). *The social context of education: Anti-racist multicultural education*. Pretoria: University of Pretoria.

Walton, E. (2016). *The language of inclusive education*. Abingdon: Routledge.

Walton, E., Nel, N., Hugo, A., & Muller, H. (2009). The extent and practice of inclusion in independent schools (ISASA members) in Southern Africa. *South African Journal of Education*, 29(1), 105–126.

Walton, E., & Rusznyak, L. (2017). Choices in the design of inclusive education courses for pre-service teachers: The case of a South African university. *International Journal of Disability, Development and Education*, 64(3), 231–248.

# 2

# ENGAGING FORCED INTROSPECTION
Teaching social justice in Critical Diversity Literacy

*Peace Kiguwa*

## Introduction

Teaching social justice in the classroom is both an affective and action-oriented endeavour. Social justice as it is taught in the classroom demands that teachers and learners relinquish deeply held assumptions and beliefs, which are often core to their identities. Social justice teaching challenges social attachments and identities in ways that demand that we become vulnerable to letting go of who we are, and that we invite new spaces of engagement. Engaging textual and other material that challenges our privilege, attachment to particular identities, and positions is a difficult thing to do. It is not only a socio-cognitive process, but also, as I have mentioned, an affective one. It is affective insofar as our emotions and psychic investments are made present in the moment of confrontation with texts, the Other, symbolic and material worlds, as well as with ourselves. It is also action-oriented in that we are called upon to do something about these affective states, as well as about how we make sense of the social world, and how we interact and make sense of others' lived experiences and everyday realities. Reflecting in depth on our immediate and broader social contexts is intrinsic to how we practise and learn about social justice and issues of diversity.

This chapter draws on the notion of 'forced introspection' as a way of reflecting on how we may teach Critical Diversity Literacy (CDL). I borrow the term from a comment made by a student in her course evaluation at the end of the course I offered. I had introduced photo-essays as an assessment tool to engage components of the students' personal and social lives, and as a means of thinking about the insertion of the social into the personal and vice versa. There were guarded mumblings that perhaps attested to a sense of confusion, mistrust, and some trepidation to engage with such an approach on the part of the students. As we worked together in preparation for the class presentations, students continually mentioned the challenges of writing and reflecting on personal narratives as opposed to straightforward theoretical analysis, which they had been trained to do in their undergraduate study. By the end of the course, students were more comfortable with this mode of reflection and were also more inclined to name and reflect on specific affective states such as anger, shame and fear as part of the social aspect of their lives. In her evaluation on the course, one student remarked: "thank you for the forced introspection". I use the term in the current discussion to elucidate the notion of a pedagogy of discomfort (Bozalek, Leibowitz, Carolissen & Boler, 2013) as fundamental to engaging critical literacy and social justice.

The chapter is divided into three sections. The first discusses CDL as social justice pedagogy. It examines the epistemology of the CDL module and its intersection with social justice as fundamental to the education project. The second section looks at a CDL course offered to a small cohort of students. It explores the course components and the objectives of critically engaging diversity in the curriculum. The last section analyses the students' reflective accounts of diversity and subjectification (i.e. the process whereby individuals come to experience themselves in particular ways and as particular kinds of subjects) through the photo-essay narrative account titled *"what does diversity mean to me?"* The section examines how students mediate and experience different practices of subjectification through the lenses of the social categorisations of race, language, gender, sexuality, culture and class, among others. I argue that a reflective mode of engaging complexities of diversity (both as concept and as identity) brings to the fore the contradictory and nuanced processes by which the individual becomes raced, gendered, classed etc. Such a reflective practice allows for an understanding of how personal and everyday experiences and modes of being are inextricably tied to the social. Here, I take seriously the psycho-social emphasis on how our everyday psychological lives and meaning-making is interwoven with social and material structures and influences. This unravelling of the micro- and macro-politics of subjectification involves affective responses from students that I argue are necessary to the conception of how to teach social justice in the classroom.

## Critical Diversity Literacy as social justice pedagogy

An important aspect of educating for social justice is the exploration of the many disjunctures in how lives are lived, depending on the societies to which these lives belong. Social justice pedagogy primarily engages the notion of change as intrinsic to any practice of social and personal transformation. This notion of change encompasses five essential components of social justice in education, which Hackman (2005, pp. 104–109) identifies as dominant within the literature on social justice and fundamental to a critical learning environment. The first component concerns the skill and capacity for content mastery. In this process, students are able to not only understand and master factual information specific to a course, but are also able to engage the historical locatedness of knowledge, and grapple with its contextual nuances. Such a process also implies that students engage a macro-micro analytic orientation to critiquing and working with knowledge. This would mean engaging the myriad ways that our personal lives are influenced by broader social and structural factors and institutions. Such an orientation allows us to explore personal dimensions of our subjectivities as inextricably bound to social dimensions. This aspect of social justice is especially significant because students require the skills to engage an array of information and knowledge as part of a process of actively participating in knowledge production.

The second component of social justice education is critical thinking around and analysis of oppression that builds on the foundation of content mastery. Freire (1996) has argued that critical thinking and analysis are processes in which individuals actively reflect on their lives and information available to them to effect personal and social change. Critical thinking and analysis involve the student moving beyond simple awareness of and mastery of subject matter, to acquiring the skills necessary to interrogate this subject matter. A social justice pedagogy framework demands that all knowledge – whether critical or not – be open for interrogation and debate. Critical thinking enables students to analyse the intricacies of power – both structural and subjective – so as to engage broader perspectives and experiences of intersubjectivity (i.e. how our identities are intertwined with other elements in our social and personal contexts) and subjectification (i.e. processes of becoming subjects). This criticality would enable students to ask questions about other possible alternatives to current social realities. Such a conceptualisation means that critical thinking goes further than merely analysing other perspectives without interrogating our own individual framing.

Action and social change is the third component, and it is especially useful in engaging with the despair that social justice and critical thinking practice may unwittingly cause. Dell and Anderson (2005), cautioning against the potential of critical social psychology to disrupt in ways that cause students to experience despair in relation to their situatedness, raise the ethical responsibility that all social justice teaching must grapple with. Students may experience frustration and despair in the face of their oppression and when they become cognisant of the broader macro-politics of such oppression. Similarly, students who enjoy some forms of privilege by virtue of their membership of specific social groups may experience a sense of frustration, guilt and hopelessness as they learn about the socio-political dynamics of such privilege. Fatalistic thinking (Freire, 1996) – the process whereby a sense of hopelessness and despair results in an apathetic response in the individual or group to social issues – is counter-productive to social change and transformation (both personal and social). This is because such thinking reinforces passivity and hopelessness in the face of social issues that are experienced as overwhelming and oppressive.

Personal reflection, which is the fourth component of social justice education, highlights the teacher's identity as critical to how students learn. Our varied and hierarchical social positioning – whether associated with our race, gender, class, sexuality and others – influences how students learn, and whether they experience the learning as hostile. This is related to the social inscriptions that students may make about our personal and social embodiment (Probyn, 2004). Continuous self-reflection is therefore a useful practice to adopt, both on the part of the teacher as well as that of the student. Self-reflection allows us to gain greater understanding of our differential privileges and oppressions, and of how these may be re-enacted in the classroom. It enables us to challenge the tendency towards normalising specific identities and social relations as 'common sense' and 'natural'.

The fifth component of social justice teaching is fostering greater awareness of multicultural group dynamics. Given that students and teachers already enter the classroom space as socially inscribed bodies that in turn have sociohistories that influence how they interact and engage with others in the classroom, attention must be paid to the unique dynamics of a class that will influence *how* subject matter can be taught. For example, my own lectures to undergraduate and postgraduate students on race and racism, gender-based violence and its intersections with social identities of race, gender, class and sexuality have been characterised by different styles of delivery that relate to the unique class composition. It is not possible to teach in the same way to all and have effective and consistent deep engagement with students. The social identities presented within the classroom space require different styles of interaction, a different pitch of the lecture, as well as different practices of disruption. Hackman (2005) notes that class composition should not determine whether a topic, however sensitive, gets discussed. Rather, the task at hand involves being attentive to who we teach and what identities are present in that moment of interaction. CDL encourages a more critical understanding of the concept of 'diversity' than the normative bureaucratic conception that many institutions and business corporations employ (Vertovec, 2014). As an academic project, CDL aims to foster a different way of conceiving what we mean by diversity as well as challenge the meanings that we attach to difference. Social categories of difference are interrogated as part of this critique. The myriad intersections and attachments whereby difference is experienced and reinforced are also interrogated. Critical Diversity Studies endeavours to highlight the intricate ways that difference functions in interrelational, fluid and destabilising ways (Steyn, 2015) such that the complexities of personal and social lives cannot be separated but must be analysed as interwoven components of everyday lives and structural forces in society (Janks, 2002).

## Critical Diversity Literacy: Towards a definition

Steyn (2010, 2015) locates CDL within a paradigmatic orientation, namely Critical Diversity Theory, which has its roots in the critical tradition of the Frankfurt School, as well as in the post-structuralist and postcolonial schools of thought. These schools of thought all espouse the notion of multiple axes of power, by which networks of social relations may be understood as interconnected via differential access to power. Furthermore, social categories of identity such as race, gender, class, sexuality etc. are understood to be fluid and complex configurations that intersect with other categories of identity. An individual never just experiences and navigates the social world in terms of an exclusive identity category, but may often experience contradictory (and harmonious) moments of interpellation with regard to more than one identity marker. For example, race may be salient for an individual in a given context. In a different context, other categories of identification such as gender, sexuality and class may become salient. Yet still in other contexts, all these identities may intersect simultaneously for the person. The multiple axes and intersectional dimensions of difference are thus at the core of a Critical Diversity approach. By this account, this approach engages difference in terms of multiplicity, intersectionality, as well as power axes.

Reading the social world by employing critical thinking and self-reflection requires critical theoretical tools that allow for such an orientation to difference. CDL may thus best be understood as a "reading practice" (Steyn, 2010, p. 54) that enables the individual to read the structures and relations of power and oppression in society. Part of this practice is developing awareness and understanding of the role of hegemonic structures and enactments of power such as whiteness, hegemonic masculinities, heteronormative social orders, and so on. This awareness and understanding in turn must be accompanied by a capacity for deconstruction and interrogation of the ways in which power structures in society may intersect and reinforce each other. It should also include a critical understanding of the sociohistory of oppression and how this history persists in contemporary society (Steyn, 2010).

CDL is a useful theoretical and analytical tool for engaging the personal as interwoven with the political (see, for example, Reygan, Walton & Osman [this volume]). It provides critical language that enables a deconstruction of the constructed configurations of identity categories, difference and social relations that are perceived to be natural and essential. The student of this approach should be able to not only perceive differently, but employ a critical vocabulary that poses questions in search of alternatives to current social realities. CDL is thus important, in that its social justice pedagogical orientation enables work towards a transformed society in which individuals do not accept the oppressive status quo as legitimate and natural.

## Curriculum design

In this section, I elaborate on the CDL course offered at Master's level at the University of the Witwatersrand by the Centre for Diversity Studies. The course is offered over a full year and is facilitated by two different lecturers in the first and second semesters, respectively. The reflections offered here concern the students' interactions and discussions on the course in the second half of the second semester. The course is offered over a thirteen-week period in this half of the academic year. The first seven weeks are devoted to traditional lecture delivery in which I introduce and discuss different themes each week, as well as work with students in preparation for the photo-narrative essay submissions at the end of the course. The last six weeks are devoted to guest lecturer input on different issues from diverse disciplinary fields of study. In the last week, students present their photo-narrative essays to the class and hand in written submissions. Twelve students were enrolled for the course over the period I am examining. Their positionality in terms of work experience in social justice projects as well as subjective locations and identifications was varied. Some students had considerable experience in the areas of transformation within institutions, and in social justice work with sex workers. There was only one male in the cohort of students. The students engaged their personal identity struggles as white, activist, black, African, migrant, and Muslim, as well as with different enactments of subjectification via body weight identity, and 'coconut', or other racial signifiers, in their personal narrative essays. In so doing, they also performed a critically reflexive analysis of linking the personal with the social and political. The course engaged critical readings and theoretical analyses of difference, power and subjectivity such as race, gender and class.

The guest lectures, too, engaged critical discussions on different, multiple and intersecting axes of power and difference, highlighting the constructed nature of identity categories as well as their intersections with other categories of belonging and exclusion. From the beginning of the course, students were introduced to photo-voice methodology, and each week's discussion employed photo-narratives to analyse and interrogate difference. The photo-voice assessment task was structured around the question: *"what does diversity mean to me?"* Students were required to submit a written photo-narrative essay at the end of the course on this topic. One of the core learning outcomes of the course was that students are equipped to think critically about the project of difference within the broader context of the personal and political struggle for social justice. They were also required to demonstrate knowledge and understanding of the nature of the relationship between subjectivities, the subject, the political and the everyday. Finally, students were required to demonstrate understanding of the intersection of structural and subjective oppression as well as demonstrate understanding of the complexities of social transformation.

Following Leibowitz, Bozalek, Carolissen, Nicholls, Rohleder and Swartz (2010), along with Boler and Zembylas (2003), the course adopted a pedagogy of discomfort – which involves the conscious facilitation and nurturing of discomfort as necessary to learning. This facilitation of discomfort must occur within an environment that is not hostile to difference or alternate perspectives. It is the responsibility of the teacher to allow for different perspectives to emerge within the classroom and to work with students towards critically reflecting on their own social situatedness and perspectives, as well as those of others. One could argue that learning and shifts in identity and knowledge are more effectively produced through discomfort. By an environment that is not hostile to difference, I refer to a space where students are able to delve into their unique and collective social identities as part of an intricate and hierarchical system of power. They should be able to do this without a need to sanitise or hide uncomfortable affective dimensions of subjectivity. They should be able to experience epistemological and ontological breaks in deeply entrenched ways of being and doing as part of re-learning. For example, white students should be able to confront their social embodiment in whiteness, engaging the role of affect in constituting racial subjectivities. Such engagement with the affective and material embodiments of our subjectivities is a difficult exercise to undertake. The teacher's task and responsibility here is important as students are never prepared for the emotional task that such an analysis unearths, and the initial response may often be to retreat and dissociate from further reflection and engagement. To counteract this defensiveness, I have worked individually with students who struggle with such personal and social analysis of their lives. The small class size of the cohort enables intimate contact sessions between lecturer and student. These consultations highlight how much of learning about social justice destabilises individuals' sense of comfort and identity. The course becomes almost a kind of journey that is undertaken with intermittent moments of resistance and openness. The students develop emotive relationships with the textual aides used. These responses to texts reveal how the student is experiencing and engaging with their discomfort.

The next section discusses some of the students' reflections on the photo-voice assessment task, highlighting the value of an engaged pedagogy that incorporates dimensions of the affective and subjective domains of teaching for social justice and diversity studies. The thematic reflections engage different dimensions of *recognition, confrontation, re-reading the social* and working through *affective embodied configurations*.

## "I went through life impervious to my difference": *Recognising axes of difference and power*

Moments of recognition and awareness of hegemonic identities and their intersection with symbolic and material resources of power started to feature in the students' reflections on their own identities and positionality. These moments of recognition were underpinned by reflections on a prior disregard for the social significance of difference in whatever form: race, gender, class, sexuality etc. A necessary outcome of engaging CDL is the ability to read and recognise different nexuses of power in society and how these reinforce certain identities as dominant and hegemonic, and others as subordinate. Such awareness is central to the task of understanding how relations of power are maintained in society as well as understanding the more intricate processes and complexities of resistance and transformation. Reflecting on the different moments of her lived experience and sudden confrontation with difference, one Muslim female student[1] noted in her photo-essay:

> I went through life impervious to my difference, consciously unaware of my otherness ... it is a peculiar sensation to realise that one's difference is not celebrated but is granted negative connotations in a world that proclaims to celebrate difference and to grant its citizens the freedom of choice.

Each of the reflections describe this moment of recognition as not only deeply hurtful but also shrouded in a profound sense of disillusionment. This moment makes visible the individual's personal positioning and relation to themselves, and engenders a realisation that one's social locatedness is simultaneously entangled with the Other.

Disillusionment and frustration come about as a result of realising that one's social identity is not only denigrated but also that those re-enactments of identity take place within a social and symbolic order that valorises some identities as dominant and normal. Blackness in the new South Africa is increasingly negotiated in relation to other embodied forms of blackness from the rest of the continent. National citizenship and what it means to be a 'different kind of black' in the post-apartheid context reveal that negotiations and resistances of racialised subjects are made possible by re-essentialising categories of blackness. In reflecting on the racialised meanings of language and identity as a middle-class, educated black female, one student observes:

> With the majority of white people I meet, one of the first things that they comment about is how well I speak and then ask where I am from as the assumption is that I could not be a South African due to my accent and the mastery of the English language. There are times I want to scream and ask if they know that nearly half of the white people in Europe don't speak 'good' English.

The dynamics of a cosmopolitan identity that is not tied down to essentialised and stereotypical meanings of blackness is revealed by new configurations of power and exclusion which emerge within a post-apartheid context. These racial configurations that do not meet the stereotypical social meanings of blackness are experienced as liberating on the one hand, and constraining on the other. The ensuing tensions and conflicts become part of a process of constant re-negotiations of one's ascribed 'foreign' identity in relation to the Other.

Citizenship and what it means to belong is further complicated in another student's reflection on what it means to be 'South African' and to experience deep alienation related to language and identity. Reflecting on the role of language and place as cultural signifiers of belonging, she laments her inability to converse in an indigenous language thus:

> It was expected of me, that when someone asked me *O tswa kae?* (Where do you come from?), *Ko gae ke kae?* (Where is home?) or *O wena mang?* (Who are you?), I should have the ability to confidently answer. But often times, there was great hesitation caused by an anxiety and nervousness with knowing that I could not respond in the language that they spoke but also that I could articulate where home was for me in a single phrase and ultimately that I could not fulfil their expectations.

In my own reflection as part of the group project, I also reflect on this troubled relationship with language and what this means for how I have navigated certain spaces and relationships. As a monolingual black woman, my relationship to language has been marked by internal and external conflict and tension that are tied up with how I make sense of what being black and African means today:

> ... whenever I think of language in a conscious way... I invariably think about community. Exclusions from but also inclusions into particular communities. Some of these communities have excluded me on the grounds that I wasn't black or African enough – whatever these mean. And others I think have accepted me precisely for the same reasons.
> *(Author's own reflections on language and subjectification)*

The micro-politics of belonging and non-belonging remain key sites for thinking about how hegemonic identities, via cultural signifiers of race, class, gender, language and so on, function to maintain constructs of difference as natural. Recognition is simultaneously entangled with intricate processes of surveillance and self-surveillance that further constrain how we view ourselves. Reflecting on her struggle with body weight and beauty ideals of the thin woman, one student captures this tension between awareness and/or recognition and internal psychic state:

> I have always been fat. Bar that year in matric. I have always been soft, no angular edges, little elephant elbows. No delicate birdlike wrist bones, or collar bones, or ribs breaching my surface. I have always been fat... but I have been S T A R V I N G.

This reflection highlights how internalisations of social constructs of difference and hegemonic identities may position us in ways that reinforce feelings of emptiness as well as constant self-surveillance. Recognition of difference and denigration of one's social identity is also fraught with other intersections with social categories that are imbued with valorised forms of cultural capital. These embodiments in turn make it possible to re-signify denigrated identities as desirable at different moments. As one student notes in her reflection:

> I began to understand that, in society there is [sic] certain types of stories [...] that are ascribed to you [...] manipulation in accent could be used as a form of [...] currency in a sense to gain access to certain spaces as well as to be seen as educated and intelligent, hegemonic spaces like the workplace or educational institution. But then also to gain access to non-hegemonic spaces [...] to be seen as a certain type of black.

## "Forceful removal of the veil": *Confronting the Other*

All the reflections discuss interlocking moments of recognition and awareness of difference that are made salient through direct confrontation with the Other. These moments of confrontation with others also become moments of confrontation with oneself in the sense that they comprise a moment of truth in which the individual must (internally) consider particular courses of action. When confronted with hegemonic displays of power and difference, one is left with both a sense of estrangement and realisation that one's difference (and resultant estrangement) can become a site for violent erasure. The following two reflections on recognising and confronting two hegemonic re-enactments of difference illustrate this:

> In 1998, while I was walking with my brother in Mowbray, four black youth approached us and wanted to know why I was always hanging with this "kwerekwere"?[2] They looked at my brother and wanted to know what he was doing with "their women"? We walked away and I asked my brother not to respond. In that moment I realised that because he was darker than me they assumed that I was a South African and he wasn't.
>
> When my younger sister came home after receiving her license I was appalled and shocked to hear that the official had not allowed her to have her photo for the license taken with her head scarf on. Recounting my story I am reminded of a time when Ghandi was asked, by a magistrate, to remove his turban as he sat in a courtroom in Durban. As I think of the comparisons the irony, for me, lies in the fact that this happened twenty years into democracy. I cannot, till today, explain what it was that drove me into a confrontation with officials at the licensing department. After being treated with indifference, my anger would allow me to do anything less than confront a group of male officials. Blind with rage I walked up to them and stated that my Hijaab or the fact that I am a woman did not mean that the laws of the constitution did not apply to me. At that moment, I was no longer me, an individual with my own identity and achievements. Rather, I was the subject of a single story, a victim of history, a sum of the stereotypes which defined me as I stood before this group of men trying to justify my choices and my existence.

These reflections portray the sense of estrangement that is experienced in moments of direct confrontation with the Other based on one's ascribed difference. In both these accounts, difference is constructed and made visible through a racialising lens, and race intersects with other markers of difference such as gender and religion. The accounts highlight the processes of subjectification, and how subjects become nothing more than their physical embodiment of difference and are in turn made to feel inferior and different from the norm. In the first account, the subject engages this recognition but also recognises the strategic import for keeping silent and not engaging with the Other. Also, recognising the interwoven layers of hegemonic masculinities that make it possible to speak of women's bodies as belonging to male persons, the second student reflects on this moment thus: "the notion that as a woman I was 'theirs' is [...] problematic". This process of subjectification illustrates the epistemic violence of representation in which bodies are accorded freedom and legitimacy to *just be* in one's agentic mode of self-presentation and embodiment. This account also highlights the continuous process of negotiating and re-presenting oneself in a world that does not recognise the legitimacy of one's mode of existence, even in so-called mundane configurations such as style of dress. Du Bois (1903) relies on the metaphor of the veil to describe this state of double consciousness of black subjects. Being black for him means living with certain experiences and myths and stereotypes. These myths and experiences have their roots not in individual biology but rather the historically racist society with which one is confronted (Kiguwa, 2014). "The veil" refers simply to the colour line. However, this metaphor is useful for understanding other forms of subjective fragmentation in society that are marked by a sense of looking at oneself through the eyes of the Other. In this case, we can also speak of a metaphorical veil (Kiguwa, 2014).

Engaging the veil also means choosing how we confront the Other. This may mean embracing silence, as in the first account of confrontation, as well as 'playing along' as a strategy of survival. In my own photo-reflection, I discussed my navigation and negotiations of physical and social spaces that become gendered and hegemonic in their reinforcements of heteronormative identities. Navigating social spaces as a black lesbian queer woman, always in confrontation with different practices of the heteronormative social order, means that I negotiate different strategies of capitulation and resistance in my interaction with the symbolic and material world. The ease with which we normalise our everyday moments of violent interactions and identifications is at the heart of the photo-voice methodology. Through forced introspection, students and teachers are forced to confront these normalisations and interrogate others' and our own participation in the everyday. Social enactments of the self and social inequalities are revealed to be so taken for granted that we cease to consider these as violations. Through photo-voice, we are able to re-engage our world in order to tell our stories and account for our participation in that world. In the preceding narrative accounts, a student is forced to confront how she is positioned by others as a Muslim and exercise agency in how she responds to such positioning. Photo-voice methodology demands that we tell the story of our world and ourselves, however uncomfortable this is.

## "It is transformative to see yourself outside... the vision of dominant hegemonic eyes": Re-reading the social

The reflections highlight the tensions and internal conflicts that characterise moments of subjectification and confrontation with the Other. In his elucidation of the veil, Du Bois (1903) argues that this confrontation with the material and metaphoric veil may be the catalyst for further repression and denial of one's subjectification via double consciousness and internalisation of a status quo. On the other hand, it may also be the catalyst for second sight, i.e. a state of consciousness that enables the subject to see and relate to the world with an insight which peers into the intricacies and relations of power within society. Second sight in this sense may function both as a blessing and curse that positions one with the existential tools necessary for transformation and personal and social change, but which can simultaneously heighten one's sense of alienation and distance from the world. For Du

Bois, both the veil and second sight are fundamental to how agency is conceptualised, and to personal and social liberation.

At certain moments and phases of putting together the photo-essays, a grappling with different states of consciousness was evident in how the reflections highlighted tensions of seeing ourselves via a hegemonic social meaning system. At other moments, insight into how our personal experiences and accounts intersected with broader socio-political processes came to the fore. We were thus able to begin conversations about how we could think through the social, and also think through how the social was evident in us. Thus, although our personal and social realities did not necessarily change, a sense of personal transformation was often evident in the accounts and re-telling:

> There comes a time when you realise that no amount of assimilation, hiding, making people feel comfortable about who you are so that they can tolerate you, and no amount of suppression of fear about rejection or not belonging will ever make you less black or less desirable from the eyes of others. You realise that when you imitate or assimilate, what you really are is a cheap imitation of something else. I decided I would rather be an authentic and valuable reality of myself.

Similarly, embracing the veil and one's social ascription as different can be a practice that re-positions the subject at the centre, no longer passive in the face of discrimination and oppression:

> Reclaiming for me is to choose to unapologetically don the Hijaab and to go about my daily life wearing it.... For me it says, "I have a right to live my life as I choose to live without justifying it to ease your fears or misconceptions".

In these moments of reflecting on the social and how deeply woven this is into our lives, the transformative function of agency in how we positioned and re-presented ourselves emerged. The exercise was also a means to thinking about the broader structures and relations of power and the different and often messy entanglements that accompany this. Throughout, students were challenged to think about their moments and positions of subordination as well as their positions of privilege. For example, they might consider what it means to be embodied as a light-skinned black person in a context where xenophobia is primarily directed at dark-skinned individuals, or to experience discrimination in terms of one's body weight and simultaneously to be privileged as a white subject in a racially hierarchical society. They may also consider the ways in which gender intersects with enactments of xenophobic violence, for example foreign-identified black men may be subjected to different and life-threatening forms of violence.

## "This anger has not yet silenced my voice": *Working through affective embodied configurations*

Reflecting on the psychic wounds caused by multiple and continuous processes of subjectification – whether through the lens of race, citizenship, sexuality, religion and culture etc. – the reflective narratives highlighted the importance of affect in how we live our lives and make sense of the social. Teaching social justice in the classroom is not always possible without this engagement with the affective dimensions of identification and subjectification. Engaging with such dimensions is necessary in order to work through the challenges, defences, resistances and feeling of being 'stuck' in key moments and experiences. Another layer of the reflective essays therefore entailed identifying our different affective configurations and re-enactments in thinking about how we are differentially positioned and how we become specific subjects.

Underlining most of the narratives were emotions of shame and anger that exemplified how processes of subjectification are fraught with these emotions. More than this, strategies of defensiveness were evident in how we all engaged with some aspects of the course – whether reading a text or listening to accounts from our peers that challenged our own lived realities and understandings of the world. Thinking critically about our different investments in particular subject positions in our conceptualisations of power and knowledge was also necessary during the course of compiling the photo-essays. Moments of deep anger were present in thinking about different moments of subjectification and the intricate ways that these personal realities are interwoven with symbolic and material structures. The myriad of emotions attests to the complicated and nuanced processes of transformation and assuming agency in how one thinks about the socio-political world.

Interestingly, the importance of acknowledging and working through particular affective states such as shame and anger was seen to be both strategic and useful for change. In some accounts, it is only because of the register of shame that a process of active resistance was made possible. For instance, one student narrated how her sense of personal shame and being shamed by others about her dark skin tone and hair became a catalyst which caused her to embrace a politics of resistance and a postcolonial reading of herself and others. Similarly, the use of anger as a stepping stone to challenging and fighting back against an oppressive order is voiced. Speaking of her sense of frustration and helplessness in the face of oppression and discrimination against herself and others, one student notes: "I am encouraged because this anger has not yet silenced my voice into a sense of apathetic amnesia and justification for why things are as they are."

Similarly, this sense of anger is functional in reclaiming one's personal identity separate from the denigrated social construct:

> In retrospect I can say that it was anger that motivated me to stand up and voice myself when I felt as though my dignity and rights were being impinged on [...]. So yes, my response to the discrimination I felt was anger and I articulated this anger.

Just as I began by paraphrasing Du Bois (1903), I conclude by echoing the sentiments of Lorde (1981). I speak here as a Hijaab-wearing Muslim woman. I am not set upon destruction but upon survival. I have suckled the wolf's lip of anger and I have utilised it for illumination, laughter, protection, fire in places where there was no light, no food, no sisters, and no quarter. I am not a goddess or matriarch, neither am I a fiery finger of judgement or a tool of flagellation. I am a woman forced back on my woman's power. I have learned to use anger and bruised, battered and changing I have survived and grown.

## Conclusion

This chapter has discussed a project of forced introspection in a CDL class that incorporated photo-essays to engage the interconnectedness of personal lives with social structures and relations of power. The reflections highlight the complexities of how we meet each other not only in the classroom but also in the everyday world. While this exercise was useful in thinking about the social more generally, it also provided a platform for understanding how our different social positionalities result in different axes of privilege and oppression. Students were challenged to think about the multiple and layered identities that they embody and how these emerge in different contexts that either reinforce or challenge identities.

Students' resistances, reflections and insights demonstrate educational praxis in ways that have a bearing on how we teach social justice in the classroom. Learning is thus more than a socio-cognitive process but encompasses bodily, emotional, identification and attachments to our positions as social configurations. These configurations are sociohistorical and are imbued with entrenched sociohistories that may impede learning in the present moment. I argue that affect is central to a process of introspection and is necessary to engaging social justice work in the classroom. Emotions and affective states are fundamental to how both students and teachers embrace and/or resist certain knowledges in the classroom and also how we engage with certain texts and listen to the stories of others.

Lastly, these emotions may be important for instilling a sense of indignation at injustice and taking on agentic roles in our personal and social lives. The textual readings prescribed in the course were not always accessible to the students because of the dense theoretical language they sometimes employed. Other readings were inaccessible due to their troubling affective content (many students responded to the emotive dimensions of the Biko and Fanon readings, for example, and other texts triggered deep and perhaps buried emotions of shame and anger and were initially engaged with superficially). Some readings evoked a sense of despair. Others ignited feelings of hope and passion for social justice. For all these reasons, I introduced a process of personal response pieces to each of the readings as a means of engaging and bringing to the fore these emotions. We all set up different relationships to the texts and to different phases of the photo-voice procedure. Some photos evoked memories and stories of resistance, challenges, normalisation of violence, personal agency and so on. Photo-voice methodology allowed for different introspections to emerge within the personal written essays as well as within the classroom. Our introspections were not always welcome, even to ourselves, because it meant confronting and acknowledging unwelcome configurations of ourselves and our relationships to the socio-political world. And yet, these reflections opened up new ways of re-engaging with this world.

## Acknowledgements

To my students in Critical Diversity Literacy: I thank you for the forced introspection.

## Notes

1 Also see www.irtiqa.co.za/she-who-is-veiled/ for the student's blogged reflections on this topic.
2 This is a derogatory term used to refer mainly to African foreigners.

## References

Boler, M., & Zembylas, M. (2003). Discomforting truths: The emotional terrain of understanding difference. In P. Trifonas (Ed.), *Pedagogies of difference: Rethinking education for social change* (pp. 110–136). New York: Routledge.
Bozalek, V., Leibowitz, B., Carolissen, R., & Boler, M. (2013). *Discerning critical hope in educational practices*. New York: Routledge.
Dell, P., & Anderson, I. (2005). Practising critical psychology: Politics, power and psychology departments. *Critical Psychology*, 13, 14–32.
Du Bois, W. E. B. (1903). *The souls of black folk*. Chicago: A. C. McClurg and Co.
Freire, P. (1996). *Pedagogy of the oppressed* (revised edition). New York: Continuum.
Hackman, H. W. (2005). Five essential components for social justice education. *Equity & Excellence in Education*, 38(2), 103–109.
Janks, H. (2002). Critical literacy: Beyond reason. *The Australian Educational Researcher*, 29(1), 7–26.
Kiguwa, P. (2014) 'Telling stories of race: A study of racialised subjectivity in the post-apartheid academy', unpublished Doctoral thesis, University of the Witwatersrand, Johannesburg.
Leibowitz, B., Bozalek, V., Carolissen, R., Nicholls, L., Rohleder, P., & Swartz, L. (2010). Bringing the social into pedagogy: Unsafe learning in an uncertain world. *Teaching in Higher Education*, 15(2), 123–133.
Probyn, E. (2004). Teaching bodies: Affects in the classroom. *Body & Society*, 10(4), 21–43.
Steyn, M. (2010). Critical diversity literacy: Diversity awareness in twelve South African organisations. *Innovative Issues and Approaches in Social Sciences*, 3(3), 50–82.
Steyn, M. (2015). Critical diversity literacy: Essentials for the twenty-first century. In S. Vertovec (Ed.), *Routledge international handbook of diversity studies* (pp. 379–390). London: Routledge.
Vertovec, S. (2014). *Routledge international handbook of diversity studies*. London: Routledge.

# 3

# DECONSTRUCTING HETERONORMATIVITY AND HEGEMONIC GENDER ORDERS THROUGH CRITICAL LITERACY AND MATERIALS DESIGN

A case in a South African school of education

*Navan N. Govender*

## Introduction

On 25 February 2016, I searched for the phrases 'Homophobia in South Africa', 'Transphobia in South Africa', 'Gender violence in South Africa' and 'Gender diversity in South Africa' on Google. I found that 712,000 results appeared for homophobia in South Africa, 119,000 for transphobia, 3,640,000 for gender violence and 5,470,000 for gender diversity. In each case, there was a mix of search results: from online articles and web posts, to blogs and scholarly work. While I did not go through the millions of results individually, their headlines suggested a rather bleak picture of South Africa in relation to issues of sex, gender and sexuality. Terms such as 'violence', 'inequality', 'corrective rape', 'silence' and 'injustice' dominate the pages. From patriarchy to heterosexism, South Africa seems flooded with separatist discourses that use both violence and silence to maintain hegemonic norms.

Statistics South Africa (SSA) has released a report on the ways in which many South Africans see gender. The report *Gender Series Volume II: Education and Gender, 2004–2014* reveals that the majority of the country's citizenry believe that gender and sex are the same (SSA, 2015), and the document only includes the findings related to literacy, access to education and competence of girls and boys. While such reports reveal significant and persistent gender inequalities between South African boys and girls in terms of education, they overlook the range of biological sexes, gender identities and sexual identities that contribute to the lived inequalities of so many South Africans. SSA works with a normative, conflated understanding of sex and gender, and does not provide a report on sexual diversity. There is a profound silence that surrounds gender and sexual diversity in the SSA reports; however, one online article from my Google search did engage with the role of education in dealing with sexed, gendered and sexual diversity: *Homosexuality in South African schools: Still largely a silent taboo* (Davis, 2015).

This article resonated with how I sought to use the design of my own educational materials to deconstruct and reconstruct the hegemonic gendered and sexual order by considering my pedagogical choices and their meaning potential in the literacy classroom, as well as in initial teacher education. This article draws on Bhana's (2015) study *Under Pressure: The Regulation of Sexualities in South African Secondary Schools*, where she outlines the stereotypes and problematic beliefs that are held about lesbian, gay, bisexual, transgender, intersexed, plus (LGBTI+) identities, if indeed they are considered at all. Here, the problem that South Africa faces is not just one of phobia, but also of *difference* and *certainty*.

How South Africans deal with difference, and therefore diversity, influences what social justice might look like in this context. Therefore, methods of engaging with diversity as a resource need to create spaces and conversations that allow South Africans to move beyond preconceived certainties. The classroom can become such a space, and teachers and learners must dare to engage with difficult conversations. In the words of Paolo Freire, "A pedagogy will be that much more critical and radical the more investigative and less certain of 'certainties' it is" (cited in Freire & Macedo, 1987, pp. 358–359). Any critical orientation to teaching and learning is fundamentally about developing awareness. Many influential researchers across the fields of critical theory (Eagleton, 1988; Gramsci, 1975a, 1975b; McLellan, 1977), critical pedagogy (Freire, 1970; hooks, 1994; Kumashiro, 2002), critical literacy (Janks, 2010; Morgan, 2002; Vasquez, 2008) and critical language awareness (Fairclough, 1989, 1992; Halliday, 1976; Janks, 1993) discuss notions of awareness, or consciousness of diverse ways of seeing, doing, thinking and being. As a result, these theoretical perspectives contribute to what it means to be 'critical' by engaging with the relationship between language, literacy and power across contexts.

Critical literacy, an interdisciplinary product of these schools of thought, seeks to engage with the politics of language, literacy and power. It also seeks to develop awareness of the social, political and cultural constructions that govern people across space-time. The approach therefore requires those involved to let go of their certainties, their undeniable truths, and to step out of their own shoes in order to learn alternative ways of seeing. This is easier said than done. In this chapter, I aim to engage with what it means to practise critical literacy, as a teacher-educator and teacher, by focusing on the design of educational materials. Using a workbook that I designed for teaching issues related to sex, gender, sexuality and the conflations between them, I reflect on the processes required for producing critical educational materials. The materials themselves were designed to be copy-ready for use in secondary English classrooms; however, they were also used in a critical literacy course with pre-service English teachers' initial teacher education. It is important to note that gender and sexual diversity is but one controversial topic that needs to be confronted.

I propose the use of 'critical reflexivity' (Elliston, 2005) when analysing pedagogical choices and their effects. This method asks researchers and teachers to consider how their own identities and pedagogical choices affect the collection and analysis of data. To use critical reflexivity when teaching and when designing educational materials, one must become hypervigilant of one's own practices and treat one's own work as the data to be analysed. This is not merely to justify the actions of the teacher-researcher; rather it is a task that entails "locating the 'experiences' about which one writes within fieldwork pragmatics and drawing out their sociocultural insights, theoretical ramifications, and significances" (Elliston, 2005, p. 42). Reflection thus becomes a process for engaging with the ways in which theoretical positions emerge in pedagogical practice. In the sections that follow, I outline my methodology and the theories related to representation and critical literacy in relation to gender and sexual diversity.

## Methodology

The data presented in this chapter includes the copy-ready, activity-based workbook that I designed for secondary English classrooms in South Africa, which was also used to teach a second-year critical literacy course at a Johannesburg university for initial teacher education. Bachelor of Education students who choose English as a major or sub-major are required to take the course. The workbook uses critical literacy to address issues related to sex, gender, sexuality, and the conflations between them in representation as one example of a social issue that can be confronted in classrooms.

Critical reflexivity becomes a tool for qualitatively analysing the workbook in order to theorise my own pedagogical choices and the processes involved in making those choices. Such an analytical tool enables one to step outside one's own practice and evaluate that practice in relation to relevant theory. It is a 'queering' that makes something "strange unto itself" (Elliston, 2005, p. 44) in order to reveal its constructedness. Over and above the reconceptualisation of practice (pedagogy), critical reflexivity also allows one to step out of one's own knowledge base and evaluate one's practice in relation to a framework of knowledge (epistemologies), despite one's own political and cultural positions.

Freire (in Elbaz, 1988) explains that critical reflection is paramount to good teaching, and that teachers need to engage with critically reflective practices in order to develop a pedagogy that is responsive to the socio-cultural contexts that it works in and for:

> Freire speaks of a problem-posing education as a collective process in which participants reflect on their situations, coming to perceive them as 'objective-problematic situations' and acquiring the ability to intervene in reality as they become more aware of them. This process is seen as analogous to the decoding of "an enormous, unique, living 'code' to be deciphered".
> *(Freire, 1970, p. 103 cited in and discussed by Elbaz, 1988, p. 174)*

Turning pedagogy into an 'objective-problematic situation' is not an easy task. It requires asking the questions that matter: Why did I make these choices? Whose interests do I serve through this text/pedagogy? Who do I choose to empower or disempower, and why? Who do I choose to foreground, background or silence? And, what is my text/pedagogy doing to me, my learners and even my context? (adapted from Janks, 1993, p. iii). Answering these critical questions means developing an awareness of how we, as teachers, use pedagogy and text (both its design and selection) to position our lessons, potentially foregrounding our own ideals about education, representation and identity.

Freire discusses three steps involved in making the critically reflexive turn: sympathetic observation, dividing and reintegrating the total situation, and then (re)structuring a programme of educational action (Elbaz, 1988, p. 174). The first step includes observing, identifying and recording a situation as a 'problem' (Elbaz, 1988; Freire & Macedo, 1987). The situation to be reflected on is thereby made into an object for observation and analysis. The second step requires that the observed situation be analysed for contradictions, or 'limit-situations'. The purpose of this step is that any disjuncture between representation (in texts and pedagogy) and the lived experiences of teachers and learners be identified and named. Finally, the third step requires an action to be taken. This means the redesign of texts (Janks, 2005, 2010; New London Group, 2000) or the reconceptualisation of pedagogy in order to engage better with cultural context. Here, teachers and learners are required to take their learning, unlearning and relearning of reality and use it to transform their limit-situations. For materials design, this step means redesigning materials in more socially just and responsive ways that are conscious of new or alternative ways of thinking, new knowledge, new experiences and realities.

In the following sections, I present a summary of my workbook by making reference to the theories related to critical literacy as well as those related to sex, gender and sexual identity in representation. Thereafter, I critically reflect on the processes involved in producing the workbook. In this section, I consider the role of text selection, content and pedagogy in materials design by mapping out the decisions that I had to make and correct as I designed the workbook.

## The workbook

The workbook that I designed for use in secondary schools as well as in a critical literacy course for pre-service teachers comprises four main sections: 'Language', 'Policing and Subversion', '(Re)Design', and 'Social Impact'. Each section identifies a general theme or process linked to *doing* critical literacy (Janks, 2010; Janks et al. 2013). That is, it follows a process of deconstructing current texts and representations, looking at the positioning power of texts, as well as alternative representations, transforming normative representations, and finally developing an awareness of the social impact that language and representation has on socio-cultural circumstance and experience (Janks, 2014; Janks et al., 2013). Throughout the workbook, a variety of gendered and sexual identities are explored: from heterosexuality and hegemonic cisgender types, to gay and lesbian identities, to bisexual and transgender identities that are often sidelined in even the queerest of spaces.

## Language

The words we employ to speak about sex, gender and sexuality can be slippery. Over time, words shift in connotation as a result of shifting socio-cultural circumstances and power relations (Barthes, 1957; Freire & Macedo, 1987; Janks, 2010). The objective in this first section of the workbook is to consider what language we use to speak about sex, gender and sexuality, and how the meanings of those words have been conflated in various ways, across languages and the cultures and ideologies that inform them. This involves taking into consideration how speaking about men and women might actually mean speaking about masculinities and femininities, what it means to name gender nonconforming people, and which identities have not been named in a language. Engaging with language critically therefore means unpacking what language reveals about who matters.

## Policing and subversion

In the second section of my workbook, I focus on how the language of policing, heteronormativity and compulsory heterosexuality is used "to examine heterosexuality as a political institution which disempowers women" (Rich, 1993, p. 227) as well as people who identify as Lesbian, Gay, Bisexual, Transgender, Intersex, Plus (LGBTI+). This section thus seeks to promote practices that are "critical of privileging and Othering" (Kumashiro, 2002, p. 44). Moreover, this section also looks at occurrences of subversion (Butler, 1993, 2006) as ways of expanding imagination beyond prescriptive gender performance.

## (Re)Design

In the third section of the workbook, I have chosen to move from abstract discussions on heterosexuality, heteronormativity and compulsory heterosexuality to more specifically observable instances of power relations. It begins with an analysis of a common restroom sign that is normative in every way: there are two figures (male and female), two colours (pink and blue), and markers of differentiation (the dress and shoulder width). The question is whether these are representations of sex, gender or sexuality or a conflation of them. Furthermore, users of these materials are asked to conceptualise what gender-neutral restroom signs might look like, and how these redesigns position readers in new ways.

## Social impact

Any critical approach to education aims to be socially transformative (Janks, 2010; Kumashiro, 2002; Morrell, 2008; Morgan, 2002; Vasquez, 2008). The same is true of a critical literacy pedagogy, in which the idea of social impact is worked with in two main ways: first, it is understood that every text is positioned and positioning. Therefore, every text works to position its readers and to influence their ways of thinking about the world. Second, texts and their meanings can lead to a range of social responses such as anti-homophobia movements, or organisations bent on preserving 'traditional marriage' as between a man and a woman.

## Processes of production

Following Giroux's (1987) understanding of literacy work in education, I have aimed to construct the workbook from the understanding that:

> ...literacy [has] to be viewed as a social construction that is always implicated in organizing one's view of history, the present and the future; furthermore, the notion of literacy [needs] to be grounded in an ethical and political project that [dignifies] and [extends] the possibilities for human life and freedom.
> *(Giroux in Freire & Macedo, 1987, p. 2)*

However, in order to construct a workbook that organises views of history, normativity and critically deconstructive practices, a number of processes need to occur. From brainstorming and experimentation to the exploration and application of different theoretical approaches, I have been involved in several processes that informed and influenced my design choices for the workbook.

In an attempt to understand the processes of production (Fairclough, 1989, 1992) of my workbook, I have mapped my own design process from initial conception to final product. Thereafter, I have used this map as a framework for discussing some of the defining decisions that I had to make within each of these phases and continuing processes:

The term 'processes' connotes ongoing activity; however, Figure 3.1 illustrates that within the overall process of production there are three main phases, with two

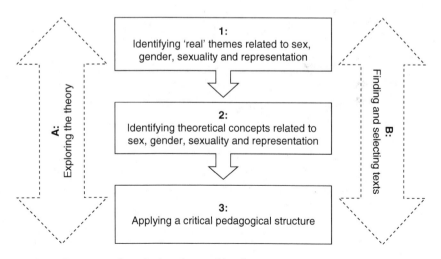

**FIGURE 3.1** Processes of producing the workbook

continuous processes alongside. Here, I understand the term 'phase' to represent defining parts of the overall process that end or are transformed to give rise to a new phase. There are three main phases: 1. Identifying 'real' themes; 2. Identifying theoretical concepts; and 3. Applying a critical pedagogical structure. Each phase led onto the next until the final workbook was produced. It is possible that more phases could be added in relation to the intentions of the designer over and above the constant need to review and redesign texts (Janks, 2005, 2010). What is important to note, then, is that these three main phases were influenced, even directed, by my simultaneous and ongoing engagement with theories related to sex, gender, sexuality and representation ('A' in Figure 3.1) and the everyday texts that represent these theoretical perspectives ('B'). These two processes locate my workbook, and me, in a theoretical and social context.

## Identifying 'real' themes

Often what is thought of as normal is something that has been *made* more apparent through repetition – I am constantly bombarded with sexualised texts when I wake (clock radios blaring news reports or radio-hosts' discussions on celebrity gender performance), while making my way to work (billboards looming over high-density streets and highways advertising elusive products hiding behind beautiful, intertwined and oppositely sexed bodies), and when I come home (where television shows present nuclear families and the heteronormative promiscuity of their children). And this is just one example of my middle-class South African experience, in which I need to look, and look carefully, to find truly subversive representations – or, at the very least, equitable representations of the categories I inhabit as a gay, male, Indian, twenty-something academic in South Africa. What is significant to note through this daily journey is the presence of sexualised materials that have become commonplace. More significantly, however, are the power relations between genders (Connell, 1995) and the silencing of non-heterosexual identities or practices (Rich, 1993) that is evident throughout these taken-for-granted texts. This is a kind of social policing that confines human imagination to patriarchal and heteronormative tidiness.

It was easiest, then, to begin by locating texts for analysis. From these texts, a normative representation could be identified (Janks, 2014) which could be deconstructed to help both (student) teachers and learners understand the various ways in which normativity and socialisation work through language. The following extract comes from a section in the workbook on families that was designed during this phase:

In this section, it is the family restroom sign that identifies 'families' as a topic for the workbook. This is a highly sexual topic; normatively and historically, families have come to represent units for reproduction and are therefore 'naturally' heterosexual (Dasgupta, 2000 in Connell & Messerschmidt, 2005; Goode, 1982). I have made definite choices regarding what kinds of imagery to use, taking into account how visible sexual attraction or intimacy are made in the workbook. It is not that I chose between images with sexual intercourse and those without; rather that the decision considered certain, everyday intimacies: holding hands, kissing, hugging, and gazing. Because the workbook is intended for secondary classrooms, I chose representations that I considered 'appropriate' for adolescent learners, which was conflated with my fears of what *might* be considered inappropriate by teachers and parents.

For example, one text that I use in the critical literacy course with student teachers, and not in the workbook, is an online post by an unknown author. It shows three greyscale Kodak photographs. All the images are of couples (one opposite-sex couple and two same-sex couples) photographing themselves in a mirror while kissing. These images are a parody of normative texts that only represent heterosexual acts of intimacy as publicly acceptable. These images are anchored by the text: "i'm sorry but i can't see the difference". While this text is not pornographic, I still found myself fearing how learners and teachers might respond to same-sex intimacy. I used the image in lectures with pre-service teachers, alongside the workbook. Such issues of risk and safety need to be considered and more questions need to be asked about what risks might be necessary in the classroom or in teacher education, and how safety might reproduce problematic norms (Govender, 2017).

While elements of the section from the workbook presented in Figure 3.2 might be useful, it does still contain some fundamental design flaws which are

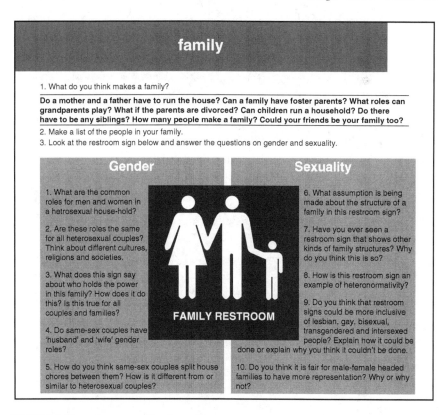

**FIGURE 3.2** Phase 1 extract: Family

characteristic of other sections constructed during this design phase. These flaws are largely due to a lack of theoretical cohesion: firstly, the activities do not always reflect the theory effectively and thus cover the content on sex, gender and sexuality by focusing on 'feelings' rather than informed criticism. Secondly, theory is sometimes incomplete, which means that the links between activities and theory can be haphazard. Although it was useful to begin designing my critical literacy workbook by situating it in authentic, recognisable topics, this was not nearly enough. These topics and ideas for activities further needed to be situated in sound theoretical approaches and understandings.

## *Identifying theoretical concepts*

Theories on sex, gender and sexuality constitute a vast terrain of knowledge and perspectives. Compounding this are theories of power, of semiotics and the functions of language and representation, as well as a myriad of pedagogical approaches and theories on what it means to take a critical stance in education. These theories can be combined in different ways to construct critical literacy curriculums (Ferreira, 2009; Janks, 2010; Janks et al., 2013; Kumashiro, 2002). However, bringing these fields of study together also allows us as teachers, learners and students to ask the right kinds of questions about texts, everyday interactions, and the ways we construct ourselves and others through language.

It is imperative that educational practice be located in sound theoretical understandings of the world and ways to be in it. This second phase therefore involved reconsidering my initial designs through various theoretical lenses. Deciding what theory to draw on and what texts to use, and when, became a process of compromise. Some texts are only useful for illustrating one theoretical concept, and while some theories include important concepts, it is difficult to find an authentic text that is appropriate for the classroom. I therefore began to realise that design involves negotiation between text, theory and interest.

In the initial design of the workbook, sections were delineated according to what I identify as 'real themes'. However, theories on sex, gender, sexuality and representation name concepts in different ways. Constructing theory-driven materials rather than theme-based materials is useful for a critical literacy approach. Once a concept is taught, students should begin to apply it to their own lives to bring real and relevant issues back into the classroom (Vasquez, 2000, 2001). I therefore began to reorganise the activities in the workbook using theoretical concepts as my guide, moving, adding and removing activities according to the knowledge and skills I thought learners would need. Thus emerged the four sections of the workbook: 'Language', 'Policing and Subversion', '(Re)Design', and 'Social Impact'.

Theory did not just influence how I separated sections and main ideas. It also influenced how I understood sex, gender and sexuality in relation to gender performance, power and representation. As this understanding changed, so too did the content that I wanted to include and the ways in which I represented that content. For example, in the first section of the workbook, *Language*, I was determined to present students with a visual representation of the relationships between sex, gender and sexuality that moved beyond cisgender and heteronormative models. Drawing on queer theory's agenda to dispose of essentialised binaries (Jagose, 1996), I began designing a model for thinking about sex, gender and sexuality, and the conflations between them. This model, most importantly, also needed to be flexible enough to include a vast array of (nonconforming) identities.

From Butler's (2006) gender performance to the more empirical research by Tucker (2009), Gevisser and Cameron (1994), and Msibi (2014), scholars have revealed the myriad of gendered and sexual identities across the globe, and in South Africa. Engaging with this scholarship required that I *un*learn my own gendered language that came so easily, and which also sternly resisted change. This engagement also involved the use of identities, and the language(s) used to express those identities, that are particular to a South African context (Francis & Msibi, 2011; Luyt, 2012; Msibi, 2012, 2014; Tucker, 2009). The following figures show the progression of the way I mapped sex, gender and sexuality in order to come to terms with them and their conflations. Next to each diagram, I have given a rationale for their construction, and the shifts in representation:

Diagrams in chronological order:

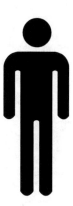

**FIGURE 3.3** The universal man

1.

Initially, I started with the 'universal man' concept. In deconstructing this symbol, I wanted students to recognise the presence of male dominance in representation, that it establishes an 'original' gender, of which femininity is a copy, as well as an 'original' sexuality, where homosexuality and bisexuality are constructed as distorted copies of an authentic heterosexuality (Butler, 1993). However, this does not map sex, gender and sexuality.

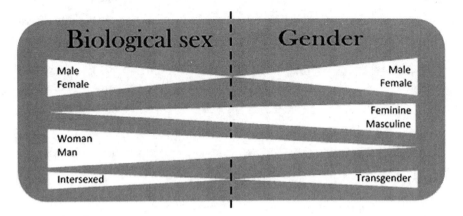

**FIGURE 3.4** Sex/gender model

2.

I then tried to separate the concepts by categorising them according to 'biological sex' and 'gender'. In order to represent the conflation in which words for gender are used to signify biological sex, I used the tapering effect given by the triangles in the diagram. I imagined that meanings could be stretched and pulled into new spaces while still holding on to their original denotations. Words that refer to biological sex had been pulled and conflated with gender while still maintaining some sense of their original reference to sex.

However, there are two significant problems with this representation. Firstly, it neglects any representation of sexuality, and secondly, this representation essentialises the identities that it does include. There are only three distinct sexes and two genders, and a representation of transgenderism that negates its diversity.

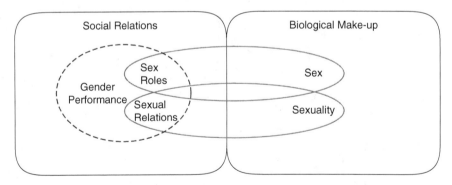

**FIGURE 3.5** The interactions between Foucault's (1984) *Social Relations and Sexual Relations* being enacted through Butler's (2006) *Gender Performance* (Reproduced)

3.

This representation is based on Foucault's (1984) theorisation of the interaction between social relations and sexual relations (see Spargo, 1999), as well as Butler's

(2006) theory of gender performance. I aimed to show in this diagram how our social relations are influenced by our sexuality, and vice versa. That is, the socio-cultural value systems that govern our sexual relations can be transposed onto our social relations. We see this in the condemnation of celebrities who come out as gay in controversial ways, such as Caster Semenya, or in the serious stigmatisation of early childhood teachers who come out as gay or lesbian. But, this representation is still insufficient. It still maintains the binary between the biological and the social. It also misrepresents sexual relations as a form of gender performance, maintaining a problematic conflation.

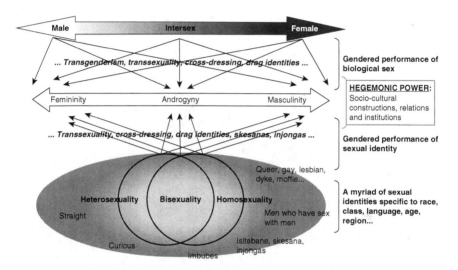

**FIGURE 3.6** The identity gem – mapping sex, gender and sexual identities

4.

The final model for representing sex, gender and sexuality is the 'identity gem'. It encompasses sex as a continuum but also includes biological variations in sexed identities such as intersex. Gender, too, is rendered as a continuum, and spans masculinity, femininity and androgyny. Finally, sexuality, which includes interconnections between and beyond heterosexual, bisexual and homosexual identities, is represented within a cloud of self-identified sexualities by different communities. The spaces between these categories signify the gendered performance of either sex or sexuality. They are socially and culturally bound practices, and the deviances from those practices, that make sexed and sexualised identities (in)visible. However, it is also within this space of gender performance that the gendered hegemonies of our time, place and culture police identities. Furthermore, transgenderism, transsexuality, cross-dressing, drag, skesana (active sexual partner) and injonga (passive sexual partner) identities have been included as possible gendered performances of sexual identity.

## Applying a critical pedagogical structure

The structure and sequencing of the workbook emerged from the relationship between social justice and educational praxis. That is:

> How can teachers work together in the interests of developing critical subjectivity among themselves and their students that can begin to rehabilitate the pathological development of homophobic discourses in current school policy and practice? Further, how can teachers and students develop a collective praxis that takes up in a politically charged and pedagogically progressive way the contradiction between social relations of homosexuality and the social form of "alterity" (one's relationship to the "other")?
>
> *(McLaren, 1995, p. 109)*

Such questions are not new. They have manifested in response to various forms of injustice with regard to race, class, language and gender. Education bent on social justice should not fixate on theoretical possibilities of equity, but on the development of critical and socially equitable *practice*. This is evident in one example from the workbook that was discussed with the pre-service teachers in the critical literacy course. In this example, a McDonald's (2013) advert was used in conjunction with a series of questions. These questions, posed to learners in the workbook and discussed with the pre-service teachers in the university course, have been constructed using Fairclough's (1989) model for critical discourse analysis. Fairclough (1989, 1992) distinguishes between 'Description', 'Interpretation' and 'Explanation' as interrelated parts of the critical discourse analysis process. Each part is also known as 'Text', 'Processes of production and reception', and 'Conditions of production and reception', respectively, which are represented diagrammatically as three boxes set within each other. Each box, or part of the critical analysis process, represents an overarching idea about texts and how they work as positioning constructions. From a concern with the text itself, to meaning-making processes when producing and reading the text, to the socio-cultural situatedness of the text itself and the meanings made available by the context, this model allows us to construct questions that pertain not only to the text but also to how texts work in society and in relation to power. Table 3.1 illustrates how Fairclough's (1989) model was used to apply a critical pedagogical structure:

Students move from dealing with the text (scene-by-scene) to thinking about authorship and readership as well as context and social impact. For example, in the first scene, which comprises two frames, students have to begin reading the text by identifying what is taking place and where it takes place. They then move onto answering a question on how they relate to the meanings that these first two questions pose, and then finally considering the positioning power of the text. Similarly, concepts such as Rich's (1993) compulsory heterosexuality and McCarl Nielson, Walden & Kunkel's (2000) gender violations have been used to create sections and activities in the workbook.

**TABLE 3.1** Applying a critical pedagogical structure

| Frame number as it appears in the workbook. | Questions from the workbook on the McDonald's (2013) 'come as you are' advertisement: |
|---|---|
| *Text: Description* | |
| 1–2 | Where does this scene take place? How do you know? |
| 3–6 | What is the boy looking at? |
| 14–15 | Who is the boy talking to? How do you know? |
| | Is this slogan a command, statement or question? |
| *Processes of Production & Reception: Interpretation* | |
| 1–2 | Is this scene easy to relate to? |
| 3–6 | Are you making an assumption? Explain. |
| 7 | What kind of relationship does the boy have with the person on the phone? |
| 8–10 | |
| 11–13 | What evidence do you have to support your answer? |
| 14–15 | What is the effect of 'silencing' the voice on the phone? |
| | Why do you think the boy has to hang up? What does this suggest about his relationship with the person on the phone? Describe what you think a 'ladies' man' is. |
| | How is the father's speech in frame 12 an example of heteronormativity? Do you think the father realises he is excluding gay, lesbian and bisexual people? |
| | What does the boy's facial expression in frame 13 suggest about what he thinks about his father's comments? |
| | What effect does this have on you as the reader? |
| *Conditions of Production & Reception: Explanation* | |
| 1–2 | What do you think this advert is trying to do to you (or make you think)? |
| 8–10 | |
| 8–10 | Do your parents/guardians or older siblings often compare you to themselves? Why do you think people do this? |
| 11–13 | |
| 14–15 | Why would the father boast about being a 'ladies' man'? What does it say about the kind of man he is? What does it say about the kind of man he would want his son to be? How do you think a 'ladies' man' would view women? |
| | What power/authority do women have against this kind of man? |
| | Who is being foregrounded and who is being silenced? What assumption could the father be making about romantic relationships in schools? |
| | What, then, does McDonald's want you to think about their restaurant? |
| | This advert was aired in France. Find out about the rights for gay, lesbian, bisexual, transgender and intersexed people in France at the time the advert was aired. Do you think this could be aired in South Africa? Why or why not? |
| | Go to www.youtube.com/user/TheYoungTurks to find out how some Americans responded to this advert. |

It is imperative to place knowledge and skills development in any educational setting, from the classroom to the lecture theatre, into theoretical perspective. Such perspectives enable particular kinds of text selection, topic analysis and questioning. Choosing to apply a critical pedagogical structure enables teachers, and eventually their learners, to ask the critical questions of power, as well as attempt to answer them.

## Conclusion

The need for critical literacy education is well documented (Janks, 1993; Janks et al., 2013). However, the design of critical educational materials to support teachers and practice is also a vital project. As such, it is important to think carefully about how these materials are designed in order to do critical literacy and transform literacy education. In this chapter, I have outlined some perspectives on critical literacy as well as the theories related to sex, gender, sexuality and the conflations between them as one example of a social justice issue for classrooms. I then critically reflected on the design process of a workbook I designed by mapping out the pedagogical decisions I made, unmade and remade during its production.

Importantly, critical reflexivity also takes consideration of "the dialectical relationship between reflection and action" (Elbaz, 1988, p. 178):

> To the extent that a teacher is able to analyse the situation in depth and perceive its inherent contradictions, [his/her] ability to act to change that situation is enhanced. But insofar as [he/she] sees no options for action that will bring about change, [his/her] very ability to perceive the situation will in turn be limited.
>
> *(Elbaz, 1988, p. 178)*

Elbaz's (1988) discussion of the limits of reflective work in teaching suggests the need to recognise that all designs and redesigns are both positioned and positioning (Janks, 2010). Over time, new texts and representations will become available, and old ones will become history. The need to engage in critical reflection and (re)design is thus a continuous one. It goes hand-in-hand with the need to constantly reimagine social contexts and political concerns. Therefore, design processes are continuous, where teachers design curriculums, teach, reflect, redesign, teach, reflect, and so on. Perhaps, then, a print-based workbook is not enough to engage with this process. Rather, an online, participatory format would be more appropriate. Furthermore, initial teacher education must engage pre-service teachers with critical reflexivity as a practice. This would include the critical analysis of educational materials as a concrete method for engaging with the need for continual (re)design of teaching practice, resources, contexts, identities, and even epistemologies. The fluidity of knowledge and what it means to teach and learn should be embodied in the very changeability of teaching practice and thought.

# References

Barthes, R. (1957). *Mythologies*. 1972. Trans. A. Lavers. New York: Hill and Wang, 302–306.

Bhana, D. (2015). *Under Pressure: The Regulation of Sexualities in South African Secondary Schools*. Braamfontein, South Africa: Modjaji Books.

Butler, J. (1993). Imitation and Gender Insubordination. In H. Abelove, M. Aina Barale & D. M. Halperin (Eds.). *The Lesbian and Gay Studies Reader* (pp. 307–320). New York & London: Routledge.

Butler, J. (2006). *Gender Trouble*. New York: Routledge Classics.

Connell, R. W. (1995). *Masculinities*. Sydney: Allen & Unwin.

Connell, R. W. & Messerschmidt, J. W. (2005). Hegemonic Masculinity: Rethinking the Concept. *Gender and Society*, 19(6), 829–859.

Davis, R. (2015). *Homosexuality in South African Schools: Still Largely a Silent Taboo*. Retrieved from *The Daily Maverick* website: www.dailymaverick.co.za/article/2015-02-17-homosexuality-in-south-african-schools-still-largely-a-silent-taboo/

Eagleton, T. (1988). *Against the Grain: Selected Essays*. London & New York: Verso.

Elbaz, F. (1988). Critical Reflection on Teaching: Insights from Freire. *Journal of Education for Teaching*, 14(2), 171–181.

Elliston, D. (2005). Critical Reflexivity and Sexuality Studies in Anthropology: Siting Sexuality in Research, Theory, Ethnography, and Pedagogy. *Reviews in Anthropology*, 34(1), 21–47.

Fairclough, N. (1989). *Language and Power*. London: Longman.

Fairclough, N. (Ed.). (1992). *Critical Language Awareness*. London: Longman Group UK Limited.

Ferreira, A. (2009). Reading Pictures. In A. Ferreira (Ed.). *Teaching Language in the South African Classroom* (Chapter 14). Braamfontein: Macmillan.

Foucault, M. (1984/1992). *The History of Sexuality: An Introduction*. Trans. R. Hurley. Harmondsworth: Penguin Books.

Francis, D. & Msibi, T. (2011). Teaching about Heterosexism: Challenging Homophobia in South Africa. *Journal of LGBT Youth*, 8(2), 157–173.

Freire, P. (1970). *Pedagogy of the Oppressed*. Trans. M. Bergman Ramos. New York: Continuum.

Freire, P. & Macedo, D. (1987). Rethinking Literacy: A Dialogue. In A. Darder, M. Gevisser, & E. Cameron (Eds.) (1994). *Defiant Desire*. Johannesburg: Ravan Press.

Gevisser, M. & Cameron, E. (1994). *Defiant Desire*. Johannesburg: Ravan Press.

Goode, W. (1982). Why Men Resist. In B. Thorne and M. Yalom. (Eds.). *Rethinking the Family: Some Feminist Questions*. New York: Longman.

Govender, N. N. (2017). The Pedagogy of Coming Out: Teacher Identity in a Critical Literacy Course. *South African Review of Sociology*, 48(1), 19–41.

Gramsci, A. (1975a). *Prison Notebooks: Volume I*. In J. A. Buttigieg (Ed.) (1992). Trans. J. A. Buttigieg and A. Callari. New York: Columbia University Press.

Gramsci, A. (1975b). *Prison Notebooks: Volume II*. In A. Buttigieg (Ed.) (1996). Trans. J. A. Buttigieg and A. Callari. New York: Columbia University Press.

Halliday, M. A. (1976). *System and Function in Language: Selected Papers* (ed. G. Kress). Oxford: Oxford University Press.

hooks, b. (1994). *Teaching to Transgress: Education as the Practice of Freedom*. New York: Routledge.

Jagose, A. (1996). *Queer Theory: An Introduction*. New York: New York University Press.

Janks, H. (Ed.). (1993). *Critical Language Awareness Series*. Johannesburg: Witwatersrand University Press and Hodder & Stoughton Educational Southern Africa.

Janks, H. (2005). Deconstruction and Reconstruction: Diversity as a Productive Resource. *Discourse: Studies in the Cultural Politics of Education*, 26(1), 31–43.

Janks, H. (2010). *Literacy and Power*. New York: Routledge.

Janks, H., Dixon, K., Ferreira, A., Granville, S. & Newfield, D. (2013). *Doing Critical Literacy: Texts and Activities for Students and Teachers*. London: Routledge.

Janks, H. (2014). Critical Literacy's Ongoing Importance for Education. *Journal for Adolescent and Adult Literacies*, 57(5), 349–356.

Kumashiro, K. (2002). *Troubling Education: Queer Activism and Antioppressive Pedagogy*. New York & London: Routledge.

Luyt, R. (2012). Constructing Hegemonic Masculinities in South Africa: The Discourse and Rhetoric of Heteronormativity. *Gender and Language*, 6(1), 47–77.

McCarl Nielson, J., Walden, G. & Kunkel, C. A. (2000). Gendered Heteronormativity: Empirical Illustrations in Everyday Life. *The Sociological Quarterly*, 21(2), 283–296.

McDonald's. (2013). *Come As You Are*. Banned television advertisement. Retrieved from YouTube: www.youtube.com/watch?v=bUekXg_tK2M

McLaren, P. (1995). Moral Panic, Schooling, and Gay Identity: Critical Pedagogy and the Politics of Resistance. In G. Unks (Ed.). *The Gay Teen: Educational Practice and Theory for Lesbian, Gay, and Bisexual Adolescents*. New York & London: Routledge.

McLellan, D. (1977). *Karl Marx: Selected Writings*. Oxford: Oxford University Press.

Morgan, W. (2002). *Critical Literacy in the Classroom: The Art of the Possible*. New York: Routledge.

Morrell, E. (2008). *Critical Literacy and Urban Youth: Pedagogies of Access, Dissent, and Liberation*. New York & Abingdon: Routledge.

Msibi, T. (2012). 'I'm used to it now': Experiences of Homophobia among Queer Youth in South African Township Schools. *Gender & Education*, 24(5), 515–533.

Msibi, T. (2014). The Teaching of Gender & Sexuality Diversity Issues to Pre-Service Teachers at the University of KwaZulu-Natal: Lessons from Student Exam Responses. *Alternation Special Edition*, 12, 385–410.

New London Group. (2000). A Pedagogy of Multiliteracies: Designing Social Futures. In B. Cope and M. Kalantzis (Eds.). *Multiliteracies*. London: Routledge.

Retief, G. (1994). Keeping Sodom out of the Laager. In M. Gevisser and E. Cameron (Eds.). *Defiant Desire*. Johannesburg: Ravan Press.

Rich, A. (1993). Compulsory Heterosexuality and Lesbian Existence. In H. Abelove, M. Aina Barale & D. M. Halperin (Eds.). *The Lesbian and Gay Studies Reader*. New York & London: Routledge.

Spargo, T. (1999). *Foucault and Queer Theory*. Cambridge: Icon Books.

Statistics South Africa (SSA). (2015). *Gender Series Volume II: Education and Gender, 2004–2014*. Pretoria: Statistics South Africa.

Tucker, A. (2009). *Queer Visibilities: Space, Identity and Interaction in Cape Town*. Oxford: Wiley-Blackwell.

Vasquez, V. (2000). Our Way: Using the Everyday to Create a Critical Literacy Curriculum. *National Council of Teachers of English*, 9(2), 8–14.

Vasquez, V. (2001). Constructing a Critical Curriculum with Young Children. In B. Comber and A. Simpson (Eds.). *Negotiating Critical Literacies in Classrooms*. Mahwah, New Jersey & London: Lawrence Erlbaum Associates, Publishers.

Vasquez, V. (2008). *Negotiating Critical Literacies with Young Children*. New York & London: Routledge.

# 4

# THE ROLE OF DEVELOPING PRE-SERVICE TEACHERS' PEDAGOGICAL REASONING TO SUPPORT CONTEXTUALLY RESPONSIVE TEACHING

*Lee Rusznyak and Alfred Masinire*

## Introduction

In South Africa, like many other countries in the global South, pre-service teachers come from vastly diverse communities. After graduation, these teachers then secure employment in a wide range of schooling contexts. It is thus imperative that by the time they qualify, pre-service teachers are able to teach in diverse contexts. For them to respond in pedagogically appropriate ways within the possibilities and constraints of different contexts, learning about and for pedagogic responsiveness needs to be considered as an essential part of the professional development that pre-service teachers undertake. In this chapter we argue that in order for pre-service teachers to foster the pedagogic reasoning necessary to teach in diverse contexts, programmes need to construct multiple opportunities for pedagogic reasoning that prompt pre-service teachers to consider the implications of context in relation to their developing levels of content and pedagogic knowledge.

## Cultural sensitivity, contextual responsiveness and learning to teach

In the global North there is a large body of research documenting various approaches to preparing teachers for contextually responsive teaching (e.g. Goodwin, 1997; Becket, 1998; Littleton, 1998; Sleeter, 2001). Most of these studies focus on promoting culturally sensitive teaching in contexts where prospective teachers are of a different race, linguistic background, religion, culture and/or socio-economic background from the learners they teach. In one influential study, Villegas and Lucas (2002) provide a framework which describes salient features of a culturally responsive teacher so as to centre diversity issues in teacher education. They argue that teachers should possess a socio-cultural consciousness that enables them to hold affirming views of learners from diverse backgrounds, have the capacity to use their knowledge about learners to support and extend their knowledge construction, and be committed to being agents of change who will make schools increasingly responsive to all learners. While this body of literature provides a useful framework to think about learning to teach in culturally responsive ways, much of this literature considers the preparation of White, English-speaking, female and middle-class pre-service teachers to teach learners of different racial, ethnic and/or socio-economic backgrounds within the American context. Very little research considers the preparation of teachers whose biographical backgrounds are often similar to those of the learners they teach, but who are expected to have the capacity to teach diverse learners in widely varying contexts.

Two of the dominant approaches informing the conceptualisation of pre-service teacher education programmes hold very different implications for how pre-service teachers should develop contextually responsive teaching practices (Matsko & Hammerness, 2014; Rusznyak, 2016). Preparing teachers using a *contextually specific approach* (geared towards particular contexts, such as rural-based schools) assumes that some contextual differences are so pedagogically significant that the set of knowledge and skills required are fundamentally different from those needed by teachers who teach in any other school setting. This stance is located in a wider philosophical position that insists that teaching practices are so contextually embedded that they cannot be imagined, studied and developed outside of the context in which they happen (Carr, 2006).

The concept of place-conscious pedagogies is often used as a framework for thinking about how place influences peoples' identities and lived experiences (Gruenewald, 2003). The concept of place, it is argued, needs to form a central construct in teacher education programmes, along with related concepts, such as rurality, which should be understood historically, politically, and on its own terms, and not as having deficits in relation to urban contexts (Moletsane, 2012). Advocates of this approach argue for a rural education that provides hope and possibility, and contend that quality education "should fit rural people to a rural future through orientating curricula more closely to community needs" (HSRC, 2005, p. 141). They thus argue that there are strong urban biases in most pre-service teacher education curricula, and hence teachers are seldom taught to link general concepts within the curricula to locally specific issues and concerns (e.g. Balfour, Mitchell & Moletsane, 2008; Mukeredzi & Mandrona, 2013). It is argued that this compromises teachers' ability to be pedagogically responsive within non-urban school contexts. While some call for specialised curricula and teacher education programmes that focus specifically on the realities of rural communities, others argue that such a narrow contextual emphasis will ultimately further marginalise already vulnerable communities (Gardiner, 2008).

A decontextualised approach to teacher education emphasises teaching as a practice with shared conceptual knowledge, which in turn informs choices undergirded by an understanding that contextual and learner responsiveness is required of every teacher (Gonzalez, McIntyre & Rosebery, 2001). In this approach, pre-service teacher education curricula are designed around powerful ideas that enable prospective teachers to work productively within the challenges and the opportunities in diverse contexts in which they may teach. Darling-Hammond (1997) for example, regards the sine qua non of education to be "whether teachers know how to make complex subjects accessible to diverse [learners]" (p. 294). Good teaching is characterised by a pedagogic responsiveness to learner diversity and works within the possibilities of the contextual reality. Proponents of contextually responsive approaches to pre-service teacher education argue that the particularities of local contextual knowledge can be acquired relatively quickly in situ through experience and community engagement. However, the non-intuitive insights that decontextualised education theory provides cannot be acquired through experience, and are most effectively acquired through formal study (Rusznyak, 2015). Furthermore, there is such vast variation within and between schools that are regarded as 'rural' or 'urban' that it would be impossible to prepare teachers for every contextual eventuality, given that upon qualification, teachers from the same programme find employment in vastly different schooling contexts.

It is our contention that a binary opposition between contextually specific and decontextualised approaches to pre-service teacher education is unhelpful in thinking about what it takes to produce contextually responsive teachers. Both theoretically and contextually grounded knowledges are essential for the professional development of prospective teachers. Exclusive focus on preparing teachers to teach in the current conditions of schooling (sometimes called the realities of the classroom) closes down possibilities for change. A strong focus on an idealised notion of schooling without an understanding of how to work effectively within the current contextual realities sets newly qualified teachers up for frustration (Gravett, Henning, & Eiselen, 2011; see also Kigua (this volume)). The challenge is thus for pre-service teacher programmes to both equip prospective teachers with the skills and knowledge to teach well under existing contextual conditions, and to help them acquire the deep conceptual knowledge of teaching and schooling to formulate a vision of what a more equitable and functional schooling system could look like. Pre-service teachers need to be empowered to discern what is needed on various levels (ranging from classroom practice to school management to challenging structural inequalities) to bring about educational transformation (Walton & Rusznyak, 2017). When pre-service teacher education curricula provide a stand-alone module on understanding the present contexts of schooling, prospective teachers may not necessarily make meaningful connections between contextual learning and the professional learning that is contained throughout the rest of the programme (Rusznyak, 2016). If an exclusively decontextualised approach to pre-service teacher preparation is taken, it is unlikely that prospective teachers will easily imagine how the practices of teaching might be operationalised within the contextual realities in which they work.

It is therefore not sufficient that the theoretical and contextual aspects of teaching are covered as discrete components of a curriculum. They need to be brought into relation with one another at some point. To support the development of pre-service teachers' pedagogic reasoning, they need access to conceptual knowledge that enables them to have powerful insights into contextually bound incidents. We therefore reiterate Robinson and Zinn's (2007) call for a coherent approach to pre-service teaching that regards contextual responsiveness as a fundamental part of pedagogically responsive teaching. This needs to be intentionally designed into the curriculum as systematic learning that takes place over time, so that prospective teachers interrogate their own histories of schooling and the assumptions of teaching that they have formed. They also need opportunities to observe and analyse teaching practices in diverse contexts. They further need opportunities that require them to account for the pedagogic choices they make in relation to the possibilities and constraints they encounter when teaching diverse learners in different contexts.

## Preparing teachers for contextual diversity in South Africa

Contextual diversity assumes a particularly complex texture in South Africa. Zinn and Keet (2010, p. 75) argue that diversity "sits uneasily in South Africa, as it has to locate itself within a context in which diversity has been a foundation for separateness, or apartheid". The imperative for attending to diversity in South African education arises from constitutional obligations undergirded by principles of equity, social cohesion and restorative justice. This imperative is made more urgent by systemic failures that perpetuate the continued marginalisation of rural-based schools, which is illustrated by the slow rate at which the Department of Basic Education implemented a directive to ensure that all schools have basic levels of infrastructure (DBE, Department of Basic Education, 2013).

With the desegregation of institutions and the movement of teacher education into the higher education sector, urban universities in South Africa began to admit a far greater proportion of Black students coming from township and rural schools (Mabokela & King, 2001). National policy required that previously segregated schools be accessed by learners with diverse ethnic, racial, class, gender, dis/ability and sexual identities. Twenty years into democracy, some important progress has been made in terms of the provision of basic education to all learners under 15 years of age, but many structural inequalities have yet to be adequately addressed (Maringe & Prew, 2015). For the most part, teacher education programmes have remained urban biased and seem not to have responded quickly to this student demographic change (Masinire, Maringe & Nkambule, 2014). Given this imperative, current legislation governing the provision of pre-service teacher education expects that prospective teachers "be exposed to concrete experience of the varied and contrasting contexts of schooling" (Department of Higher Education and Training (DHET), 2015, p. 18), so that they are able to "analyse different [teaching] practices" across a variety of schooling contexts and learn to "teach in a manner that includes all learners" (DHET, 2015, pp. 12, 64). South African teacher education programmes thus have an urgent moral and legal obligation to ensure that qualifying teachers are able to teach in the diverse contexts that characterise schooling in South Africa.

Preparing teachers for contextual diversity is particularly crucial where the majority of public schools do not yet have basic levels of infrastructure. In the present South African reality, contextual diversity is thus linked to vastly inequitable material conditions. Engaging with this continued inequality requires that pre-service teachers learn to take cognisance of the variation in experience, daily lives and learning needs of the children they teach. Importantly, they should not accept inequality as inevitable or acceptable, but their teaching should nevertheless work within the possibilities offered by vastly different and unequal material conditions. There is a growing body of research on the preparation of educators for diverse contexts in South Africa. However, there is very little research on the experiences of pre-service teachers who come from disadvantaged school contexts and the extent to which their coursework and experiences of learning to teach in urban (and often more affluent) contexts adequately prepare them to teach in their schools in their own communities. In one study on preparing teachers for diverse contexts, Robinson and Zinn (2007) found that while teacher educators from three universities are committed to ensuring that prospective teachers recognise and respect diversity, their initiatives to prepare pre-service teachers for diverse classrooms were largely individual and atomistic, and did not foster a shared and coherent approach at programmatic and curricular level.

One example of a coherent curriculum intervention aimed at preparing teachers for diverse schools in the South African context is reported on by Amin and Ramrathan (2009). They researched the impact of an initiative designed to reframe pre-service teachers' memories about schooling in South Africa, and to disrupt assumptions about what constitutes 'normal' conditions of schooling. Their intervention recognises that pre-service teachers in the South African context need formal opportunities to reconsider what they have learnt in their past histories of schooling. Pre-service teachers in their first year of study visited a number of schools in both familiar and unfamiliar contexts, and were then required to demonstrate how they would adapt lessons for use in each of those contexts. The researchers found that participants in their study reconsidered their assumptions about 'normal' schooling and expressed interest in undertaking subsequent practicum sessions in environments substantially different to those in which they had been schooled. However, when asked to adapt particular lessons for suitability in the various contexts they had visited, the researchers found that participants' understanding of contextual diversity was "limited to descriptive understanding" and this understanding "did not translate and integrate into thinking about how to teach in diverse contexts" (p. 75). For the most part, pre-service teachers in their study "taught in [different school contexts] exactly the same way, with the only difference being a modification and adaptation of teaching resources" (p. 75). While their understanding of schools in different contexts was developed, their ability to analyse and adjust teaching practices in different contexts remained elusive. The literature reviewed here reflects the need for further research to understand how best to structure programmes for preparing pre-service educators to teach in diverse contexts.

## Conceptual framework for the study: Episodes of pedagogic reasoning

Teaching that is contextually responsive and inclusive of all learners depends on teachers developing the ability to engage in conceptually informed and pedagogically reasoned practice. The importance of pedagogic reasoning in informing teachers' classroom action was emphasised in Shulman's (1987) influential work on the knowledge bases of teaching. Teaching had been regarded as the technical management of classroom environments that set up a series of stimulus/response/reinforcement cycles that prompted appropriate observable behavioural responses. By contrast, teaching conceptualised as pedagogically reasoned action requires that teachers draw on diverse knowledge bases (of content knowledge, learners and contexts, and of pedagogic options) to make considered choices for appropriate classroom action that advance learning. Pedagogical reasoning requires that teachers choose their teaching approaches in relation to the content to be learnt, the curriculum that guides knowledge selection, the learning needs of the children, and the context in which schooling takes place (Ball & McDiarmid, 1989).

In this chapter, we draw on the work of Horn (2007), who uses episodes of "pedagogical reasoning" to analyse the conceptual resources that teachers bring to their practice in order to promote equity-geared reforms. Horn (2007) defines *episodes of pedagogical reasoning* as units in which "teachers describe or raise questions about teaching practice that are accompanied by some elaboration of reasons, explanations or justifications" (p. 46). In her study, Horn sought to identify instances of pedagogic reasoning in relation to inclusive teaching in mathematics education from teacher-to-teacher talk. In our study, we use the reflections of pre-service teachers on their practicum teaching in a community context familiar to their own, but in schools that differ in significant ways from ones in which they had previously attended.

## Context of the study

The findings reported in this chapter are drawn from a broader project investigating the experiences and pedagogic learning of a group of South African pre-service teachers undertaking practicum placements across diverse (urban, township, rural and special) schooling contexts (Rusznyak & Walton, 2017). The participants in this study were a group of 23 third-year pre-service teachers registered for a four-year Bachelor of Education degree in an urban-based university. Pre-service teachers in that cohort were drawn from a wide range of communities, with 48% coming from township schools, 18% from rural schools, and 34% from suburban and inner city schools.

In their first year of study, pre-service teachers attended their first practicum session in a school just ten weeks after commencing their degree. During the ten weeks preceding their practicum, coursework required pre-service teachers to articulate and then interrogate their beliefs about teaching acquired during their own experiences of schooling (Rusznyak & Walton, 2014) as they were formally introduced to a conception of teaching as mediation of knowledge. This yielded significant and valuable reflections, given that their own experiences of being learners took place in an outcomes-based curriculum, where the role of content knowledge was severely undervalued (Allais, 2010).

For their first practicum, pre-service teachers were assigned to a range of well-functioning (formerly White) suburban, inner city and (formerly Black) township schools that had a track record of providing supportive learning environments for pre-service teachers and have a strong culture of teaching and learning (Christie, Butler & Potterton, 2007). Pre-service teachers were required to complete an observation assignment in which they had to describe the school, and analyse the ways in which teaching and learning in that context is similar to or different from the teaching and learning at the school/s they attended as learners. From their second year, students were required to develop rationales for their design of their lessons (Rusznyak & Walton, 2011). The rationale requires pre-service teachers to include a justification of how they have considered the nature of the content knowledge, the pedagogically significant aspects of learner diversity and their choice of teaching and learning strategies.

By their third year of study, pre-service teachers had completed half of their subject content, pedagogy and educational theory courses (including courses on learning theory, sociology of education, philosophy of education, understanding learner diversities and inclusive education from a social justice perspective). In conjunction with their third-year university-based coursework on diversity in society and the use of inclusive pedagogies, pre-service teachers were encouraged to undertake sessions of teaching practicum in a context unfamiliar to their own experiences of schooling (which may be in a rural, inner city, township or suburban area), or in a school of a different type to those that they had gone to for practicum sessions (for example, a special school). Pre-service teachers who had demonstrated the ability to organise productive learning experiences within a well-managed classroom were encouraged to take an unsupervised practicum session in a local school within the communities from whence they come.

## Methodology

Data for this chapter was drawn primarily from three sources, namely the response to the observation tasks that pre-service teachers completed in their first year of study, as well as the focus group interviews and reflective journal entries from their third year. During their third year of their initial teaching degree, participants were invited to a focus group discussion before they went to rural school placements, and a second interview within a month of returning to campus. In the first focus group discussion, questions sought to uncover their expectations of the placement, particularly in terms of what they expected to learn about teaching in a context they were familiar with as learners, but not as prospective teachers. We also asked participants about the ways in which they thought teaching in rural school contexts would be both similar to and different from teaching in the urban school contexts they had already experienced. After their return, participants were asked to describe the extent to which they felt prepared for teaching within that rural context, the aspects of teaching they enjoyed, those they found challenging and those that surprised them, and the ways in which they had adapted their teaching to the demands, challenges and possibilities of that context.

We are aware that participants may feel pressurised to contribute socially acceptable responses in focus group settings (Nederhof, 1985; Fisher, 1993). To complement and elaborate on participants' focus group contributions, we draw on the reflective journal entries that participants wrote during their placements in the rural schools. The value of keeping a reflective journal is well documented, and it is a means by which pre-service teachers can reflect on their experiences, and give an account of their pedagogic thinking and action during the course of the practicum (Larrivee, 2000; Ezati, Ocheng, Ssentamu & Sikoyo, 2010). The journal is also one of the ways we, at our university, assess pedagogic thought in relation to content knowledge, learner characteristics and contextual responsiveness (Nilson, 2008; Shulman, 2015). We need to acknowledge that our dataset is limited to what participants wrote in their journals and volunteered during the focus group discussions. Amid the complexity of classroom life, many decisions are made during a teaching day, and not all of them will be explicit subjects of reflection. An absence of empirical data does not necessarily mean that pedagogic reasoning was not present in that teachers' practice. Our findings are thus both partial and provisional.

In this study, we seek pedagogic reasoning in relation to the ways in which pre-service teachers adapted their classroom practices to a different set of contextual demands in order to teach in rural schools. Identifying episodes of pedagogic reasoning under the broad concept of pedagogic responsiveness to learning needs in the context, we were able to identify five main ways in which participants in our study demonstrated the pedagogic reasoning that enabled them to become responsive to the context of schooling. These themes are: pedagogic responsiveness with respect to learner understanding; local knowledge and experience; schooling structures; resourcing; and finally, community context. We consider evidence for episodes of pedagogic reasoning to be present when pre-service teachers described a contextually related incident, observation or concern, and proceeded to provide a full rationale for the pedagogic choices made to address that issue. We consider evidence for pedagogic reasoning to be limited when a partial explanation is provided. We seek to understand the kinds of conceptual resources student teachers employed to analyse and respond to the opportunities and constraints of challenging contexts. In this chapter, we first review the pedagogic responsiveness of the participants broadly, then we focus specifically on one participant, Zodwa. She was selected as a focus for this study because her dataset was extensive, and her reflections exemplify many (but not all) of the issues raised by the larger group of participants.[1]

## Findings

### 1 Engagement with contextual diversity when participants were in their first year of study

In their first year of study, we found that all participants in this study were able to describe the school context in which they were placed. Nearly all participants included in their descriptions the state of the school infrastructure, the sizes of the classes, the demographics of learners, language of instruction and the nature of the discipline systems employed. The second part of their observation assignment required pre-service teachers to describe the similarities and differences between the teaching and learning in this school context and that of school/s they had attended. For 42% of participants in this study, their responses to this question focused on differences in school routine (for example, when the school has assembly, and how learners move between classes) and differences in the available resources used during lessons (including access to textbooks, television and computer facilities).

Despite introductory coursework on the mediation of knowledge, a significant portion of participants found it difficult to distinguish between differences in teaching and learning, and differences in the school context itself. Of the participants in the study, 58% (including Gertrude, Sandy, Ntombi and Zodwa) drew on concepts introduced in university-based coursework to describe how teachers linked learners' everyday experiences to the content knowledge they were mediating, and how they developed understanding systematically. Zodwa, for example, recalls how as a learner "we were just given information in lessons. If you did not understand, our teacher would not really explain. [In this school] the supervising teacher goes step by step to [build up understanding of] the knowledge". Several participants (including Zodwa) noticed a difference in pedagogy in that learners in the urban schools often worked in pairs and small groups, a strategy seldom used during their schooling. Numerous participants noticed how learners were encouraged to provide examples, discuss their prior knowledge and ask questions. This had been different to the expectations of them as learners in the schools they had attended. The analysis of our data suggests that the first-year pre-service teachers in our study were able to notice and articulate contextual differences with respect to school routines and infrastructure, but nearly half found it more difficult to articulate an analysis of the pedagogic action of teachers between contexts.

## 2 Engagement with contextual diversity when participants were in their third year of study

In their third year of study, we found that participants were able to describe both school contexts and pedagogic approaches in much more nuanced ways. More than that, they were better able to recognise and articulate the implications of learner diversity and school context for their teaching. While not all participants reported successful implementation of interventions arising from their pedagogic reasoning, we found that all participants in our study were able to notice the implications of diversity for teaching. In addition, most accepted pedagogic responsibility for enabling learning within the constraints and possibilities of the context. For half of participants we found written evidence in their journals of them justifying their chosen pedagogic responses to the learner and contextual diversities they encountered. Although the others had not explicitly written their reasoning in their journals, they were able to elaborate on the reasons for their pedagogic choices when asked to do so during the focus group discussions.

## 2.1 Pedagogic responsiveness to the availability of resources

For some participants, the use of visual resources when teaching in a rural school was crucial to providing learners with ways of accessing the knowledge – but their focus was on enabling the learning, rather than on the straightforward application of a classroom technology. For example, participants found that their lessons needed to have visual support and engaging resources to enable learners to visualise what they were learning about, as Anna explains: "or else all I got from them were blank stares". She "…realised the importance of gathering resources over time. I never really valued my resources because they have never been this essential". A technical aspect of teaching that Zodwa had to become familiar with during this practicum was the use of a chalkboard as the primary technology available for representing knowledge to learners. She believes that she quickly "…got used to using chalk, and learnt to make a success of it". Similarly, when Wattson found no chemicals in the science laboratory, he brought salt from home to teach a lesson on electrolytes. A point raised by several participants is explained best by Wattson, who "…learnt that [resources] don't have to be fancy to influence teaching but something relevant (such as newspapers, wall charts, magazines and models) for developing deep understanding". However, participants were adamant that "…resources alone do not assure learners' access to knowledge". Anna realised that in addition to appropriate resources, her "…questioning had to be helpful in guiding the learners' thinking". The use of appropriate resources was therefore regarded more as a means to an end than the essence of what it means to teach in a contextually appropriate manner. Participants in their third year regarded their use of available resources as something that they used to represent knowledge to the learners, but did not regard the resources they used to be the essence of what it means to teach effectively.

## 2.2 Pedagogic responsiveness to learner understanding

Using concepts from university-based coursework to analyse and interpret the teaching practices she observed, Zodwa describes an incident in which she observed a teacher instruct a learner to read a text out loud. When the learner struggled to do so, she was surprised that the teacher "…just ignored the mistakes". At first, she "…assumed that it was a strategy that the teacher was using". However, by the end of the lesson she expressed concern that "…all the mistakes were still [left] unattended". She draws on concepts acquired from university-based coursework and previous practicum experiences to pose the question "…how are learners supposed to '*gain epistemological access*' to knowledge if they don't know if they are right or wrong in what they are doing in class?" She describes how "…normally in situations like this, one would expect some form of teacher sensitivity to be applied trying to understand the anxiety of the learner... As a teacher, one is expected to assist and correct the learner's mistakes". In her analysis of the incident, Zodwa demonstrates her capacity to consider the affective experiences of learners in the learning situation. In addition, she draws on theoretical constructs to think critically about the pedagogic value of prevailing practices in relation to the overall purpose of teaching.

Most participants noticed a larger discrepancy between learners' proficiency in their home language and their proficiency in the language of learning and teaching (LOLT) than they had encountered in urban-based schools. Participants (including Helen, Lerato and Andile) explained concepts to learners in their home language so they could "...understand better". Others (such as Grace, Anna, Samuel, Nkosi and Zodwa) reasoned that their purpose was both to enable conceptual understanding and to advance learners' ability to articulate their understanding of those concepts in the LOLT. As Samuel explains, "...I found myself explaining difficult terms in isiZulu.[2] When I asked questions, I encouraged learners to answer [in their home language]. Then I'd help them [express their ideas] in English. So I ended up teaching Mathematics and English together". During the first lesson Zodwa taught in the rural school, she realised that her pace had been too quick, as learners' level of understanding of English (as the LOLT) was not what she had assumed it to be. She described how she "...knew [she] had to go back to the drawing board and plan a new way of going about [teaching] this lesson". She discussed her concern with other teachers, asking them how they sought to address the barriers to learning experienced by the children in the school. Reflecting in her journal, she rejected an explanation reportedly given to her by one teacher at the school that "...these learners are lazy and don't want to learn". She was emphatic that the effectiveness of her teaching depended on learner understanding: "If learners don't understand what I'm saying, then the purpose of my lesson is not achieved, and it wouldn't matter if I went to class or not". In analysing her journal entries, we notice how she intentionally adjusted her lesson pacing. She stated that teaching is "...about getting through to all the learners even if it takes a whole week to do that. As long as by the end, I have taught them what they needed to know". In this way, we see Zodwa making a carefully considered pedagogic decision to adjust pacing to prioritise learner understanding over curriculum coverage.

Many participants observed that learners in their allocated classes experienced difficulty when reading texts. Whereas Andile continued to meet curriculum pace expectations by avoiding reading tasks in the lessons he taught, others (particularly Zodwa and Gertrude) planned intensive reading tasks with structured support to develop learners' reading competence. Zodwa designed reading tasks in every lesson that she taught "...to engender a love of reading, to increase learners' confidence in engaging with written texts", and to provide opportunities for learners to "...practice their ability to read for information". From these examples, we see that although participants encountered similar barriers to learning, the manner in which they addressed them differed. The pedagogic choices required trade-offs to be made between curriculum coverage and learner understanding. It became clear that to address this meaningfully, teachers of the intermediate phase needed more knowledge about teaching reading than they were getting from their pre-service teacher education curriculum.

## 2.3 Pedagogic responsiveness to local knowledge and experience

Numerous participants specified how they had used contextually relevant examples and brought pictures or other visual resources with them to class to introduce unfamiliar places and objects to learners. However, few pre-service teachers wrote explicitly about the relevance of the prescribed content to the lives of the learners in the classes they taught. They accepted the national curriculum uncritically as determining the topics they needed to teach. This, we believe, is probably appropriate given their stage of professional development. Anna was the only pre-service teacher in the group who wrote extensively on the choice of a literature book for a class of Grade 10 learners learning English as a First Additional Language. In her reflective journal, she describes how she realised that her introductory lesson was not sufficiently engaging learners. She writes, "...I literally took a moment, looked around and I thought the main thing they understand is that their parents go to work every day yet their opportunities are so limited". On the basis of this thought, Anna reconceptualised her unit of lessons, making explicit links between an important theme of the novel and the lived realities of the learners she taught. We found numerous examples of participants designing an approach, quickly realising that it did not work as they had hoped, and having the capacity to think through different pedagogic possibilities and enact them with more success.

## 2.4 Pedagogic responsiveness to school organisation and structures

Some participants (like Hope, Zodwa, Lerato and Gertrude) grappled with how to manage large classes when there was insufficient seating in the classrooms. Zodwa expressed concern that learners stand during her lessons because there are "...not enough chairs and tables to accommodate them". She "...knows that learners need support", but finds that physically moving around the classroom is "...very difficult because of the limited space". She reflected on how this arrangement impacts the quality of teaching and learning, saying "...how does a 30-minute lesson work in a class of 75–80 learners? How does one go around and make sure that all learners have enough understanding, or even to see if they have done the work?" She made different pedagogic choices in order to work more productively within the structural limitations of large classes and short time periods. She sometimes split the class in two and taught half the class while the rest worked on a given task. She would then repeat the lesson to the other half of the class. This modification of her teaching, she reasoned, would enable her to "...get to all [learners], and assist them when they don't understand". While the long-term sustainability of this arrangement is doubtful, she thoughtfully finds ways to mitigate some of the contextual challenges by adjusting time and space variables.

## 2.5 Pedagogic responsiveness to community obligations

Many participants (including Mary, Gertrude, Lerato, Bheki, Eve, Nkosi, Sandy, Wattson, Sipho and Zodwa) explicitly considered the pedagogic implications of the home circumstances of children in their classes. They expressed awareness that many learners lived with elderly relatives who were not all able to provide support with homework tasks. Few had easy access to computer facilities or the internet, and most were required to do domestic/agricultural chores after school. Typically, participants ensured that "…all learning tasks could be finished in scheduled class time". In this context, participants drastically reduced the amount of homework given to learners, or even eliminated it completely.

In their reflections, participants (including Zodwa) drew on concepts from their university-based coursework to consider the conditions under which children are schooled. Zodwa, for example, drew on Morrow's (2007) distinction between the formal and material elements of teaching to describe the school where there are only two toilets available for 800 users, and Grade 1 classes are held under a tree. She asked, "How does one expect these kids to learn? Every child has the right to formal education in a safe environment, but for learners at this school, this is far from a reality". She was challenged by having to "…get used to the reality of seeing learners come to school barefoot every day in cold weather". She was also "shocked and surprised" to see how learners are permitted to write notes for different subjects in one exercise book. She employed the ideas of Morrow (2007) when she commented that "…not every child who has formal access to schooling is guaranteed epistemological access to education". She admits that teaching in a context where structural inequalities led to untenable material conditions in the school had been "an emotional battle" for her.

## Discussion

Internationally, it is recognised that learning to teach is a complex process, which in some sense is both a personalised journey of becoming (Korthagen, 2004; Flores, 2006) and a communal induction into the best-known practices of the profession (Morrow, 2007). Learning to teach in the South African context has additional complexities in that many communities live in areas that still reflect the geographical, economic and racial legacies of apartheid. In many ways, the findings of our study confirm those of Amin and Ramrathan's (2009) study: that in their first year of study, pre-service teachers were well able to describe contextual differences between schools, but their analysis of the pedagogic implications of that diversity was limited. This is developmentally appropriate, given the limited time pre-service teachers have had to develop their content and pedagogic knowledge, their understanding of inclusive pedagogies and their understanding of theories of learning. It is upon this knowledge that the development of their ability to engage in pedagogic reasoning rests. With conceptions of teaching that are based primarily on their personal experiential knowledge, it is unsurprising that at first, pre-service teachers find it difficult to imagine pedagogic responsiveness to contextual diversity in more than technical ways. We agree with Amin and Ramrathan's (2009) argument that pre-service teachers should not be provided with "*idealised conceptions of schools*" (p. 76). However, we strongly argue that an 'idealised conception of *teaching*' should be part of their professional development. An idealised conception of teaching should be one which considers the mediation of content knowledge to diverse learners in ways that are inherently contextually sensitive and responsive. Once a more formal conception of teaching has developed, together with deeper content and pedagogic knowledge, our findings show pre-service teachers who are more able to draw on theory to analyse the teaching and learning that they observe. Furthermore, we found that they are better able to imagine pedagogic possibilities to the learning needs of the children they teach in ways that go beyond mere technical adjustments.

## Conclusion

It is widely accepted that content knowledge and educational theory need to be systematically organised in pre-service teacher education programmes for optimal professional learning. In this chapter, we argue that a sequence in which pre-service teachers engage explicitly with the conceptual knowledge of teaching alongside contextual responsiveness to diversity is just as important. We raise the question of how conceptual knowledge of teaching can best be organised in relation to pre-service teachers' awareness and experience of contextual diversity. The kind of pedagogic reasoning that is required to enable newly qualified teachers to teach in diverse contexts is unlikely to develop from the individual efforts of teacher educators. Rather, opportunities for contextual awareness and for pedagogic reasoning in context need to be systematically constructed into the overall design of pre-service teacher education curricula. Moreover, the progression from observation of contexts, to comparative analysis of pedagogic practices, and ultimately opportunities for pedagogic reasoning and contextual responsiveness need to consider the overall professional learning of pre-service teachers.

## Acknowledgement of grants

This work was supported by a practice-based research grant from the School of Education, University of the Witwatersrand.

## Notes

1 An overview of the professional learning of the participants is reported in Rusznyak and Walton (2017).
2 isiZulu is an indigenous African language and one of the eleven official languages of South Africa.

## References

Allais, S. (2010). Outcomes-based education: understanding what went wrong. In Y. Shalem & S. Pendlebury (Eds.), *Retreiving teaching: Critical issues in curriculum, pedagogy and learning* (pp. 27–40). Cape Town: Jutas.

Amin, N., & Ramrathan, P. (2009). Preparing students to teach in and for diverse contexts: A learning to teach approach. *Perspectives in Education*, 27(1), 69–77.
Balfour, R., Mitchell, C., & Moletsane, R. (2008). Troubling contexts: Toward a generative theory of rurality as education research. *Journal of Rural and Community Development*, 3(3), 95–107.
Ball, D., & McDiarmid, G. W. (1989). *The subject matter preparation of teachers*. Issue Paper 89–84. Michigan: National Centre for Research on Teacher Education.
Becket, D. R. (1998). Increasing the number of Latino and Navajo teachers in hard-to-staff schools. *Journal of Teacher Education*, 49(1), 196–205.
Carr, W. (2006). Education without theory. *British Journal of Educational Studies*, 54(2), 136–159.
Christie, P., Butler, D., & Potterton, M. (2007). *Report to the Minister of Education: Schools that work*. Pretoria: Government Printer.
Darling-Hammond, L. (1997). *The right to learn: A blueprint for creating schools that work*. San Francisco, CA: Jossey-Bass.
Department of Basic Education (DBE). (2013). *Minimum uniform norms and standards for public school infrastructure*. Pretoria: Government Gazette.
Department of Higher Education and Training (DHET). (2015). *Policy on the minimum requirements for teacher education qualifications, as revised 2014*. Pretoria: Government Gazette.
Ezati, B. A., Ocheng, M. K., Ssentamu, P. N., & Sikoyo, L. N. (2010). Enhancing quality of student teachers' practices through reflective journal writing during school practice. *Perspectives in Education*, 28(2), 31–40.
Fisher, R. J. (1993). Social desirability bias and the validity of indirect questioning. *Journal of Consumer Research*, 20(2), 303–315.
Flores, M. (2006). Being a novice teacher in two different settings: Struggles, continuities, and discontinuities. *Teachers College Record*, 108(10), 2021–2052.
Gardiner, M. (2008). *Education in rural areas*. Braamfontein: Centre for Education Policy Development.
Goodwin, A. (1997). Historical and contemporary perspectives on multicultural education. In J. King, E. Hollins & W. Hayman (Eds.), *Preparing Teachers for Cultural Diversity* (pp .5–22). New York: Teachers College Press.
Gonzalez, N., McIntyre, E., & Rosebery, A. S. (2001). *Classroom diversity: Connecting curriculum to students' lives*. Westport, CT: Heinemann.
Gravett, S., Henning, E., & Eiselen, R. (2011). New teachers look back on their university education: Prepared for teaching, but not for life in the classroom. *Education as Change*, 15(sup1), S123–S142.
Gruenewald, D. S. (2003). Foundations of place: A multidisciplinary framework for place-conscious education. *American Educational Research Journal*, 40(3), 619–654.
Horn, I. S. (2007). Fast kids, slow kids, lazy kids: Framing the mismatch problem in mathematics teachers' conversations. *Journal of the Learning Sciences*, 16(1), 37–79.
Human Sciences Research Council (HSRC) (2005). *Emerging voices: A report on education in South African rural communities*. Johannesburg: Nelson Mandela Foundation.
Korthagen, F. (2004). In search of the essence of a good teacher: Towards a more holistic approach in teacher education. *Teaching and Teacher Education*, 20, 77–97.
Larrivee, B. (2000). Transforming teaching practice: Becoming the critically reflective teacher. *Reflective Practice*, 1(3), 293–307.
Littleton, D. M. (1998) Preparing professionals as teachers for the urban classrooms: A university/school collaboration model. *Action in Teacher Education*, 19(4), 14–28.
Mabokela, R. O., & King, K. L. (Eds.) (2001) *Apartheid no more: Case studies of Southern African universities in the process of transformation*. London: Bergin & Garvey.
Maringe, F., & Prew, M. E. (2015). *Twenty years of education transformation in Gauteng 1994 to 2014*. Cape Town: African Minds.

Masinire, A., Maringe, F., & NkambuleT C. (2014). Education for rural development: Embedding rural dimensions in initial teacher preparation. *Perspectives in Education*, 32(3), 146–158.

Matsko, K. K., & Hammerness, K. (2014). Unpacking the "urban" in urban teacher education: Making a case for context-specific preparation. *Journal of Teacher Education*, 65(2), 128–155.

Moletsane, L. (2012). Repositioning educational research on rurality and rural education in South Africa: Beyond deficit paradigms. *Perspectives in Education*, 30(1), 1–9.

Morrow, W. (2007). *Learning to teach in South Africa*. Pretoria: HSRC Press.

Mukeredzi, T. G., & Mandrona, A. R. (2013). The journey to becoming professionals: Student teachers' experiences of teaching practice in a rural South African context. *International Journal of Educational Research*, 62, 141–151.

Nederhof, A. (1985). Methods of coping with social desirability bias: A review. *European Journal of Social Psychology*, 15, 263–280.

Nilson, P. (2008). Teaching for Understanding: The complex nature of pedagogical content knowledge in pre-service education. *International Journal of Science Education*, 30(10), 1281–1299.

Robinson, M., & Zinn, D. (2007). Teacher preparation for diversity at three South African universities. *Journal of Education*, 42, 61–81.

Rusznyak, L. (2015). Knowledge selection in initial teacher education programmes and its implications for curricular coherence. *Journal of Education*, 60, 7–29.

Rusznyak, L. (2016). Making conceptual connections visible to students in professional programmes: the case of initial teacher education. *South African Journal of Higher Education*, 30(2), 205–225.

Rusznyak, L., & Walton, E. (2011). Lesson planning guidelines for student teachers: A scaffold for the development of pedagogical content knowledge. *Education as Change*, 15(2), 271–285.

Rusznyak, L., & Walton, E. (2014). Using metaphors to gain insights into South African student teachers' initial and developing conceptions of being a teacher. *Education as Change*, 18(2), 335–355.

Rusznyak, L., & Walton, E. (2017) Could practicum placements in contrasting contexts support the preparation of pre-service teachers for an envisaged inclusive education system? A South African study. *International Journal of Disability, Education and Development*, 64(5), 463–482.

Shulman, L. (1987). Knowledge and teaching: Foundations of the new reform. *Harvard Educational Review*, 57(1), 1–22.

Shulman, L. (2015). PCK: Its genesis and exodus. In A. Berry, P. Friedrichsen, & J. Loughran (Eds.), *Re-examining pedagogical content knowledge in science education* (pp. 3–13). New York: Routledge.

Sleeter, C. (2001) Preparing teachers for culturally diverse schools: Research and the overwhelming presence of whiteness. *Journal of Teacher Education*, 52(2), 93–106.

Villegas, A. M., & Lucas, T. (2002). Preparing culturally responsive teachers: Rethinking the curriculum. *Journal of Teacher Education*, 53(20), 19–32.

Walton, E., & Rusznyak, L. (2017). Developing responsive and inclusive teaching: Implications for the design of pre-service teacher education courses in South Africa. *International Journal of Disability, Development and Education*, 64(3), 231–248.

Zinn, D., & Keet, A. (2010) Diversity and teacher education: Explorations of a social justice framework. In K. Sporre & J. Mannberg (Eds.), *Values, Religions and Education in Changing Societies* (pp. 75–91). Dordrecht: Springer.

# 5

# DIVERSITY OF TEACHER AUTONOMY IN RESPONSE TO CURRICULUM REFORM

Towards a humanistic focus on teacher education

*Jing Xiao and Ora Kwo*

### Introduction: Educational reform in a global context

Over the last two decades, within a climate of globalisation, educational reform has become a global phenomenon in response to rapid social changes. As a result, administrators and teachers are expected to stay alert to ways in which their institutions can become more competitive in response to shifting social and economic circumstances. Within the Chinese context, schools are under pressure to remain accountable with regard to their adherence to policy within these altered circumstances, and Kwo (2007) has raised questions about institutions' adherence to policy, particularly insofar as policy expectations might interfere with professional autonomy. She has observed that accountability systems, which professedly are intended to bring about enhanced performance rooted in autonomous learning, often result in teachers being overwhelmed with paperwork.

A prominent feature of current global educational enquiry is the question of how education can enhance sustainable development. The four pillars of education, identified by UNESCO's International Commission on Education for the Twenty-First Century (Delors, 1996), are advocacy for learning to know, learning to do, learning to live together, and learning to be. The last two tend to be neglected, despite their importance to citizenship and sustaining peace. In an attempt to rethink education for the common good, UNESCO's 2015 report refocused on these neglected pillars. The statement which best reveals this refocus is the report's assertion that "Sustaining and enhancing the dignity, capacity and welfare of the human person, in relation to others and to nature, should be the fundamental purpose of education in the twenty-first century" (p. 36). This constitutes a return to an awareness of the importance of cultivating the inner self, as well as cultivating healthy relationships, in education.

Alongside economic reforms which opened up the Chinese economy in response to the demands of globalisation, China launched *suzhi* (quality) education reform in 1999 to equip the next generations to be successful in an increasingly marketised and globalised society (Zhang, 2013). The aim of cultivating well-rounded people with *suzhi* education reform resonates with UNESCO's four pillars of education. This chapter aims to assess *suzhi* education reform alongside the curriculum reform of College English, which was launched nationwide in 2007. By examining the assumptions undergirding the curriculum document, the chapter reports on how teachers' autonomous states were manifested in their diverse responses to perceived institutional pressures. The chapter therefore looks at the tension between the challenge to innovate and the pressure for accountability to policy stipulations.

## Learner autonomy for College English curriculum reform

The study took place at a time of curriculum reform for College English (CE), a core course for first- and second-year undergraduate students not majoring in English. The course has textbooks which are standardised across the country, and spans four semesters, the last of which prepares students for what is called the Band 4 College English Test (abbreviated as CET-4). It is a standard examination administered nationwide which all students are expected to pass before graduation. Three major aims are identified in the official CE reform document (2007):

- improve students' English language competence;
- facilitate students' autonomous learning capacity;
- cultivate students' morality and cross-cultural awareness.

Unlike the former CE Syllabus, the document which laid out the CE reform characterises teachers as accountable agents for curriculum delivery. Unfortunately, this document does not address the gaps between external expectations and teachers' own lived experiences. Learner autonomy is a dimension that was newly introduced in the CE curriculum reform, and the underpinning assumptions made with regard to learner autonomy are that (a) teachers are autonomous, and (b) teachers can facilitate learner autonomy. Both assumptions can be examined by looking at teachers' responses to contextual challenges amidst competing expectations. As pointed out by Kwo (2007, p. 211):

> As teachers are expected to be the frontline agents for educational reforms, it is essential to understand the truthful inner picture about their capacity and sustainability in adapting to changes that impact on their *learning and development*.

Among the competing expectations that CE teachers confronted amidst curriculum reform is the assumption that they would meet both long-term and short-term educational goals. Examining teachers' responses to such competing discourses can reveal their autonomous learning patterns within this period of education reform. We wished to engage with teachers' unfiltered and authentic impressions, and to gain a clear picture of teacher autonomy we asked them about their perception of the institutional pressures they face while they facilitate learner autonomy.

The CE reform document emphasised learner autonomy as a foundation for independent learning. It espoused a student-centred focus, and stated that it was the responsibility of teachers to cultivate students' own English learning strategies. Teachers were also expected to facilitate web-based learning, a platform in which students can determine where and when they want to learn. Here, they can progressively complete online learning tasks according to their diverse levels of learning competence. This chapter addresses how CE teachers conceptualise learner autonomy in the context of the CE reform in a study which looked at how teachers learned from facilitating learner autonomy.

## Perspectives on teacher autonomy

The concept of teacher autonomy is not defined as only one thing in scholarly literature. One prevailing paradigm highlights teachers' perceived freedom in making professional decisions. Autonomy is related to teachers' independence to make professional decisions at their own discretion within the classroom (Street & Licata, 1989). In a similar vein, Little (1995, p. 178) has defined such autonomy in teachers as a "strong sense of personal responsibility for their teaching, exercised via continuous reflection and analysis [... and] affective and cognitive control of the teaching process". The concept is extended to reflect the ability to improve one's own teaching through one's own efforts (Lamb & Reinders, 2008). This paradigm defines teacher autonomy as the responsibility to fulfil self-directed professional goals, but ignores the inherent tension between such a sense of ownership and responsibility and the interpretation of externally prescribed accountability, thus missing the complexity of teaching and learning.

Another paradigm defines teacher autonomy as freedom from external control and constraints (Benson, 2000; McGrath, 2000; Shaw, 2002). This perspective takes teachers as qualified authorities in the instructional process because they have considerable expertise. They have a right to organise the learning process at their own discretion, and the network of impersonal school rules stops at the classroom door because teachers can formulate their own personalised flexible rules to operate within their classrooms (Franklin, 1988; Hanson, 1991). This view of teacher autonomy addresses tensions between responsibility and accountability within the classroom, but unfortunately still polarises teachers' inner self from the external environment, and perpetuates the perceived external constraints.

## Teacher autonomy reconsidered

These two prevailing paradigms of teacher autonomy tend to ignore the subtle but critical presence of administrative accountability that can distract teachers from professional responsibility and give rise to tension between accountability and responsibility. The study reported on here was driven by a desire to find a balance between teachers' dual commitments to professional responsibility and administrative accountability. Autonomous teachers may be considered dynamic learners because within the shift of curriculum reform, they take responsibility to learn with the learners, and do so within administrative constraints, so as to be genuinely accountable.

This chapter is concerned with various degrees of teacher autonomy. The highest level of teacher autonomy comprises an optimal balance between professional responsibility and administrative accountability, while the lowest involves ignorance and neglect of the tension between them. An understanding of the nuances of teacher autonomy requires a close examination of the diversity of teachers' inner lives.

## Research methodology

The primary research question for this study is *How is teacher autonomy manifested in teachers' responses to perceived institutional pressures against facilitation of learner autonomy?* As a qualitative case study following the approach advocated by Patton (1990) and Merriam (1998), its objective was to understand experiences that people 'lived' or 'felt' in their worlds. The study aimed to examine teachers' lived experiences in the context of CE curriculum reform.

### An ethical stance for validity

With ethical approval at an institutional level, and with informed consent from participants, one of the researchers took on the role of a participant-observer. As suggested by Merriam (1998, p. 101), the significance of participant observation was explained to the participant teachers and their students, and a concerted effort was made to ensure that classroom observation was unobtrusive. Rapport with the participant teachers was developed in order to optimise the validity of the qualitative data. Interviews were conducted with receptive and non-judgmental listening, and these were followed by validation of transcribed data with interviewees. The collection and analysis of data were made more robust by teachers engaging in several rounds of dialogue to reach deeper self-understanding.

### Research participants

The research site was what is called a 'normal' university in Beijing, China, and such universities traditionally specialise in preparing students to be future teachers. Multiple-case sampling on "conceptual grounds" was adopted from the approach of Miles and Huberman (1994, p. 29), in recognition of the fact that autonomous teachers are dynamic learners who actively engage with curriculum reform. Participants were CE teachers, and were selected because of their readiness to commit to curriculum reform, and proof of this commitment was corroborated by:

- documented verification of their effort for curriculum enactment;
- contributions they had made to faculty discussion on curriculum reform; and
- their research publications on curriculum reform.

From a two-month pilot study, six teachers were purposefully shortlisted according to the degree of their responsiveness to curriculum reform. All were willing to participate in the main study, and they varied in their epistemological orientations. Four believed in transmission teaching, among whom was Li, who was chosen because of his strong view that students have limited capacity for knowledge production. Chen and Gu were also purposefully chosen for their clearly articulated views on students. Chen was confident that students have the potential to construct knowledge, while Gu considered students to be contextual knowers. Li held a bachelor's degree, Gu held a Master's degree, and both specialised in English linguistics. Chen's Master's degree was in English language education. The participants' age and the duration of their teaching experience were not regarded as major factors affecting teacher autonomy, and therefore did not affect selection. Gender balance was considered so as to ensure maximum variation sampling (Creswell, 2002), which strengthens in-depth case studies.

## Data collection

Data were collected through pre-observation interviews, class observations, and post-observation interviews. Pre-observation interviews provided a holistic view of teachers' responses to learner autonomy as a major aim of the curriculum reform under investigation. Four class observations were conducted for each teacher to observe each of the four content areas of the curriculum, namely reading, writing, translation, and listening-speaking. The primary purpose of the class observations was to detect critical unexpected moments, and teachers' lived stories were gathered thereafter in interviews to reveal the gap between teachers' expectations and their realities. At least one post-observation interview was conducted after each class observation to explore the specifics of the observed unexpected moments, and to review previous interview texts to trace parallel themes among the cases.

## Data analysis

Data analysis and interpretation took place in four stages. The first involved documentation of the three cases with narration of the data-collection process in chronological order, and this narration was accompanied by the transcribed and translated raw data with field notes that identified aspects of significance related to the research question. The second stage constituted a move from chronological data compilation to derivation of themes for data analysis. Themes were clustered and re-clustered hierarchically, and sub-themes were extracted in a rigorous process of data-reduction. The third stage involved a review and re-construction of themes. The identification of parallel themes between cases, in turn, led to a new round of data re-clustering within each case. Data were condensed with the elimination of unparalleled themes, followed by identification of common themes for all three cases so that analysis could be conducted across all cases. The fourth stage was a cross-case analysis, which aimed to track different levels of teacher autonomy manifest in teachers' responses to perceived institutional constraints against facilitation of learner autonomy. Data were then further analysed in terms of teacher diversity manifest at different levels of autonomous learning.

For the presentation of the findings, data sources are abbreviated as 'pre-o' for pre-observation interviews, 'c-o' for class observation, and 'post-o' for post-observation interviews. The discussion is subdivided under parallel themes.

## Findings on teachers' responses to perceived institutional pressures

The three cases are discussed according to the four parallel themes that emerged, namely workload, research, examination, and teaching quality. A brief analysis of each case will be presented below.

### The case of Li

### Workload pressure: Group tutoring as a strategy

For Li, facilitation of learner autonomy resulted in an increased workload. He said:

> The web-learning platform entails individualised tutoring and demands investment of a large amount of time. I check out each student's learning plan, and offer suggestion on revised planning and advice on their learning problems. I want to stay in touch with students on their learning needs and propensity, in order to teach more efficiently to address individual learning differences. (pre-o)
>
> I have two classes and over 100 students, and six sessions every week. […] I am short of time to talk with students individually, but I do not want to ignore them. For the sake of efficiency, I tutor students in groups according to the pace of their learning progress. As I offer individual tutoring to those in need of instant help, students receiving group tutoring complained that I did not give them equal attention. I could only explain why those students need more attention. What else can I do? (pre-o)

Li's perception of his workload reveals his commitment to the facilitation of learner autonomy. The reform document recommends face-to-face tutoring, which inevitably results in an increased workload. Beyond the curriculum demands of responding to students' autonomous web-learning progress with individualised feedback, Li took heed of learning differences, and extended the scope of his tutoring. Despite his extensive effort, he was obliged to resort to group tutoring as a strategy to reduce his workload. Students' complaints about being given unequal attention in his tutorials suggests Li's limited understanding of the nature of group tutoring, and of the complex dynamics of community learning. In this instance, more needy students may benefit from learning from peers if tutoring can be tailored to provide a space for effective community learning.

## *Research pressure: Competition between teaching and research*

Li viewed research as a hindrance to the facilitation of learner autonomy, saying:

> The inadequate preparation for a session is partly due to the pressure of research. If I spend more time on research, my time for teaching is reduced accordingly. It is hard to balance between teaching and research. (post-o)
>
> Teachers are evaluated by research outcome. I am worried about the thin outcome of my research, but I comfort myself that it takes time to do substantial research. I am trying to combine teaching and research. After all, teaching has already consumed much time. [...] Research tends to outweigh teaching. [...] I think it is unjust to evaluate teachers by research. (post-o)

Li's responses with regard to research pressure reveal his struggle. In spite of his awareness of the complementary relationship between research and teaching, he perceived research as being in competition with teaching in terms of time allocation. Li's struggle to balance teaching and research reflects the need for the reform to include the improvement of teaching techniques and enhancement of research activities. Li was aware of the outcome-based expectation of teachers' research output. Like many teachers, he was left to navigate these complex demands on his own.

## *Examination pressure: Dilemma and complaint*

Li's teaching of reading, writing, and translation was congruent with the form of the CET-4 examination. He used multiple-choice questions for checking students' reading comprehension, a writing template in line with CET-4 writing requirements, as well as translation exercises in vocabulary teaching to prepare students to handle the translation section of CET-4. When asked about the relationship between CET-4 examination and learner autonomy, Li commented:

> CET-4 inhibits cultivation of moral quality, an aspect of learner autonomy. Students' main goal is to pass the exam, thus neglecting the moral dimension of education. I then reminded students of the importance of moral values. What else can I do? [...] I think it is unreasonable to hold CE teachers accountable for students' CET-4 test scores. (post-o)

Li's response shows his awareness of the conflict between the two discourses in the curriculum document: CET-4 examination as a short-term learning goal and learner autonomy as a long-term goal. He found no alternative to cultivating students' moral quality but to merely remind them of the importance of moral quality, even though he did not know precisely what this entailed. In addition, Li's critique of teachers being held accountable for students' CET-4 test scores indicates his sense of external pressure. A correlation could be observed between his resistance to the pressure put on teachers and the oppressive nature of his knowledge-transmission teaching style. However, he did not appear to be aware of this correlation.

## Pressure for teaching quality: Justification for transmission teaching mode

Li viewed comments from the course reviewers as another source of external pressure affecting the quality of the learner autonomy he could facilitate:

> I felt pressurised when receiving a criticism from the course reviewer: my class practice lacked teacher-student interaction for facilitating learner autonomy. What does it mean? I talked a lot? I think the dualist view of teacher-talk and student-talk is wrong. To me, interaction means teachers' communication with students, understanding of students' individualised learning needs and adapting content and techniques accordingly. (pre-o)
>
> Is it valid to evaluate student-teacher interaction by the amount of teacher-talk? I think it is too formalistic, without considering the reality of those students who are still habituated in being fed by teachers. Teacher-student interaction means guiding students to think and reflect. For instance, in my teaching of an article on thanksgiving, I asked students to extend gratitude to people around them, in order to cultivate them to become mature people. (pre-o)

Li's justification of his transmission teaching style is based on his rejection of the definition of "student-teacher interaction in facilitation of learner autonomy". He challenged what he perceived to be an overly simplistic time-allocation view of teacher-talk and student-talk. He proposed that interaction should involve teachers' detailed feedback to students and should be more organic than the authoritative view which limits teacher-student interaction to rounds of question-answer. Li's response was not reconstructed into knowledge due to a lack of critical dialogue between Li and the reviewer. Li and the reviewer seemed to be judgmental of each other. The reviewer's critique was not responsive to Li's conception of student-teacher interaction, and Li's justification sounded more self-defensive than a seeking of understanding. If the review process could have included mutual listening, there would have been an opportunity for Li's concerns to have been turned into knowledge.

## The case of Chen

### Workload pressure: Complaint regarding class size

Chen, a female CE teacher, identified workload as a pressure which hinders her facilitation of learner autonomy, saying:

Diversity of teacher autonomy 77

> I do not have enough time to tutor each student's autonomous reading. [...] Though I have singled out 100 short articles for supplementary reading, I cannot check whether they have done it. I can only ask students to submit reading journals at the end of a semester. (pre-o)
>
> Class size has a major impact on the effectiveness of tutoring individual students for autonomous learning. With over 60 students in each class, I can only randomly check their reading progress. [...] Students' inability to think deeply is partly attributed to a lack of individual guidance in a large class. (pre-o)

Chen's complaint about class size reflects a typical dilemma teachers face. The reform document suggests group tutoring as a strategy for facilitating autonomous learning, and therefore does not recognise teachers' concern that tutoring can hamper the cultivation of autonomy. Teachers' opinions around such contextual challenges speak to the uncertain relationship between autonomy and guidance. Though Chen initiated a supplementary reading task to facilitate learner autonomy, she viewed tutoring chiefly as mere "checking" of students' learning outcomes in line with outcome-based learning, rather than probing into their diverse needs to overcome reading difficulties.

## *Research pressure: Frustration caused by limited research capacity*

Chen considered research as a major challenge. She said:

> I am willing to do research, but I do not know exactly how to do scholarly research. [...] What can I do? I can read more theories, and write about theory application. [...] I want to become a doctoral student, so that the supervisor can point out a direction for me to do research systematically. (pre-o)
>
> I do not have time for research, because of the intensity of teaching workload from curriculum reform. [...] I am really frustrated by my limited research capacity. [...] With more doctorate holders recruited to the faculty, my pressure is mounting. I may be isolated as inferior. (pre-o)

In Chen's view, the dominant discourse in publications on CE prioritises theories, and is characterised by summary, with little critical understanding and little application in practice. Chen's reliance on a supervisor to "point out a direction" indicates her perception of research as something to be directed by an authority. Her feeling of isolation from colleagues who hold PhD degrees signals her vulnerability and fear of being marginalised. Such fear is rooted in the judgmental nature of the dominant institutional culture, in which qualifications are given undue importance. Unfortunately, this results in an environment where teacher development is not viewed as a process of growth through learning in practice. An understanding of teacher development in this context is limited to the acquisition of higher degrees.

## Examination pressure: Compromise between competing demands

Chen regarded the CET-4 examination as a constraint against learner autonomy, saying:

> Students view the course instrumentally for passing CET-4, paying little attention to autonomous learning. Autonomy is even taken as a burden to them […] also on CE teachers who are accountable for students' examination scores. (pre-o)
>
> Without CET-4, I would give students more freedom. I would help them to look at a topic from different angles by reading at least 10 supplementary articles. However, even without CET-4, students' lack of thinking capacity would be problematic for in-depth discussion. (pre-o)

Chen's approach to competing discourses reflects her internal conflict. She asserted that CET-4 examination inhibits learner autonomy and is an imposition to teachers. She has found no compatibility between examination demands and learner autonomy. Apart from CET-4, Chen held students' thinking capacity as salient for in-depth discussion, which in turn requires teachers to have honed their critical and constructive thinking capacity. In this light, examination may not be as much a pressure hampering learner autonomy as one that hampers teachers' own dialogical capacity.

## Pressure for teaching quality: Dichotomy between experience and theory

Chen held a vague view on teaching quality and desired support. She said:

> Theoretical knowledge is regarded as crucial for teaching quality. […] I want to obtain more knowledge from teacher training programmes, but find them not useful. […] Teachers are not supported to do research with relevant theories. (pre-o)
>
> Without a solid foundation in theory, I am just an ordinary teacher who can only talk about learner autonomy from personal teaching experience. I am not a qualified college teacher. […] My teaching stays at an experiential level, weak at the theoretical level. I want to become an excellent teacher, with abundant knowledge of theories. (pre-o)

Chen here reflects her view of experience and theory as diametrically opposed. By encouraging teachers to facilitate learner autonomy through research, the reform document tends to presume that teachers have the capacity to do research without institutional support. Teacher training programmes which merely provide textual information leave Chen feeling helpless. Despite her eagerness to develop knowledge of theories, she may hardly go beyond her here-and-now experiential learning without acquiring the habit of critical dialogue. She seemed powerless to critically integrate experiences for knowledge construction.

## The case of Gu

### Workload pressure: Efficient tutoring by discernment

Gu elaborated on how she managed workload pressure, saying:

> We need to tutor students' web-based and classroom-based learning, each learning mode with its set of textbooks. Tutoring for students' web-based learning was burdensome with much preparatory work, which distracted me from helping students handle obstacles against learner autonomy. [...] I just tutored students by monitoring how they finished textbook exercises. (post-o)
>
> As I try to build a relationship between the two modes of learning, I noticed the overlapping topics in both textbooks. I then realised that I can use different learning materials for the same topic. [...] My multiple-angled marking can help students further construct their understanding of the topic, as I can tutor them in an informed way. (post-o)

Gu's merging of web-based and classroom-based textbooks increases her opportunities to find ways to synergise the various learning mediums. Her initiative to establish a relationship between the various textbooks resulted in her feeling less burdened. Gu's transformation was attributed to her relational learning which enabled her to respond to teaching demands by generating an enhanced system. The change in Gu's approach to tutoring, which increased her autonomy, came about as a result of her claiming responsibility beyond what the reform demands. The reform document requires teachers to tutor students' web-based learning by monitoring their completion of textbook exercises. By integrating workloads, Gu had time to tutor students for knowledge construction, rather than merely checking on them.

### Research pressure: Synergy between teaching and research

Like others, Gu perceived research as a constraint to facilitating learner autonomy. She said:

> I used to split research from teaching [...] As I explore more on educational problems, my perspective changes. Genuine educational research is not about borrowing others' theories, but an inquiry into one's own experience. At the same time, teaching, by nature, is inquisitive research. [...] I believe that genuine research will naturally lead to external recognition, such as reward of promotion. (pre-o)
>
> I was once worried about my slow pace in publication, under the current 'publish-or-perish' reality. I notice that some teachers are preoccupied with publication regardless of seeking true quality of research. [...] I do not follow

that trend of quick publication for career promotion. I want to be driven by my conscience to serve education. (pre-o)

Gu's altered perspective on the relationship between teaching and research opens up her autonomous learning capacity. She managed to establish an equilibrium that runs counter to the dominant view that teaching is opposed to research. Gu's drive for research is indicative of her autonomy, because she would employ such research to uphold her values. Her learning stance enabled her to see that the ultimate goal of research should be to serve students, and this has freed her from the constraints of performance discourse. Her understanding came with her critical thinking, which is essential for meeting research demands without "worry".

## Examination pressure: Cultivation of students' higher-order thinking

To this teacher, the CET-4 examination was perceived to be a hindrance to learner autonomy. Gu explained:

> Most of the examination papers are presented as multiple-choice questions. Closed items often discourage students from deep thinking. Such items are not congruent with the call for learner autonomy. [...] A mere focus on CET-4 can enslave both teachers and students. (pre-o)
>
> As I know more about how the CET-4 certificate impacts on students' job-hunting, I am sympathetic with students on the pressure. [...] I do not give up learner autonomy for CET-4, but try to harmonise both. My teaching in the first three semesters focuses on training students' capacity for higher-order thinking, a critical dimension of learner autonomy. Such training lays the groundwork for students' capacity for meeting examination requirements. (pre-o)

Gu is aware of the tension between the CET-4 examination and learner autonomy. The gap between reform requirements and reality is addressed with autonomy, which comes about when an inner space for critical understanding is nurtured. This critical capacity will enable learners and teachers alike to grapple with competing discourses. Gu's effort to respond to examination pressure without foregoing learner autonomy is based on her own nurtured capacity to handle competing discourses. With an understanding of students' need for the CET-4 certificate, Gu was able to nurture learner autonomy and ensure the examination tasks were completed.

## Pressure for teaching quality: Pursuit of external-internal harmony

Gu felt that the external criteria for teaching quality may not be congruent with the facilitation of learner autonomy. She commented:

I had thought that my dialogical approach would help me win the Faculty teaching award. To my disappointment, my teaching was described as not practical, while the winners were praised for application of interesting language teaching techniques. [...] I was frustrated, wondering why teaching excellence was all about techniques. [...] I then realised that the depth of the concept of learner autonomy has not been widely understood. (pre-o)

I have been through a rough time in blaming the problematic criteria for teaching quality. [...] I then realised that my blaming came from my own blindness. It suddenly dawned on me that I had forgotten how I had grown into a more mature teacher. [...] Looking back, I am grateful for this experience, through which I learned to attain inner peace. (pre-o)

Her struggle with the external criteria for teaching quality captures how she operates in a way that is independent of the dominant judgmental discourse. As she pondered the concept of teaching excellence, her frustration triggered inquiry. Despite a lack of a dialogic environment, Gu's inner dialogue enabled her to gain insights from the dissonance she experienced, and also to gain understanding of her own limitations. She discovered that her resentment was rooted in her self-judgment. Gu's new awareness enabled her to establish an inner equilibrium, despite the judgmental culture in which she is situated.

## Cross-case analysis of teachers' responses to perceived institutional pressures

Table 5.1 summarises and captures the overlapping features of all individuals at three developmental levels.

**TABLE 5.1** Summary of teachers' responses to perceived institutional pressures

| Teachers' perceived institutional pressures | Li | Chen | Gu |
|---|---|---|---|
| Workload pressure | Group tutoring as a strategy | Complaint about class size | Efficient tutoring by discernment |
| Research pressure | Competition between teaching and research | Frustration at limited research capacity | Synergy between teaching and research |
| Examination pressure | Dilemma and complaint | Compromise between competing demands | Cultivation of students' higher-order thinking |
| Pressure for teaching quality | Justification for transmission teaching mode | Dichotomy between experience and theory | Pursuit of external-internal harmony |

## Teacher autonomy manifested as diverse developmental levels

The following presents a cross-case analysis that captures the overlapping features of the individuals, and three developmental levels of teachers' responses are identified and discussed here.

### Level 1: Dilemma amidst competing discourses

At a preliminary level of response to perceived institutional pressures, teachers face an impasse amidst competing discourses. Li felt helpless about students' complaints regarding a lack of equal access to his time, and gave a weak explanation to justify his providing selective attention to more needy students within the time constraints. Likewise, Chen's complaint about large class size reveals a lack of autonomy to handle workload pressure. Considering the accountability to CET-4 as a burden, she has limited capacity to negotiate between the competing discourses.

### Level 2: Relational understanding of reform demands

At a higher level of response to perceived institutional pressures, teachers can draw a tenuous surface relationship between competing reform demands. Li struggled to establish a complementary relationship between teaching and research, and Chen struggled to associate the experience of teaching with theories. Chen also heeded the gap between reform expectations and reality, by noting high demands on teachers for publication outputs and her own limited research capacity. Consistently, a sense of helplessness prevailed.

### Level 3: Dialogic accommodation of competing discourses

At this level, Gu manifests her capability to accommodate reform discourses with internal transformative dialogues. Gu initially had an antagonistic view of CET-4, and did not believe that examination is an accountability indicator. However, she was determined to negotiate a relationship between discourses. Reflecting on her journey, Gu moved beyond complaining about external pressures. Autonomy is therefore about claiming responsibility to identify and harmonise tensions between competing discourses.

## Teacher diversity in autonomy as manifested in a process of learning to be

Teacher diversity rarely appears in scholarly literature on diversity. When it is addressed, the concept is often understood to reflect differences with regard to age, race, and ethnicity. In light of the findings of this study, teacher diversity can also be understood in terms of different levels of autonomous learning. As the highest level of teacher autonomy necessitates a mature understanding of the self, teacher diversity can reflect the points along a process of cultivating the self through 'learning to be'.

## Perception of constraint from dominant external discourses

The teacher in a preliminary state of autonomous learning has not yet cultivated an inner value system in their initial response to dominant external discourses. One cannot develop one's own voice without a system of constructing and developing knowledge within an internal discourse. A teacher is not an empty vessel to be loaded with expectations ready for fulfilment. Without an independent inner value system, a teacher cannot discern the nature of learning opportunities underpinning unresolved problems paradoxically imposed by the external discourses. Training can often involve mere immersion in information and a hierarchical structure of top-down delivery. This approach neglects the true meaning of autonomy.

## Space for inner exploration

As a teacher is listening to and cultivating their inner voice, a space is created to probe contextual challenges, and this in turn enables contextual learning to take place. Through raising questions which may be superficial to begin with, a journey of seeking from within can begin. In this process, outside support is not as salient as the drive from within. This is a journey towards an integration of competing discourses and resolving tensions. Inevitably, this journey features feelings of helplessness and struggles in recognition of conflicting discourses. When a teacher is engaged in this state, their sense of inadequacy may become the catalyst for stretching the boundary.

## Critical awareness of self and environment

At this level of maturation, a teacher becomes critically aware of the dominant discourses and problems of their inner state. As expressed by Shor and Freire (1987, p. 13), "the dominant ideology 'lives' inside us and also controls society outside […]. We can gain distance from our moment of existence." An autonomous teacher is liberated from what appear to be controlling external discourses, and refuses to be distracted from maturing professionally. Despite a limited capacity to deconstruct the internalisation of dominant discourses, an autonomous teacher can rise above inner disequilibrium, and take responsibility to understand what is going on both internally and externally.

## Towards a humanistic focus for teacher education

A critical goal of teacher education is to facilitate teachers to become autonomous learners. Given that teachers are diverse beings grappling amidst their own varied states of learning, teacher education must respond to these diverse states. Less autonomous teachers lack the capacity to construct contextual knowledge to authentically understand problems, while more autonomous teachers rely on their independent inner value system to engage with the environment to seek deeper understanding of problems. Teacher education that ignores such developmental stages could fail to accommodate different learning needs, or even hinder teachers' further learning. An awareness of teacher diversity is critically important for those who are involved in teacher training. To become autonomous, each teacher has to be responsible for a process of liberating the self to explore diverse inner resources instead of merely imbibing a ready-made fixed prescription. As pointed out by Confucius in *Analects*, learning requires an understanding of unity within diversity ('he er bu tong'). Findings from this study resonate with an appeal for a humanistic focus in teacher education, in which teacher diversity is recognised and valued for a shared journey of learning to serve younger generations. Just as teachers are expected to mature in carrying responsibilities with professional autonomy, teacher educators and curriculum policy makers must respect such autonomy by cultivating a humanistic environment for their own learning.

## *Sustaining diversity of inner resources*

The conventional teacher education paradigm prioritises objective knowledge, as teachers are often seen as cogs in the education machinery for standardised knowledge transmission. If education is to be achieved as a journey of learning to be, as recommended by UNESCO (1996, 2015), all educators need to respect teachers and students as diverse human beings, each with unique experiences to contribute to society. For teachers to establish the autonomy described in this chapter, there is a need for the humanisation of relationships, and a valuing of teachers' inner voices, which need to be released from externally- and internally imposed pressures. Authentic inquiry into contextual challenges must be safeguarded, and struggles through problem-solving and conflict resolution should not be regarded as weaknesses in the flow of managerial discourse. According to ancient Chinese Taoism, authenticity is to name the unnameable with which we are on course (Graham, 1989, p. 497). Whenever knowledge is considered fixed and certain, contextual challenges are ignored and struggles are silenced. Whenever the focus is on performativity, diversity which stems from spontaneity and authenticity is neglected. To pursue a humanistic focus, teacher educators also need a learning space to activate inner resources, where educational beliefs are tested and reinforced into an ever-growing value system.

## *Cultivating unity of shared responsibility*

The drive for teachers' inquiry into contextual challenges comes from their commitment to educational values and to educating students. As elucidated by Confucius in *The Great Learning*, "the object of a Higher Education is to bring out the intelligent moral power of our nature" (Gu, 1915, p. 1). In this sense, teacher autonomy necessarily involves the responsibility of inquiry. Unity brought about by a moral quest ensures that diversity can converge from various sectors. Only with such unity can all educators come together to learn to become better professionals. A humanistic focus can result in the creation of a safe and encouraging environment where diverse teachers and teacher educators carry out inquiry to actualise growth in a process of learning to be. Teacher education cannot neglect the state of teachers' inner voices, which is more than a system of values, but is a state of awareness that must be nurtured.

## Conclusion

This chapter has focused on a quest to understand teacher autonomy from a review of teachers' responses to perceived institutional pressures which hinder learner autonomy. It was found that teacher autonomy manifests in diverse ways, from conforming to and struggling with administrative accountability, to commitment to nurturing the young. Teacher diversity can be conceptualised as a process of developing inner resources and values. A maturing teacher is capable of transforming tension into harmony, and is driven by a moral commitment to serve students. The neglect of a moral drive has been remarked on by Greene (1978, p. 60):

> Educators and educational reformers have been continually tempted to test the rationality of what they have done by the effectiveness or efficiency of what has been accomplished, not by looking critically at their presuppositions [...]. They have seldom looked at the question of whether their actions were intrinsically right. Facts have been easily separated off from values; decisions have been made on grounds independent of moral propriety.

Teacher diversity, which in this study is understood to reflect different levels of teachers' inner state, may invite a review of the efficiency discourse in teacher education. Under the College English curriculum reform, autonomous learning is not to be taken for granted. It is teachers' critical awareness of conflicting values, along with a moral drive, that can prompt them to establish harmony between professional responsibility and administrative accountability. An understanding of teachers' various states of autonomy might prompt policy makers to look into how to create a safe environment conducive to helping teachers to reach self-understanding. We contend that professional dialogue in a safe space can release suppressed voices and yield dynamic learning in teachers.

## References

Benson, P. (2000). Autonomy as a learner's and teachers' right. In B. Sinclair, I. McGrath & T. Lamb (Eds.), *Learner autonomy, teacher autonomy: Future directions*. London: Longman, 111–117.

Committee of the Syllabus of College English (1999). *The Syllabus of College English* (modified). Shanghai: Shanghai Higher Education Press.

Creswell, J.W. (2002). *Educational research: Planning, conducting, and evaluating quantitative and qualitative research*. Upper Saddle River, NJ: Merrill Prentice Hall.

Delors, J. (Chairperson) (1996). *Learning: The treasure within*. Paris: UNESCO.

Franklin, H.L. (1988). *Principle consideration and its relationship to teacher sense of autonomy*. Doctoral dissertation, University of Oregon.

Graham, A.C. (1989). *Disputers of the Tao: Philosophical argument in ancient China*. La Salle: Open Court Publishing Company.

Greene, M. (1978). *Landscapes of learning*. New York: Teachers College Press.

Gu, H. (1915). *The translation of the Great Learning*. www.thomehfang.com/suncrates6/higher%20education.pdf

Hanson, E.M. (1991). *Educational administration and organizational behavior* (3rd ed.) Boston: Allyn and Bacon.

Higher Education Department, Ministry of Education of P.R.C. (2007). *College English Curriculum Requirements*. Shanghai: Shanghai Foreign Language Education Press.

Kwo, O. (2007). Creating a learning space for educators: Policy development for accountability systems. In D. Louis & J.C. Cheryl (Eds.), *International research on the impact of accountability systems*. (*Association of Teacher Education Yearbook XV*). Toronto: Rowman & Littlefield, 207–224.

Lamb, T. & Reinders, H. (Eds.) (2008). *Learner and teacher autonomy: Concepts, realities, and responses*. Amsterdam: John Benjamins.

Little, D. (1995). Learning as dialogue: the dependence of learner autonomy on teacher autonomy. *System*, 23, 175–181.

McGrath, I. (2000). Teacher autonomy. In B. Sinclair, I. McGrath & T. Lamb (Eds.), *Learner autonomy, teacher autonomy: Future directions*. London: Longman, 100–110.

Merriam, S.B. (1998). *Qualitative research and case study applications in education*. San Francisco: Jossey-Bass Publishers.

Miles, M.B. & Huberman, A.M. (1994) *Qualitative data analysis*. Thousand Oaks, CA: Sage Publications.

Ministry of Education of P.R.C. (1999). *Decisions on furthering educational reform and advancing suzhi education*. http://old.moe.gov.cn/publicfiles/business/htmlfiles/moe/moe_177/200407/2478.html

Patton, M.Q. (1990). *Qualitative evaluation and research methods*. Newbury Park, CA: Sage Publications.

Shaw, J. (2002). Team-teaching as negotiating autonomy and shared understandings of what we are doing. *Symposium of the Scientific Commission on Learner Autonomy*.

Shor, W. & Freire, P. (1987). *A pedagogy for liberation: Dialogues on transforming education*. Westport, CN: Bergin & Garvey.

Street, M.S. & Licata, J.W. (1989). Supervisor expertise: Resolving the dilemma between bureaucratic control and teacher autonomy. *Planning and Changing*, 20, 97–107.

UNESCO. (1996). *Learning: The treasure within*. Paris: UNESCO.

UNESCO. (2015). *Rethinking education: Towards a global common good?* Paris: UNESCO. http://download.ei-ie.org/Docs/WebDepot/UNESCOReport_RethinkingEducation.pdf

Zhang, H. (2013). *John Dewey, Liang Shuming, and China's education reform: Cultivating individuality*. Lanham, MD: Lexington Books.

# 6

# EDUCATING IN DIVERSE WORLDS

The immigrant Somali parent as a strategic partner of South African education

*Doria Daniels*

## Introduction

According to the Education White Paper 6 on building an inclusive education and training system (Department of Education, 2001), educational transformation should lead to a more just and democratic society through the promotion of equity and equality. This view reflects a respect for individual human rights and social justice, and has its roots in the international human rights movement. Parallels can be seen between what the Education White Paper 6 espouses and the Universal Declaration on Human Rights (1948) and the UNESCO Convention against Discrimination in Education (1960). Several such government policy documents argue for each child's right to basic education and promote schools as inclusive environments, which is what the South African state envisions for its schools. What these policies do not engage with, however, are the practicalities and the challenges that learner diversity poses to education and to development. They also do not address the complexities of race, ethnicity and culture. Instead, they rest on the expectation that education, as a formalised system (Jarvis, 2004), will equip those who participate in it with the confidence to enhance their abilities to make informed decisions about life's issues. This paradigm positions schools as enabling environments where equitable opportunities exist for students to develop and become socially and economically empowered (Vila, 2000). The South African Department of Basic Education supports an inclusive approach to education (Department of Education, 2001) and advances a philosophy that sees learner diversity as a positive, and positions the classroom as a space that has to be managed to the advantage of all learners (Tobin & McInnes, 2008). However, educators' lack of acknowledgement of the diverse home backgrounds of children makes them engage with learners as if they come from a homogenous background. For me, this approach is problematic as it does not accommodate the knowledges that immigrant learners might bring from their home contexts, that benefit their educational success.

The accumulated body of scholarly work on inclusion distinguishes between the terms 'integration', 'assimilation' and 'inclusion'. Integration is defined within a social and political discourse as the provision of equal access for all children to an education system (Swart & Pettipher, 2016), while assimilation refers to the child's adaptation to the existing learning environment. Where inclusion differs from these two constructs is in the positioning of the school system as a critically reflexive environment that addresses the educational needs of all of its learners. Schools are expected to be open to the probability of change, and willing to adapt their environment in order to meet all of their students' needs (Engelbrecht, 2006; Gibb, Tunbridge, Chua & Frederickson, 2007; Oswald, 2010; Ntombela, 2011; Higham, 2012). In practice, however, attempting to establish inclusive school environments is pointless without awareness of the principles of social justice, educational equality and educator responsibility towards embracing diversity (Dyson, 2001). Rankin's research (2003; see also Hurtado, Carter & Kardia, 1998; Suarez-Balcazar, Orellana-Damacela, Nelson Portillo, Rowan & Andrews-Guillen, 2003) on educational experience shows that minority students feel isolated and unwelcome, and that they continue to experience discrimination and differential treatment in the educational environment. It is especially the learners whose ethnicity differs from that of the majority, or those whose home language differs from the language of instruction, who have disempowering experiences in education.

South Africa has a history of inequality and segregation, and one would expect educators in this context to now be sensitised with regard to learner ethnicity, cultural background and educational experience (Walton, 2012). My experience as an educator, however, has shown me that the inclusion discourse on educational transformation continues to be in response to special needs education and to South Africa's racial history, and limited attention is given to ethnicity, culture and language. The changed demographic composition of urban government schools should make critical dialogue about ethnic and cultural diversity an unavoidable part of inclusive education discourse. Though teacher-training programmes provide students with theoretical knowledge on how to advance inclusive goals, they contain limited practical opportunities for trainee teachers to experience the challenges of the multilingual and multicultural classroom prior to qualifying. When they start their careers as teachers, they are then not equipped to prioritise the development of equitable measures that give minority learners a fair chance to achieve. A number of studies have found that when educational problems present themselves in classrooms with minority students, teachers tend to link the classroom problems and the poor educational performance of such students to a lack of parental involvement (Harris, 1985, in Lareau, 2000). However, teachers seldom know the parents or the home contexts of their students. International research on immigrant parent involvement shows that when teachers talk about these parents, they tend to misrepresent them (Lareau, 2000; Lareau & Weininger, 2003; Waterman, 2008; Li, 2010). When educators adopt a deficit understanding of the immigrant parent, they advance a mindset that the root of the problem is in immigrant home environments and that these parents should be trained on how to assist in the education of their children. Educators are then more likely to underestimate or simply dismiss the cultural and social capital that such families have accumulated and are contributing to the education process (Lareau & Weininger, 2003).

The community, and the family, is essentially a social world with an "accumulated history" and cultural wealth, according to Bourdieu (1986, p. 241). Yosso (2005) has argued for the recognition of the cultural wealth that minority and poor communities have and contends that it should be valued as an alternative form of social capital, as it could lead us to understand the practices of such communities. Bourdieu's (1986) understanding of the concept of social capital is as a system or network of elaborate interactions that benefit those who have access to it in society. Bourdieu's theoretical work on cultural and social capital (1986, see also Lareau & Weininger, 2003) is a useful tool to explain how the life world and cultural experiences of children from middle-class homes aid their adjustment to school and their academic achievement. It also facilitates an understanding of how the exchange of resources within and beyond the complex networks or systems of social interactions (Lareau & Weininger, 2003) privilege middle-class children. I find Bourdieu's paradigm to be a useful lens as it encourages reflective thought about the ways in which parents invest in their children beyond the normative understanding of parent support. It also helps me understand the ways in which parents value their children's education and what they do to support it. A shortcoming of Bourdieu's framework is that it does not, however, capture the cultural capital that is unique to worker-class homes. My review of international and national literature on parental involvement in education has revealed that most studies focus on parents' support of the work of schools (Epstein, 2001; Singh, Mbokodi & Msila, 2004; Lemmer, 2007; Nargis & Tikly, 2010), and that few studies explore the experience of immigrant parents, specifically, or the contributions that they make to their children's education.

In this chapter, I explore the actions of certain immigrant parents with regard to their children's education in relation to the "field condition" (Nash, 1990; Bourdieu & Wacquant, 1992) that they inhabit, or in Bourdieu's (1986) words, their habitus. I use Bourdieu's key concept of habitus as my analytical lens to understand the aspects of human agency present in the immigrant homes that I researched. By studying their being in the world, educators could develop a better understanding of their individual and collective histories. For this discussion, I draw on the data from an ongoing qualitative project on immigrant parent support, of which I am the principal investigator, and an MEd study (Peters, 2014) that I supervised on the topic. Peters' (2014) study explored the various forms of support that Somali parents provide to their primary school children. She conducted her research in the same community in which I did mine, namely a working-class Somali population in the Western Cape, and I therefore identified her work as a valuable source. The chapter starts with an overview of the literature on parental support, followed by an orientation to and description of the investigation. Thereafter I present the findings and conclude the chapter with reflections and recommendations.

## Parental involvement and support in education

The South African Schools Act (SASA) of 1996 gave parents legal power to take up central roles in their children's schools. At a policy level, at least, a supportive parent-practitioner partnership is encouraged. The SASA allows parents, together with teachers, to take responsibility for the governing of schools, as well as to become collaborators towards quality education (Singh, Mbokodi & Msila, 2004; Lemmer, 2007). Internationally and nationally, research backs the merits of parental involvement in schooling, and promotes techniques for increasing it (Lareau, 2000). However, not all parents will become involved in the governance of schools. Parents' involvement in the educational management of a school is likely to be facilitated by familiarity with the school culture, and membership of hegemonic groupings at the school. Parents who are not from the dominant culture, and whose involvement in the school is limited, could be seen by the school management as unsuited to serve on the school governing body.

The research on parental involvement and support reflects three clear foci: "how" parents need to be involved, the quality of that involvement, and the centralisation of the parent-school relationship. Some research argues for a compliant and supportive role for parents, where their involvement at school is an educator-authorised involvement (Epstein, 1985; 1995; 2001; Nargis & Tikly, 2010). This paradigm seldom encourages extensive engagement of parents in the broader educational agenda; the understanding is that their role is to assist, not to partner. Research on the quality and the extent of parental involvement in schools (López, 1999, 2001; Lareau, 2000; Waterman, 2008; Li, 2010) identifies social class as a key factor which influences parental practices. Though most conceptual models on parental support concede that a family's social class exerts a powerful influence on the life chances of their children, these models fail to recognise how the cultural experiences of the middle-class home, in particular, differentially aid children's adjustment in school (Bourdieu, 1977; Lareau, 2000; Li, 2010). The resources of such homes are accumulated capital that produce vital social returns for their members in a school system that makes use of the same cultural capital. Research that centralises family-school relations has attempted to counter the stereotypical assumptions and attitudes about non-participatory parents (Delgado-Gaitan, 1992; López, 2001; Smrekar & Cohen-Vogel, 2001; Orellana, Monkman & MacGillivray, 2002) and proposes a broader framework within which parents' understandings of their role in education are researched. My ontological stance as researcher is informed by this strand of research.

## Beginning the exploration of an immigrant Somali habitus: Context, design and methodology

Since the Somali civil war in 1991, an estimated 300,000 Somalis have migrated to East and Southern Africa. As a signatory of the UN Convention for Refugees

(UNHCR, 2000), South Africa is obliged to grant any Somali refugee status and access to work, and to ensure that their children have access to schooling. The Western Cape, with its strong Muslim presence, seems to be a preferred province for Somalis to settle (Jinnah, 2010). The town where this research was conducted has five mosques, a community primary school and a high school, and is as a result a habitus that Somali immigrants could find attractive. The primary school's registry shows that the first Somali student was enrolled at the school in 2002, and that many more have enrolled since. In 2013, there were 12 Grade R pupils and 18 Grade 1 pupils from Somalia enrolled. By 2014, more than 50% of the English Grade 1 class was of Somali origin.

The narrative inquiry was shaped by a social constructivist paradigm (Creswell, 2003; Mertens, 2014). The aim of this approach was to discover how parents think about education and their own role in their children's education, and in turn, how this intersects with their participation in the host society's education system. I also wanted to gather information about their own educational history. The school's administrators facilitated my access to the first participant, and thereafter, by way of a snowball sampling process, three more participants were selected. Previous research I have conducted on cross-cultural communication has revealed how such communication can be severely hampered by language difference (Daniels, 2003). I therefore decided to limit the participants to those who could converse in English. My interactional epistemological stance towards their realities (Terre Blanche, Durrheim & Painter, 2006) informed my decision to conduct one-on-one (Patton, 2002) semi-structured interviews with four parents, all of whom were mothers. This method created interactional opportunities that aided my understanding of how they make sense of their role in their children's educational success. I also conducted two focus group interviews with educators at the school who have experience teaching Somali pupils.

## Findings

### *The participants*

The four parents that I interviewed were all in their thirties and, on average, were raising eight children. Three of the women worked as traders. Malaika operates her business from the converted front room of her house, and sells clothes, scarves and ethnic Somali food brands. Shakirah owns and manages a fruit and vegetable shop, and Amirah and her husband operate a spaza shop[1] in a neighbouring town. Table 6.1 provides demographic information on the participants.

The parents' narratives about their educational trajectory are interwoven with their experiences of the Somali war of 1991. These narratives reflect the devastating consequences of war on family stability and on educational opportunity. Amirah, then 11 years old, fled with her family of 14, on foot, to avoid being killed. She said:

**TABLE 6.1** Demographic information on the participants

| Parent | Age | In SA | Marital status | Education | Children | Work |
|---|---|---|---|---|---|---|
| Afifa | 33 | 2002 | M | None | 8 | Housewife |
| Shakirah | 33 | 2006 | M/2nd | None | 4 | Manages a fruit & vegetable shop |
| Amirah | 39 | 1996 | M | 4 years | 10 | Business with husband |
| Malaika | 39 | 1996 | M | None | 8 | Business from home |

> They were killing the kids... they were raping the girls (pause)... I can tell. We ran from village to village, from country to country. I was 11 and kept running until I was 16. They killed my father. They kill my uncles.
>
> *(AM interview, 2016)*

Her story echoes those of Malaika, Afifa and Shakirah. The families each of these women hail from fled Somalia and sought refuge in the Kenyan refugee camp on the border between Kenya and Somalia. When their village came under attack, the 11-year-old Malaika became separated from her family members and arrived alone at the refugee camp in Kenya. She only reunited with her mother a year later. Her father and other males who fled with them were killed. Malaika spent five years in the refugee camp where she met and married her husband. Shakirah's first husband was a casualty of war, leaving the 15-year-old mother to raise her daughter on her own.

South Africa's camp-free policy, and the opportunity to establish themselves anywhere in the country, was an attractive option for these refugees, and motivated their migration south. Immigrants who travelled south would board a boat in Kismayo, a port city in Somalia, and travel to Mozambique. There they would stay in hiding until an agent could transport them over land to the South African border. Malaika and Amirah arrived in South Africa in 1997, and Afifa and Shakirah came almost a decade later. Malaika and Amirah were both part of the first group of nine Somalis who settled in the town.

## Educational background of the parents

Of the four parents, only Amirah attended formal school before the war. She was seven years old when she went to school for the first time, which was a break with tradition in her family. Girls traditionally did not receive a secular education, but were educated to read the Quran. Amirah recounted how a visit from her aunt, a business person who was working in Italy, led to the girls in her family being enrolled in school. The aunt challenged her brother's decision to keep his daughters at home, and managed to convince him that basic education is an investment in a better future for them.

She (referring to the aunt) said, 'No, they must go to school. I know what I am suffering – they are not going to suffer like I did'.

*(AM interview, 2016)*

Afifa, Malaika and Shakirah's lack of access to basic education was a consequence of the war. All of them recalled both boys and girls from their communities going to school prior to 1991. In Malaika's case, her secular education was delayed because of a tradition in her family which required children to complete their religious education before they started their secular education. However, when Malaika graduated from Madrassa (Islamic School) at age 11, the country was a war zone, and the government, together with the education system, had collapsed. All four women remembered forms of cultural and social capital such as books and newspapers, and informal educational systems, being present in their homes. Though Afifa and Malaika never went to school, they grew up in homes where family members habitually recited from the Quran, and were raised by mothers who had access to basic education. Malaika remembers her mother teaching her to read in Somali, from books and other educational artefacts. One of her prized possessions is a bilingual dictionary that she brought from Somalia, which she uses often. Thus, despite their lack of secular schooling, Malaika, Afifa, Amirah and Shakirah had various forms of cultural capital which became mechanisms that guided their own decisions and actions concerning education, as the data will show.

## *English as the key to navigating and supporting schoolwork*

All four parents showed strong commitment to the education of their children despite their challenges with education that emanated from a lack of formal education. Shakirah spoke about how her lack of operational skills made her feel inferior and caused her to doubt her ability to assist her children with their schoolwork. Afifa echoed this: "I love to help them but I cannot, because I do not know how" (AK interview, 2016). Instead of giving up, these parents have started developing skills that make it possible for them to execute the sanctioned school-related activities. Their narrative constructions of education reflect that they consider English as the exclusive medium of instruction, and that fluency in English is compulsory for their role as facilitator of educational practices at home. These parents became proactive about acquiring and/or improving their own linguistic competencies in English, as the data shows.

Amirah speaks English well. She credits a teacher friend for her verbal competency in English. When this teacher opened a school in one of the Somali villages, he made use of her services as an interpreter. In return, he taught her a few English phrases. When her group arrived in South Africa, she was the only one who could speak some English. Before coming to South Africa, the other three participants had only heard English being spoken on television. As a generation of Somali women who were socialised to not mix with the broader community, limited opportunities were available to them to practise their English. All of them turned to television to learn English. Afifa, Amirah and Malaika showed an almost child-like pride about their successes in learning to speak English, and the benefits that communicating in it held for their own development, and that of their children. Malaika and Afifa accumulated an extensive vocabulary and conversational competency through watching soap operas on television. They seemed confident to speak the language with their children and with outsiders. Afifa's children were very encouraging of her effort to learn English. Supervising their homework opened up an educational opportunity for her to learn alongside her children, which speaks to the intergenerational benefits of family literacy.

## *Education as an intergenerational project*

According to Bernstein (2000), educational attainment is augmented at home through the facilitation of pedagogical time at home to do homework. The narratives of the parents contained many examples of what Bourdieu describes as the social construction of the strategies that these parents adopt to assist their children and their progress in school. The data contained many forms of cultural capital that have been accumulated in these four parents' homes through the investments they have made in their own development, and that of their children. These parents acknowledge their educational limitations when assisting their school-going children with comprehension exercises, homework and educational projects. Nevertheless, they have succeeded in creating a dialogical space that is conducive to school-related activities being executed. They mimic the supervision process that any literate committed parents would enact. Afifa gets away with it because her younger children do not know that she cannot read or write in English, or understand their homework instructions. Both Afifa and Shakirah pretend that they understand when they ask their children about homework. Shakirah's younger children read to her, even though she does not yet have the capabilities to verify whether they are reading correctly. Afifa uses her cell phone as a strategic educational tool, to encourage them to read and to strengthen their reading skills. Each of the mothers praises their youngsters for doing their homework, even though they do not always know whether the child has done the work well. Through their actions, they send out the strong message that education is important. Their narratives challenge the perception that incomplete homework, poorly done projects and incorrect answers are evidence of a lack of interest and investment from parents.

During homework time, these parents have mechanisms in place that benefit the educational project. In Amirah's home, her children come together at 17:30 in a room with a table that seats six. While they do homework or reading, she sits close by, supervising. Television and playtime are privileges that are enjoyed only over weekends, when there is no school or Madrassa. Amirah and Malaika, who are literate and semi-literate, respectively, invest a lot of time in understanding instructions to do primary school homework. Malaika's constant consultation of her bilingual Somali-English dictionary to make sense of homework problems has paid dividends in that she is now skilled enough to supervise her primary school children's homework.

Malaika and Amirah's families settled in the town more than two decades ago. In their families, an accumulated abundance of social and navigational capital (Yosso, 2005) is evident. Their older children are in high school, and have become resources that the parents use to advance the education of their younger primary school siblings. The earlier challenges that parents were reported to face in Peters' study (2014) seem to have been addressed through an exchange of resources within and between the families. What the narratives bring into focus is the intergenerational challenges that exist when immigrant parents do not yet have literacy skills, and how their children are then disadvantaged. However, knowledge about the networks and systems of exchange serves as an important source of social capital. Amirah used to employ a retired teacher from the local community to supervise her children's homework when neither she nor her husband had the skills or the knowledge to help them. Afifa is now in a similar situation, and asks high school children from her community to assist her children with their homework, paying them a small fee. She also makes use of an after-school programme that provides extra tutoring in languages and mathematics, the learning areas that her children need help with.

The educational investment that these parents make in their children extends beyond schoolwork. One of the creative ways in which Amirah builds confidence in her children is through visual documentation. Instead of just asking them to tell her about their school day, she interviews them on video or assigns them the role of newscaster or reporter on television. Each night, a different child gets the opportunity to report, on camera, what happened to them during that particular day. Afterwards, she plays back the recordings for the whole family to enjoy. With the exception of the youngest two children, a set of twins, all of Amirah's children are at school. Despite her very busy schedule, she seems to be investing a lot of time in them, and encouraging them to participate in educational activities. When she buys them books, they have to report back to her on the books' contents. On a Friday afternoon, Amirah's children visit the municipal library, accompanied by one of their parents.

## *Religious education as a foundation for life*

Malaika recalled that it was traditional in her community to first send children to Madrassa, and then to enrol them in secular education. The women that I interviewed, like the population Peters (2014) studied, all had excellent religious educational backgrounds, which suggests that this is the norm for all Somali children. The parents consider their children's education to be incomplete without religious education. They want them "to know everything" (AM interview, 2016), referring both to secular and religious education. Compared to South African Muslims, Somali adults are more knowledgeable about their religion, and engage with it as a way of life. Religious education occupies a valorised place in the education of Somalis, and parents seem to take their responsibility to transfer a religious value system to their children very seriously. Traditionally, religious education takes place at the Madrassa, and is part of children's preparation to participate in the world as adults.

Though it is impossible to duplicate the religious schooling system as it functioned in Somalia, this community's parents have succeeded in continuing the tradition of religious education for their children. They established an after-school Madrassa that all children from this Somali community attend six days a week. During the week, from Monday to Thursday, the Madrassa starts at 15:00 and continues until just before sunset. On Saturdays and Sundays, they attend classes until noon. The parents and their children therefore lead a regimented lifestyle where both secular and religious education fill their whole day. The parents' schedule for a typical weekday looks as follows:

- prepare children for school and send them to school;
- prepare and serve lunch when children come from school;
- send them to Madrassa from 15:00 until sunset;
- have dinner ready and then supervise homework with them (older children go back to Madrassa);
- continue checking their homework (from both school and Madrassa) before bedtime.

The lack of playtime during the week seemed not to concern the parents. To quote one mother, "They have the whole afternoon of Friday, Saturday and Sunday to play" (SA interview, 2016).

## Living in a changed world: Views on education

Malaika, Afifa, Shakirah and Amirah all have dreams for their children's futures. They describe their children as "a new generation who are enjoying equal opportunities in South Africa" (MH interview, 2016). After their experiences of living in a refugee camp, with no opportunity to gain an education, these parents were thankful to raise their children in South Africa. "This country is free. I have everything here. And we are safe" (MH interview, 2016). All four participants' children of school-going age are attending school. Some of Malaika and Amirah's children have graduated from high school already, and Malaika's eldest son is studying towards a degree in psychology.

The narratives contained many examples of aspirational capital that the participants have accumulated, and that they now spend on their children. These parents are engaging with education as an investment in their children's futures. Amirah says that her husband constantly uses their refugee experience as example to encourage their children to achieve academically. He tells them: "We do not want you to struggle, like your mother and I struggle" (AM interview, 2016). The parents are investing in and planning for their children's futures by buying books on the careers that their children are interested in, and becoming informed about such professions. Amirah said:

> Even now, until they finish matric, when they go to college, university… we want to be ready. Whatever it takes, we will be ready. Whatever they dream, what they want to be – we will support them.
>
> *(AM interview, 2016)*

## *Finding a way to build the parent-teacher relationship*

The teachers seem to have very limited knowledge about the backgrounds of the immigrant children. Though teachers mentioned the Somali parents who regularly visit the school, none of them knew the parents personally. The teacher narratives mirrored the findings of Epstein (1985; 1995; 2001) and others (Nargis & Tikly, 2010) on teachers' expectations of the role of parents in education. They expect parents to be amenable to communication with their children's teachers, to be knowledgeable about their children's daily school activities and homework, to volunteer their services at school functions and extra-mural activities, and to support the school generally. All of these expectations position parents in a supportive role within the school structures, but do not take the roles that they play at home into account. The pedagogical space they create at home contributes to the successes that teachers have with children in school. My analysis of the parent narratives shows that the parents that I interviewed work hard at establishing a home environment that values education. This could challenge perceptions some teachers have of parents as disinvested in their children's education, and make them see parents as potential collaborators in their children's education.

Amirah and Afifa visit the school often, and commented on the importance of mutual respect between teachers and parents. Amirah has great respect for teachers at her children's school, saying that of one of her children's teachers "teaches them to be proud of who they are" (AM interview, 2016). Amirah phrased the teacher-parent role as follows:

> The teacher is the second mother. Mother is the first teacher. Teacher and parent must work together. To raise your child and to teach the child is the same. In the house, in the school, it is the same.
>
> *(AM interview, 2016)*

This parent described the school's teachers as "the same as parents", as they "look after our children" (AM interview, 2016). She singled out the learning support teacher as a valued resource to her, despite her view that educational support should be a collaborative effort by parents and teachers.

My interviews with both the parents and teachers led me to believe that because the mechanisms and processes of engagement are not always clearly negotiated between these parties, there is often tension, frustration, and even conflict when they interact. Though teachers described Somali parents as "very eager to please" (Focus group, 2016), some teachers used it to describe what they view as Somali parents' unnecessary visits during the school day to see teachers. However, teachers justified their irritation by pointing out that these parents often bypass the secretary's office and arrive unannounced at their classes, expecting teachers to meet with them. They ignore the rules and regulations that facilitate the smooth running of the school programme. One teacher remarked that any memo, even ones that advertise an upcoming school event, lead to Somali parents turning up at their classrooms.

What the data reveals is that the typical parent's response to any note that she receives from the school is to pay a visit to the class teacher. Parents did not realise that they are disrupting the school programme, and they believed that their quickness to respond would convince the teacher that they are involved parents. They are aware of the tensions that their visits elicit in teachers, and are hurt by the responses they receive from them. Amirah explained how her visit to a teacher's class without an appointment was met with disrespect. She felt that the teacher was talking down to her when she told her: "Why did you come here? Go see the secretary first" (AM interview, 2016). What the data further shows is the lack of empathy that teachers have with parents who have limited fluency in English. What the teachers might not be aware of is that immigrant parents could be functioning in a restrictive ethnic milieu, and that the networks they are part of might not have sufficient knowledge of the highly defined, socially constructed scripts that institutionalise the relationships amongst role-players in school settings (Smrekar & Cohen-Vogel, 2001).

## Reflections and conclusions

In this chapter, I reported on the experiences of a Somali community's parents who are navigating the General Education and Training band of the educational system and attempting to support their children of primary school age. My sense-making of their facilitation of their children's educational success is framed by Bourdieu's (1986) concept of cultural capital and Yosso's (2005) community cultural wealth. When working through my data, I was struck by the differences between this community and the one that I came to know through Peters' data collection in 2012 for her study which was completed in 2014. Peters (2014) struggled to gain access to an immigrant community, who came across as edgy and suspicious of outsiders. Peters faced numerous cultural challenges in this patriarchal community, and was forced to do all her negotiations to access the community's parents through a male gatekeeper. She had to appoint a male to negotiate on her behalf. In addition, language was a major barrier as the parents could not converse in English, and this created misunderstandings, and this in turn threatened the validity of the data. As the supervisor on that study, I recommended that she appoint an interpreter who was known to the community to assist during the interviews. In 2016, four years after Peters' data collection, I interviewed parents from the same community, and was struck by how the conditions of engagement and the dispositions of community members had shifted. To me, the community seemed more settled, and English was by then a language that they conversed in with their children and others. During the interviews, I realised that two of the parents I interviewed withdrew from the earlier study before they could be interviewed by Peters.

The four parents that I interviewed were confident and comfortable conversing in English. All have been resident in the community for at least a decade, two for almost two decades. I interviewed Afifa and Amirah at a venue close to the school. Both walked to the venue unaccompanied, which speaks to the freedom of movement of women from this community. The parents' worlds spanned both private and public spaces, which is a shift from the previous situation when women from the community seldom worked outside of the home. Though mothers continue to be the primary homemakers and caregivers, three of the four parents that I interviewed were businesspeople.

The parents consider their own lack of formal school experience to be their biggest obstacle to providing optimal educational support to their children. This is similar to what Delgado-Gaitan (1991) found in her research on Latino parents: that parents who had limited or no formal literacy skills in English showed limited participation in the activities that schools value. However, my data shows that the parents are proactive in their efforts to accumulate cultural and social capital that can benefit their children's education. I found that these parents exercise agency in building their own capacity to better support their children's education. All four parents were constantly working on their functional literacy skills in English, as their work contexts bring them into contact with a diverse population. They were proactive, participated in the homework activities of their children, and linked social activities such as sending SMSs or watching television with educational outcomes.

Amirah, Malaika, Afifa and Shakirah all present with an embodied form of capital as reflected in their attitudes towards education. Their overriding motivating factor for sending their children to school was that they believe that education will lead to a better quality of life for their children. The parents value education for the opportunities it creates for their children to have a better future than the one that they left behind in Somalia. The role that they play shows that they value education and consider the schooling of their children to be a necessity. The findings show that the parents are proponents of education, and potential collaborators with the school.

What the study does point out is that when teachers lack knowledge about the home contexts of their students, they are unlikely to consider the parents as collaborators in their children's education. If teachers knew that these parents supervise their children's schoolwork, work with them on assignments and help them improve their reading, they might relinquish their negative perceptions based on the miscommunication they experience with parents due to their ignoring of rules and regulations. Knowledge about the rich cultural capital that such homes have acquired under the guidance of these parents could illustrate to teachers the broad range of educational support activities that the parents actually engage in.

Finally, there is a scarcity of equitable communicative channels through which teachers and immigrant parents can communicate. This is something that should be addressed by school management, as it is the cause of miscommunication and tension between the school and immigrant parents. It is a fallacy to assume that all parents know how schools work. A recommendation then would be that the school orientates parents who are not from the mainstream culture in the ways that the school works, and this has to be done in a language that they understand. Knowledge about how the school operates will gives Somali parents the power to navigate school spaces better, and will empower them to engage in constructive dialogues with teachers about how they support the educational project.

## Acknowledgement

I thank the National Research Foundation for their funding of my project through their Competitive Programme for Rated Researchers grant.

## Note

1 A spaza shop is an informal structure where informal traders do business in townships and informal settlements.

## References

Bernstein, B. (2000). *Pedagogy, symbolic control and identity: Theory, research and critique.* Revised edition. Oxford: Rowman & Littlefield.

Bourdieu, P. (1977). Cultural reproduction and social reproduction. In J. Karabel & A.H. Halsey (eds.), *Power and ideology in education.* New York: Oxford University Press, pp. 487–510

Bourdieu, P. (1986). The forms of capital. In J. Richardson (ed.), *Handbook of theory and research for the sociology of education.* New York: Greenwood, pp. 241–258.

Bourdieu, P. & Wacquant, L.J.D. (1992). *An invitation to reflexive sociology.* Cambridge: Polity Press.

Christian, K., Morrison, F.J., & Bryant, F.B. (1998). Predicting kindergarten academic skills: Interactions among child care, maternal education, and family literacy environments. *Early Childhood Research Quarterly,* 13(3): 501–521.

Creswell, J.W. (2003). *Research design: Qualitative, quantitative and mixed methods approaches* (2nd ed.). Thousand Oaks, CA: SAGE Publications.

Daniels, D. (2003). Learning about community leadership: Fusing methodology and pedagogy to advance knowledge development on informal settlement women. *Adult Education Quarterly,* 53(3): 189–207.

Delgado-Gaitan, C. (1992). School matters in the Mexican-American home: Socializing children to education. *American Educational Research Journal,* 29: 495–513.

Delgado-Gaitan, C. (1991). Involving parents in schools: A process of empowerment. *American Journal of Education,* 100: 20–46.

Department of Education. (2001). *White paper six. Special needs education: Building an inclusive education and training system.* Pretoria: Department of Education.

Dyson, A. (2001). Varieties of inclusion. Paper presented at the conference *VI Jornadas Cientificas de Investigacion sobre Personas con Discapacidad,* Salamanca, Spain, 17–19 March 2001.

Engelbrecht, P. (2006). The implementation of inclusive education in South Africa after ten years of democracy. *European Journal of Psychology of Education,* XXI(3): 253–264.

Epstein, J.L. (1985). Parents' reactions to teacher practices of parent involvement. *Elementary School Journal,* 86: 568–587.

Epstein, J.L. (1995). School/family/community partnerships: Caring for the children we share. *Phi Delta Kappan,* 76: 701–712.

Epstein, J.L. (2001). *School, family, and community partnerships.* Boulder, CO: Westview Press.

Gibb, K., Tunbridge, D., Chua, A., & Frederickson, N. (2007). Pathways to inclusion: Moving from special school to mainstream. *Educational Psychology in Practice,* 23(2): 109–127.

Henderson, A.T. & Mapp, K.L. (2002). *A new wave of evidence: The impact of school, family, and community connections on student achievement*. Austin, TX: Southwest Educational Development Laboratory.

Higham, R. (2012). Place, race and exclusion: University student voices in post-apartheid South Africa. *International Journal of Inclusive Education*, 16(5–6): 485–501.

Hurtado, S., Carter, D.F., & Kardia, D. (1998). The climate for diversity: Key issues for institutional self-study. *New Directions for institutional Research*, 98: 53–63.

Jarvis, P. (2004) *Adult education and lifelong learning: Theory and practice* (3rd ed.). San Francisco: Routledge.

Jeynes, W.H. (2007). The relationship between parental involvement and urban secondary school student academic achievement: A meta-analysis. *Urban Education*, 42(1): 82–110.

Jinnah, Z. (2010). Making home in a hostile land: Understanding Somali identity, integration, livelihood and risks in Johannesburg. *Journal of Sociology and Social Anthropology*, (1–2):91–99.

Lareau, A. (2000). *Home advantage: Social class and parental intervention in elementary education* (2nd Ed.). New York: Rowman & Littlefield.

Lareau, A. & Horvat, E.M. (1999). Moments of social inclusion and exclusion: Race, class, and cultural capital on family-school relationships. *Sociology of Education*, 72: 37–53.

Lareau, A. & Weininger, E.B. (2003). Cultural capital in educational research: A critical assessment. *Theory and Society*, 32: 567–606.

Lemmer, E.M. (2007). Parent involvement in teacher education in South Africa. *International Journal about Parents in Education*, 1: 218–229.

López, G.R. (1999). *Teaching the value of hard work: A study of parental involvement in migrant households*. Unpublished doctoral dissertation, University of Texas, Austin.

López, G.R. (2001). The value of hard work: Lessons on parent involvement from an (im) migrant household. *Harvard Education Review*, 71: 416–437.

Li, G. (2010). Social class, culture and "good parenting": Voices of low-SES families. In M.M. Marsh & T. Turner-Vorbeck (eds.), *Learning from real families in our school*. New York: Teachers College Press, pp. 162–178.

Mertens, D. (2014). *Research and evaluation in education and psychology: Integrating diversity with quantitative, qualitative, and mixed methods*. Thousand Oaks, CA: SAGE Publications.

Nargis, R. & Tikly, L. (2010), *Inclusion and diversity in education. Guidelines for inclusion and diversity in schools*. Madrid: British Council.

Nash, R. (1990). Bourdieu on education and social and cultural reproduction. *British Journal of Sociology of Education*, 11(4): 431–447.

Ntombela, S. (2011). The progress of inclusive education in South Africa: Teachers' experiences in a selected district, Kwazulu Natal. *Improving Schools*, 14(1): 5–14.

Orellana, M.F., Monkman, K., & MacGillivray, L. (2002). *Parents and teachers talk about literacy and success*. CIERA Report #3–20. Ann Arbor, MI: Center for the Improvement of Early Reading Achievement, University of Michigan. www.ciera.org/library/reports/inquiry-3/3-020/3-020h.html

Oswald, M. (2010). *Teacher learning during the implementation of the Index for Inclusion in a primary school*. Unpublished doctoral dissertation, Stellenbosch University, Stellenbosch.

Patton, M.Q. (2002). *Qualitative research & evaluation methods*. Thousand Oaks, CA: SAGE Publications.

Peters, L. (2014). *Somali parents' educational support of their primary school children*. Unpublished MEd thesis, Stellenbosch University, Stellenbosch.

Rankin, S. (2003). *Campus climate for LGBT people: A national perspective*. New York: National Gay and Lesbian Task Force Policy Institute.

Republic of South Africa. (1996). *South African Schools Act*. Pretoria: Government Printers.

Republic of South Africa, Department of Education. (1995). *White paper on education and training*. Retrieved from www.info.gov.za/whitepapers/1995/education1.htm

Singh, P., Mbokodi, S.M., & Msila, V.T. (2004) Black parental involvement in education. *South African Journal of Education*, 24(4): 301–307.

Smrekar, C. & Cohen-Vogel, L. (2001). The voices of parents: Rethinking the intersection of family and school. *Peabody Journal of Education*, 76(2): 75–100.

Suarez-Balcazar, Y., Orellana-Damacela, L., Nelson Portillo, N., Rowan, J.M., & Andrews-Guillen, C. (2003). Experiences of differential treatment among college students of color. *The Journal of Higher Education*, 74(4): 428–444.

Swart, E. & Pettipher, R. (2016). A framework for understanding inclusion. In E. Landsberg, D. Kruger & E. Swart (Eds.), *Addressing barriers to learning: A South African perspective* (3rd ed.). Pretoria: Van Schaik, pp. 3–23.

United Nations (1948). The Universal Declaration on Human Rights. Paris: UN.

Terre Blanche, M., Durrheim, K., & Painter, D. (2006). (2nd Ed.). *Research in practice: Applied methods for the social sciences*. Cape Town: UCT Press.

Tobin, R. & McInnes, A. (2008). Accommodating differences: Variations in differentiated literacy instruction in Grade 2/3 classrooms. *Literacy*, 42(1): 3–9.

UNESCO (1960). Convention against Discrimination in Education. Paris: UNESCO.

UNHCR (2000). *The state of the world's refugees: 50 years of humanitarian action*. Oxford: Oxford University Press.

Vila, L.E. (2000). The non-monetary benefits of education. *European Journal of Education*, 35(1): 21–32.

Walton, E. (2012). Learner support through differentiated teaching and learning. In N. Nel, M. Nel, & A. Hugo (eds.), *Learner support in a diverse classroom*. Pretoria: Van Schaik, pp. 117–140.

Waterman, R.A. (2008). Strength behind the sociolinguistic wall: The dreams, commitments, and capacities of Mexican mothers. *Journal of Latinos and Education*, 7(2): 144–162.

Yosso, T. (2005). Whose culture has capital? A critical race theory discussion of community cultural wealth. *Race, Ethnicity and Education*, 8(1): 69–91.

# 7

# EQUITY THROUGH INDIVIDUALISED AND INTERCONNECTED TEACHER EDUCATION

*Mandia Mentis and Alison Kearney*

## Introduction

If previous generations were to see the classrooms of today, one of the greatest differences they would notice is the diversity of the student population. Student diversity is a growing worldwide phenomenon (OECD, 2010) brought about by factors including immigration, a widening gap between rich and poor, greater acceptance of diverse expressions of gender and sexuality, and social movements such as inclusive education, which have advocated for the inclusion of disabled learners in mainstream school settings.

The term 'diversity' is complex and multifaceted, and refers to the variation between people in relation to dimensions such as race, ethnicity, religion, gender, sexuality, ability and socio-economic status (Spradlin & Parsons, 2008). Diversity is also context specific, and context shapes not only how it is defined, but how it is experienced and responded to (Burns & Shadoian-Gersing, 2010). Added to this is the interrelationship between diversity and identity. As Holck, Muhr and Villeseche (2016) explain, diversity is associated with the way in which individuals are perceived by others and by themselves, that is, whether they are socially classified as different, or as similar, to the majority. Therefore, "dealing with issues of diversity is always closely linked to individuals experiencing their own identity as being different or not in a particular context" (p. 1).

While historical understandings of diversity have emphasised the challenges associated with it, current understandings emphasise the opportunities that diversity brings to organisations and communities. In education, the opportunities afforded (to both majority and minority students) by diverse student populations include increased problem-solving capacity and creativity (WISELI, 2010), helping students to live in societies characterised by diversity, fostering connectedness and personal development, understanding other languages and cultures by engaging with people from different cultural backgrounds, as well as supporting learners to understand their own identity and diversity (Luciak, 2010). However, there are strong links between diversity and inequity worldwide, and data show that education systems serve some students better than others. In particular, factors such as socio-economic background, ethnicity, disability and gender are obstacles to the achievement of some students' educational potential (OECD, 2012).

New Zealand, a country of approximately 4.5 million people, is no exception to this trend. While its education system is ranked within the top 20 nations for its quality (OECD, 2015), this system is nevertheless doing less well by some students. In particular, students who are disabled, who are from minority ethnic and linguistic groups, who experience difficulties with learning and behaviour, and those affected by poverty, are most disadvantaged. They are more likely than their peers to experience exclusion and marginalisation from and within school, and less likely to attain favourable educational outcomes.

The inequity experienced by these students is evident due to a number of key indicators. For example, in 2014, students from low socio-economic backgrounds had nearly twice the unexplained school absence than their peers from wealthier backgrounds. They also experienced nearly four times the rate of school suspensions than their more affluent peers (Education Counts, 2014). Similar disparities are evident in relation to academic achievement. Only 60% of students in the lowest decile[1] schools achieved at or above the national standard for reading, whereas 88% of students from decile 10 schools achieved at, or above, national standard. Children at deciles 1–3 were four times as likely to leave school with no qualification as those at deciles 8–10 (Education Counts, 2014).

The data in relation to ethnicity is similar. In 2014, Māori[2] and Pasifika[3] students had twice the rate of unexplained school absence of their European counterparts, and only 69% of Māori and 65% of Pasifika students achieved at or above the national standard for reading compared to 84% of European students. Māori and Pasifika males were stood down or suspended from school at a rate of 5.1% (Māori) and 3.6% (Pasifika), whereas the European rate was 2.3% (Education Counts, 2014).

Disabled students, in turn, are less likely to have secondary school or tertiary qualifications than any other minority group in New Zealand (Cleland & Smith, 2010; New Zealand Human Rights Commission, 2010). They also experience other disadvantages in relation to education, with 15% of all disabled students experiencing interrupted periods of education, 8% beginning school later than other children, and 20% having to change schools because of their disability (Office for Disability Issues, 2008). In addition, disabled students experience difficulties attending mainstream schools as some schools discourage disabled students from enrolling (New Zealand Human Rights Commission, 2010).

In response to the disadvantage experienced by these learners, New Zealand is working to create more equitable education systems where *all* students belong, participate, and can learn, and where teachers feel confident and competent to meet the needs of *all* learners. There are two dimensions to equity in education – fairness and inclusion (OECD, 2008). Fairness refers to ensuring that the social or personal circumstances of learners such as gender, socio-economic status, ethnicity and ability are not barriers to the achievement of their educational potential (ibid.). Inclusion refers to ensuring that school systems support the presence, participation and learning of all learners and that all learners are accepted and valued members of the school community (Booth & Ainscow, 2011).

The importance of equitable education systems cannot be overstated, and research unequivocally shows the serious consequences of educational inequality:

> School failure penalises a child for life. The student who leaves school without completing upper secondary education or without the relevant skills has fewer life prospects. This can be seen in lower initial and lifetime earnings, more difficulties in adapting to rapidly changing knowledge-based economies, and higher risks of unemployment.
>
> *(OECD, 2012, p. 3)*

There are also strong human rights arguments for the provision of equitable education systems. For example, the United Nations Convention on the Rights of the Child (United Nations General Assembly, 1989) states that children have the right to equal opportunities of education (Article 28). The International Covenant on Economic Social and Cultural Rights also enshrines the rights of all to an education that is tailored to ensure their full development (Article 13).

## The role of teacher education in creating equitable education systems

While educational inequity is a complex social and political issue which is impacted by many factors beyond the influence of the school, the role of the teacher has been shown to be a significant 'in-school' factor that can positively influence student outcomes (Hattie, 2009; Mills & Ballantyne, 2016; OECD, 2005; The Education Trust, 2012). Some researchers have gone even further, arguing that teachers can be major contributors to the reduction and elimination of inequity, and can mitigate the social and personal disadvantage that some students experience at school (e.g. Pantic & Florian, 2015).

Given the pivotal role that teachers can play, teacher education programmes should include an emphasis on the development of collaborative skills that allow for interprofessional practice and teamwork (Barr & Low, 2013; Commission of the European Communities, 2007; Florian, 2009). They should also situate professional learning within professional communities (Best & Winslow, 2015; Cochran-Smith, 2015), include a focus on teachers taking responsibility for learning and engaging in lifelong learning (Commission of the European Communities, 2007; European Agency for Development in Special Needs Education, 2011[4]), and focus on the utilisation of online technologies (Best & Winslow, 2015; Caldwell & Heaton, 2016). Strengthening teachers' critical thinking and digital literacy skills will enable them to access, critique and share information more effectively as they work collaboratively across their discipline areas to bring about more equitable and inclusive practices in classrooms.

## Resource Teacher programme in New Zealand

Given the increasing appreciation of diversity of student populations, along with a growing recognition of the inequitable experiences of some minority groups, the necessity for a shift in teacher education has become apparent. A 'one-size-fits-all' model of teaching and learning, in which teachers replicate past practice and perpetuate status quo models, will no longer suffice to meet the challenges associated with diversity and inequity in education. We cannot continue to provide the same lecturer-directed and content-driven model of teacher training that we did in the past. A fresh model of professional education is needed that foregrounds diversity, complexity and equity. These three elements were key in the design of a professional development programme in New Zealand for Resource Teachers.

In 2010, the Ministry of Education in New Zealand commissioned a consortium partnership of two New Zealand universities to design and develop a national postgraduate programme for experienced teachers to become specialised Resource Teachers. Resource Teachers work with teachers, learners, families and other professionals to support all learners to achieve in an inclusive education system. The goals of the programme are to increase learners' presence, participation and learning in a fair and inclusive education system. Inclusive education is founded in the Education Act 1989, which stipulates that "people who have special education needs (whether because of disability or otherwise) have the same rights to enrol and receive education at state schools as people who do not" (Education Act, 1989, Section 8). New Zealand schools also have binding obligations under theNew Zealand Disability Strategy and the United Nations Convention on the Rights of Persons with Disabilities to provide a quality education for all learners. This obligation is reinforced by the New Zealand Curriculum, which foregrounds inclusion as a key principle of an education system that is "non-sexist, non-racist, and non-discriminatory", and that ensures that "students' identities, languages, abilities, and talents are recognised and affirmed and that their learning needs are addressed" (Ministry of Education, 2007, p. 9).

The Resource Teacher programme is a two-year part-time postgraduate qualification and consists of seven specialist endorsement areas. Experienced teachers can either complete the course as fee-paying students or apply for a scholarship offered by the Ministry of Education. They complete this qualification while continuing to practise in the field. The Ministry of Education allocates scholarships proportionately to different specialist areas according to perceived need, and the majority of teachers in the programme are enrolled in the Learning and Behaviour specialist endorsement (65% of students). This is followed by Early Intervention (15%), Deaf and Hard of Hearing (6%), Autism (6%), Complex Educational Needs (3%), Blind and Low Vision (4%) and Gifted (1%). Applications from minority groups are encouraged, especially Māori and Pasifika teachers, and each year of the programme has seen a growth in the number of Resource Teachers who are Deaf or Hard of Hearing, Low Vision or from minority cultural groups. The programme thus models the principles of equity, fairness and inclusion in enabling access to the programme, as well as accommodations in teaching and learning, for Resource Teachers from diverse groups.

This is the only programme in New Zealand for Resource Teachers and it caters for a new cohort of approximately 150 teachers nationally each year. Its delivery combines face-to-face meetings with online teaching and learning. There are two one-week on-campus courses at the beginning and in the middle of each year, one of which is held at the campus of a university in the North Island, and the second of which is held at the campus of a university in the South Island of New Zealand. There are also more informal face-to-face meetings held regionally up to four times a year. The block courses begin with the traditional *Pōwhiri* (a Māori welcome), which sets the tone for the culturally responsive approach of the programme, and Resource Teachers can use Te Reo Māori language for all aspects of the programme. Interpreters and note-takers are present at block courses for Deaf, Hard of Hearing and Low Vision Resource Teachers. The regional meetings are run as *Whānau* (the Māori term for 'family') groups to provide face-to-face learning exchanges that supplement the online learning. This mix of formal, non-formal, face-to-face and online learning models the differentiated and inclusive teaching and learning opportunities that Resource Teachers use in their practice.

Given that the Resource Teachers are based across the country, all coursework is available online, and *Moodle* is the learning management system and *Mahara* is the ePortfolio site. The qualification comprises four courses, two taken in the first year and two in the second. One of the courses is dedicated to the specialist area and the remaining three are generic, and principles and competencies are applied to the different specialist areas within these courses. The three common courses are: Core Theory and Foundations of Specialist Teaching, Evidence-based Interprofessional Practice, and a year-long Practicum.

While Resource Teachers do focus on a specialist area, the programme is designed to move beyond separate specialisms and focus on interconnections within and between the specialist areas by applying principles and competencies of common practice. These include professional learning and identity development, culturally responsive practice, professional inclusive practice, interprofessional practice, evidence-based professional practice (in assessment and teaching) and ethical and self-reflective practice.

The programme therefore breaks down the silos of specialisms that exist in traditional teacher education to better prepare Resource Teachers to practise in collaborative ways across discipline boundaries. As we have argued previously:

> When professionals with a range of different expertise learn together and then practice together, the result is a shared understanding and consequently better outcomes for students with diverse learning needs.
> (Mentis, Kearney & Bevan-Brown, 2012, p. 295).

The goal of the interprofessional approach is for Resource Teachers to better support all learners in the classroom with diverse backgrounds and abilities to learn and succeed.

Resource Teachers' confidence and competence to differentiate the curriculum for diverse learners is developed through providing them with the opportunity of individualising learning for themselves in the professional programme. The design of the Resource Teacher programme enables them to map personalised professional learning goals relevant to their unique teaching context. The experience of diversifying their own learning in the course better equips Resource Teachers to individualise and contextualise learning for the students they will be supporting in the classroom, and this in turn promotes equal access, participation and engagement for all learners.

Resource Teachers in the programme network with peers from their specialist areas and different specialisms to learn *with, from* and *about* each other. The aim is to identify commonalities and differences within both their professional and interprofessional communities of practice. This again models the practices they will replicate when working in and across teams of professionals, advocating for, and working with, marginalised learners and their families for more equitable educational experiences. The Resource Teacher programme is thus both individualised in terms of learning goals and interconnected in terms of networking within and across specialist areas of practice.

This personalised, professional and interprofessional approach is conceptualised to yield what is termed a T-shaped professional. At the juncture of the T is the personal or 'me', where Resource Teachers consider their personal, cultural and social context. The stem of the T is the professional, where Resource Teachers explore their specialist area in depth. The arms of the T reach outwards to the interprofessional, where Resource Teachers explore different specialist areas. This constitutes a shift from the conventional I-shaped professional, who is competent in a single discipline area, to a T-shaped professional, who crosses disciplinary boundaries. Professional learning within this interprofessional approach moves beyond being located in specialist silos to connecting and contributing with other related discipline areas. A T-shaped professional has general literacy across a broad domain of relevant knowledge along with in-depth competence in a narrower domain (Donofrio, Sophrer & Zadeh, 2010).

Resource Teachers therefore focus on the personal, the professional and the interprofessional. At the juncture of the T, Resource Teachers identify their *personal* unique learning needs and set their differentiated and individualised professional learning goals for the programme. These individual goals align with the specific core competencies of each course within the programme. The stem of the T represents the *professional* aspect, and signifies Resource Teachers interacting and dialoguing with others in their specialist area of practice, and developing in-depth specialist expertise and professional connectedness. The arms of the T reflect the *interprofessional* connectedness Resource Teachers develop through interacting with practitioners from other specialist areas both within and beyond the programme.

Equity in teacher education 109

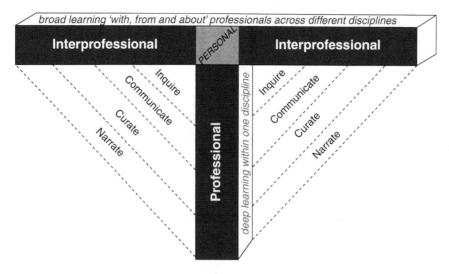

**FIGURE 7.1** The personal, professional, and interprofessional dimensions of the T-shaped learning in the programme

Figure 7.1 illustrates the personal, professional, and interprofessional dimensions of the T-shaped learning in the programme. The development of T-shaped professionals is underpinned by a learning design that provides Resource Teachers with the opportunity to inquire, communicate, curate and narrate aspects of their professional practice, which is described in the section that follows.

## Personal, professional and interprofessional – the T-shaped professional

The *inquire-communicate-curate-narrate* pedagogy progresses from comprehension to evaluation. It starts with the personal and moves to the social where Resource Teachers connect and interact with others in similar professions, as well as interprofessionally with those in different professions. Becoming members of these different communities of practice (Wenger, 1998) promotes personalised, professional and interprofessional learning that can be lifelong and lifewide.

*Personalising* their own learning equips Resource Teachers with skills and experience to then support teachers to differentiate the curriculum for particular learners with disabilities or learning difficulties to ensure relevant, appropriate and inclusive educational opportunities. *Professional* learning provides Resource Teachers with the depth of specialist knowledge necessary to address specific differences using relevant and authentic evidence-based practices. *Interprofessional* learning broadens Resource Teachers' perceptions to include and accommodate a wider range of perspectives. This in turn enables them to identify and appreciate the diversity in learners and ensure that their individual voices are heard.

Learning and networking within professional groups as well as across different communities of practice becomes particularly critical when one works in the digital age. Due to this, the programme also focuses on using new technologies to advance professional development. Thus the learning design of this programme enables Resource Teachers to:

- *Inquire* into their practice through identifying personalised learning goals which are relevant for their particular context, and map these against the competencies of the programme;
- *Communicate* with each other about practice and co-construct meaning through forum discussions both within specialist domain areas and inter-professionally across domain areas, strengthening both their depth and breadth as T-shaped professionals;
- *Curate* artefacts of evidence, resources and 'knowledgeability' to support practice, both individually and as a community of professional and interprofessional practice;
- *Narrate* a personalised professional philosophy of practice using ePortfolios, which can continually be updated after completion of the programme, ensuring lifelong and lifewide learning.

## Inquiry

Teaching for diversity and equity requires a capacity to engage in inquiry-based learning, that is, evidence-based problem-solving driven by a need to answer or resolve real-world wicked issues. The notion of inquiry-based learning has grown from an understanding that the difficult issues of our time (including diversity and inequity) will require "media literacies, critical thinking skills, systems thinking and interpersonal and self-directional skills" (Barron & Darling-Hammond, 2010, p. 200). Inquiry-based learning constitutes continuous learning, a teacher competency which has been repeatedly shown to help them meet the needs of diverse student populations and promote educational equity (Commission of the European Communities, 2007). In addition, with open access to information through the internet and sophisticated search engines, learning is shifting from a passive, transmissive model of content delivery to an interactive and transformative model where learners actively find their own solutions to current issues and contribute to collective understandings about these through their use of social media. This shift is recognised in this programme, and it therefore emphasises inquiry-based learning and focuses on developing professionals who are critically literate in using digital tools to find solutions to differentiating teaching for diversity and equity.

Inquiry-based learning can be framed as being both information oriented and discovery oriented (Levy, 2009), and this programme includes learning experiences along a continuum which spans structured inquiry (course-directed), scaffolded inquiry (course-guided), and open inquiry (self-directed). The structured and scaffolded inquiry in the programme is achieved through set competencies and course readings. The self-directed open inquiry is where Resource Teachers can generate their own unique inquiries into their practice. Resource Teachers in the programme have a range of background learning experiences (e.g. schools, early childhood centres and Ministry of Education settings). Self-directed inquiry accommodates this diversity and creates the opportunity for the teachers to design and set their own learning goals against the programme competencies, based on their current knowledge, future needs, as well as the context within which they work. Self-directed inquiry means that no two Resource Teachers on the programme have the same learning goals or curriculum activities. Differentiated and individualised learning in this professional course parallels their practice, given that Resource Teachers are required to differentiate teaching and learning for the students they work with in schools and early childhood centres (through Individualised Education Plans, for example). This course models authentic and meaningful differentiation and provides Resource Teachers with personal experience of this – as both teacher and learner.

The inquiry-based approach for the T-shaped practitioner begins with the personal, and extends into the professional and then the interprofessional. The initial focus for each Resource Teacher is their personal and cultural context, as the core of developing a professional identity begins with bringing who you are to what you do. Resource Teachers are encouraged to map their own cultural identity within their unique teaching context in order to identify their learning goals with respect to each of the course competencies. Inquiry-based learning is supported through the online course in the form of online quizzes, e-books, videos, journal articles, websites and related resources. Resource Teachers develop a deep professional understanding, as well as a broad interprofessional understanding, of their inquiry through discussing and sharing with colleagues from the same specialist area as well as comparing and contrasting with colleagues from different specialist areas. As Resource Teachers meet their learning and inquiry goals for each domain, they receive a personal digital badge on the online site, which acknowledges completion of that competency. Digital badging helps the Resource Teachers map their individualised progress through the course, and signals competence in inquiry-based learning personally, professionally and interprofessionally. Achievement in each competency area prepares Resource Teachers to work individually within their specialist area as well as interprofessionally across specialist areas to achieve equitable and inclusive education outcomes for the learners that they support in schools and early childhood settings, which they will effect through personalising learning, differentiating tasks and accommodating difference.

## Communication

The next stage involves Resource Teachers co-constructing meaning with each other through conversation and communication. The practice of teachers communicating and working interprofessionally is strongly linked to the promotion of more inclusive and equitable schools (European Agency for Development in

Special Needs Education, 2012). Diversity brings with it a need for a wide range of professionals to work together for the benefit of learners. Research shows that interprofessional education (learning with, from and about each other) facilitates effective collaborative practice (Gilbert, Yan and Hoffman, 2010).

The types of activities that facilitate co-constructing meaning and learning *with, from* and *about* each other include online forum discussions for deep and asynchronous conversations, face-to-face regional meetings, group assignments, mentoring and supervision. These forms of communication support both in-depth professional learning within specialist areas and broad interprofessional learning across specialist areas. For example, in the core paper, Resource Teachers are required to host a discussion thread in two different forums for each domain or topic area. The first discussion thread is restricted to their specialist area and is intended to develop in-depth analysis and application to specialist practice, for example, universal design for learning (UDL), or narrative assessment in the field of Autism, Blind and Low Vision, Complex Educational Needs, Deaf and Hard of Hearing, etc. The second discussion thread is more general and open to all specialist areas, for example, the different uses of UDL or narrative assessment practices across these different professional areas, to gain breadth of insight and understanding.

In the Evidence-Based Practice course, Resource Teachers work in interprofessional groups to analyse, evaluate and critically appraise various assessment approaches and programmes of practice using three sources of evidence, namely research evidence, practitioner evidence and learner evidence. This critical appraisal assignment is done across specialist areas to provide a breadth of understanding that would not be achieved if done in separate courses or in specialist silos. Learning with each other across disciplines about different assessments, terminology, interventions and programmes results in more successful teamwork in practice where professionals are required to work in inter-disciplinary teams to bring about equitable outcomes for learners with complex educational needs or from different cultural backgrounds. The blurring of the boundary between learning and practice locates Resource Teachers within authentic contexts to problem-solve real issues of equity in education.

Teachers in the programme also co-construct meaning with other teachers and professionals who are not in the programme, as well as with learners through their practicum field work. Field work is located in schools, early intervention centres, and centres for learners with sensory difficulties and complex educational needs. The programme also has close links with the Equity Through Education Research Centre (at one of the host universities) and Resource Teachers have opportunities to engage with researchers and community members of the centre both online and at the annual symposium. Resource Teachers in the programme are also encouraged to communicate more widely through publication in a New Zealand educational journal, *Kairaranga*, whose readership includes teachers and other educational practitioners. They also have opportunities to share their work by way of digital social media such as blogging, RSS feeds, and Twitter.

Networked mentoring is another example of how communication is used in the programme to develop the personal, professional and interprofessional aspects of the T-shaped practitioner. Resource Teachers map their own unique networks of support from all specialist areas rather than the more traditional model of being assigned an individual supervisor. Interprofessional mentors use the online discussion forums as well as face-to-face meetings to communicate with Resource Teachers about ethical and practice issues associated with fieldwork. In addition to the interprofessional mentoring, Resource Teachers can discuss their practicum with their specialism coordinators, peers in their specialist area, field advisors/practitioners and teachers. This flattened and networked approach to supervision and mentoring encourages Resource Teachers to be proactive in sourcing the most relevant supports when they are needed. Communicating within a network of specialist and interprofessional mentors prepares Resource Teachers for future collaborative practice. Like many other practitioners, Resource Teachers are increasingly needing to work across professional boundaries, and need to advocate for the learners they support, particularly those at the margins, to ensure their learning experience is positive and supported.

## Curation

The third aspect of learning in the Resource Teaching programme is that of knowledge curation. Resource Teachers are encouraged to manage knowledge effectively and efficiently in today's information age through digital curation. This involves finding systematic ways of collecting, sorting and critically interpreting professional bodies of knowledge to enable Resource Teachers to use this more effectively when and where it is needed – for their own learning and for designing learning experiences that best meets the needs of the teachers and learners that they will support.

Knowledge management has shifted from rows of hardback books lined up on the shelf to a more networked "community of people who contribute to the continued vitality, application, and evolution of the practice" (Wenger-Trayner & Wenger-Trayner, 2015, p. 13). Digital curations are repositories of knowledge that Resource Teachers develop individually and collectively to support themselves and others in their lifelong work in communities of practice. To practise effectively and efficiently, it is important to have systematic ways of accessing information, translating this into knowledge, and connecting through it to other people who add to the practice.

Managing digital curations through social media connects Resource Teachers to the communities of practice of which they are members, and gives them ways to seek meaning and make meaning with others. Wenger-Trayner and Wenger-Trayner (2015) talk about *"knowledgeability"* as a means of explaining the multiple ways we practise across our professional and interprofessional landscapes of practice. They note:

> Knowledgeability is a complex achievement ... Practitioners need to negotiate their role, optimize their contribution, know where relevant sources of

knowledge are, and be practiced at bringing various sources of knowledge to bear on unforeseen and ambiguous situations.

*(Wenger-Trayner & Wenger-Trayner, 2015, p. 24)*

In the Resource Teaching programme, digital curations for the T-shaped professional consist of online co-created 'glossaries' of professional knowledge as well as individualised opportunities for social networking to collate further knowledge. The course 'glossary' is created using the online *Moodle* glossary tool, which enables sharing of resources. The term for this glossary is an *e-Kete* ('kete' is the indigenous Māori term for 'basket', and the denoted 'basket of knowledge' provides an instructive metaphor for what the glossary aims to be). Resource Teachers annotate their own entries, as well as comment on and 'rate' the value and usefulness of the eKete entries of others. This results in a co-constructed and shared synthesis of knowledge, evaluated by colleagues within, and across, specialist areas of practice. The rating of peers' eKete entries gives credibility to 'practitioner knowledge' alongside 'expert knowledge' and reinforces the understanding that everybody contributes to the learning of others, and that evaluations in context by practitioners creates as valuable an evidence base as formal research. Using practitioner knowledge from the field gives Resource Teachers the confidence and competence to advocate for more equitable outcomes for diverse learners through acknowledging and valuing the partnership with learners and their families to better meet their educational needs.

Individually and collectively, Resource Teachers are encouraged to engage with relevant social media to develop 'knowledgeability' outside of the programme, for lifelong and lifewide learning. Suggested curation tools and social networking technology for Resource Teachers include ePortoflios, Google Drive, Zotero, Trello, Pinterest, Twitter, etc. Tagging, labelling and annotating the resources is part of the process, and so too is sharing curated resources with colleagues.

Thus, curation in the Resource Teaching course provides the T-professional with opportunities for both deep and broad learning. Networked curation through social media enables them to dig deeper into their specialist area within their specialist community of practice. The collaborative eKete curations in the course, as well as following and contributing to other interprofessional social networking sites, provides opportunities to interact, network and engage broadly across different specialist areas and communities of practice. T-shaped learning through digital curation is supported within the course and continues beyond the course when Resource Teachers use curation in their professional practice after completion of the qualification. Developing a habitual practice of 'knowledgeability' within specific specialist areas (depth), as well as across other specialist areas (breadth) will ensure that Resource Teachers keep up-to-date, informed and connected. This ongoing habit of curating will encourage Resource Teachers to avoiding slipping into 'one-size-fits-all' or outdated practices when working to achieve equity for all learners in diverse settings. It encourages them to think critically and reflectively when sourcing resources for the learners and teachers they support, thus ensuring evidence-based practice when differentiating the curriculum. This 'knowledgeability' involves ensuring practices and programmes are accessible, fair and inclusive to all and overcome barriers to participation, thus ensuring equity for diverse learners.

## Narration

The fourth aspect of the learning design of the Resource Teaching programme involves narrating a personalised professional philosophy. As Wenger-Trayner and Wenger-Trayner (2015) note, becoming a professional is not merely approximating a reified body of knowledge, but rather it involves "developing a meaningful identity of both competence and knowledgeability in a dynamic and varied landscape of relevant practices" (p. 23). Developing a professional identity does not just involve gaining the specific knowledge and skills to make informed decisions, but is a process of 'becoming' a particular kind of person through 'belonging' to a professional community (Wenger, 1998).

Within the programme, the process of 'becoming' and 'belonging' is facilitated through Resource Teachers narrating their learning in professional ePortfolios. Using ePortfolios, they digitally document their professional inquiries into the wicked questions of their practice, they reflect on their conversations to co-construct meaning, and they add their digitally curated eKetes of knowledgeability, thereby narrating their learning within and across specialist areas.

Reflective practice is one of the key competencies in the programme and Resource Teachers use their ePortfolios to engage in ongoing and deep reflection with regard to their learning journeys throughout the programme. They reflect on their personal context, history and culture as part of their professional identity development. Further, they identify the theorists and practitioners who have impacted and influenced their practice, and they describe the dilemmas and critical moments that informed their learning. Resource Teachers use their ePortfolios as a platform to reflect on the information amassed through self-directed inquiries, the 'ah-ha' moments of co-constructing meaning through conversations with peers, and the collective knowledgeability about practice. Reflecting on the progression from information, knowledge and meaning to appraisal and application culminates in the transformative wisdom of Resource Teaching practice. Resource Teachers map their personal, professional and interprofessional journeys in their ePortfolios through selecting artefacts which demonstrate meeting their learning goals and course competencies. Their reflections and self-assessments contribute to their overall professional philosophy, which articulates their stance as professionals in the field.

While narrating a professional identity begins in the programme, Resource Teachers continue this process using their ePortfolios after graduating from the programme. The ePortfolios are thus used to document formal learning and qualifications as well as ongoing informal professional learning and development through short courses, conferences and ongoing practice. They are used to showcase effective ongoing appraisals of continuing competency in the field and accreditation to different bodies of practice. In addition, they provide ongoing workspaces to network digitally with others to share resources and research collaboratively. ePortfolios provide Resource Teachers with the space and place to digitally narrate their ongoing personal, professional and interprofessional connectedness. Connectedness and confidence are key to their effective practice.

## Programme challenges and effectiveness

Some of the programme challenges include: (1) workload for Resource Teachers of studying while practising, (2) the difficulties working across the academic processes and systems of two universities, (3) the large cohort size of Resource Teachers, and (4) academic staff changes resulting in the need for internal professional development on the 'T'-shaped pedagogy and use of digital technologies. These challenges have largely been overcome using approaches consistent with the programme, such as (1) integrating study and practice so that assignments are artefacts taken from authentic case work, (2) hosting the online *Moodle* site external to the two universities, (3) using *Moodle* to monitor learning of large cohort sizes (e.g. through the inbuilt learning analytics), and (4) using digital teaching resources for anytime-anywhere professional development on the pedagogy of the programme.

Since the inception of the programme, there has been extensive consultation with stakeholders and professional organisations that strike a balance between professionals, academic and community groups. This has included formally eliciting feedback from the Resource Teacher participants on a twice-yearly basis, meeting with stakeholders to discuss the programme and seek feedback, providing twice-yearly milestone reports to the New Zealand Ministry of Education who fund the programme, having the teaching staff reflect on programme effectiveness, and an external independent review. Based on this consultation among staff, students, alumni, and stakeholder groups (including practising professionals, community groups, parents and people with disabilities), as well as new and emerging evidence from the literature, changes to the programme have been made. These have been in response to new government and policy initiatives, and latest evidence-based practice literature.

Feedback from participating Resource Teachers and stakeholders demonstrates the difference that the programme is making to the creation of more equitable education systems within New Zealand. Comments from Resource Teacher participants include:

> [This course] has allowed me to expand my networks and learn from and alongside a broad range of people who are all passionate about and committed to ensuring that all children receive a quality education that responds to their needs and challenges them to be the best they can be.
>
> Although it has been challenging I have most definitely become a more critically reflective practitioner.
>
> The (course) has inspired and activated my passion to embrace and address the diverse needs of all learners and has challenged my thinking of the many

different ways teachers can make a difference, especially to those with complex learning needs.

The programme underwent an external review with a review panel made up of national and international academics, stakeholders, students and practitioners. The external review stated that:

> It is clear from written and oral submissions from stakeholders, students and staff that the qualification is of high quality and is meeting the needs for which it was originally created. While the students noted that the study was challenging, they spoke of the immense and positive impact it had on their practice; their growth in understanding the theoretical underpinnings of their work and the ability to critique, reflect and challenge their actions in accordance with new learnings they encountered.

Since the beginning of the programme, 825 Resource Teachers have successfully graduated. Withdrawal and/or failure is very low (10%), and is generally due to circumstances unrelated to study. Great care is taken to weave wellbeing components into the programme and Resource Teachers are encouraged to apply this to their professional and personal lives. Research is being undertaken to investigate long-term effects of the programme, and in particular, the career trajectory of graduated Resource Teachers and their impact in the field.

## Conclusion

The individualised and interconnected approach to teacher education outlined in this chapter enables Resource Teachers to advocate in their professional work for equity in a world that is becoming more diverse and complex. The challenges of equity, diversity and human rights require teaching practices and systems that go beyond an understanding of any individual subject or discipline area, and require networking across disciplines and domain areas. An important imperative as we move towards including all learners in their local schools and communities is for professionals to work together across their professional boundaries. Creative solutions in education need educators who can move beyond their own subject silos and interact with others from related areas. Networking across disciplines is facilitated in the Resource Teacher programme through the T-shaped approach. Working across professional boundaries underpins the learning design of the programme, which facilitates a progression from using information (in inquiries) to co-constructing meaning (through communication) to 'knowledgeability' (curation) to developing professional wisdom (narrated in ePortofolios). The programme thus supports Resource Teachers to think about information and knowledge in new ways and practise wisely within and across communities of practice, to ensure relevant, equitable, appropriate and differentiated teaching and learning for all.

The Resource Teachers in this programme are invested in creating more equitable education systems. Their role and agency in this regard is significant and will require a new approach to their professional learning. This chapter has outlined one such approach. The T-shaped professional model allows Resource Teachers to personalise their own learning first, and then network with others both within their specialist area (to deepen knowledge) and across specialist areas (to broaden practice). The learning design of *inquire-communicate-curate-narrate* provides Resource Teachers with the skills and tools to search for solutions to complex educational problems, collaborate with others in teams, and co-construct a 'knowledgeability' about, and for, ongoing practice. Networking within and across professional communities of practice enables Resource Teachers to develop professional identities that are personalised yet connected, providing them with the skills and knowledge necessary to better meet their goal of achieving fair, inclusive and equitable education experiences for the students they support.

## Notes

1 New Zealand has a system of school deciles (1–10). They measure the socio-economic position of a school's student community. Decile 1 schools have the highest proportion of students from low socio-economic communities and decile 10 have the lowest proportion of these students.
2 Māori are the indigenous people of New Zealand.
3 Pasifika is a term to denote peoples of the Pacific region.
4 The European Agency for Development in Special Needs Education is now known as The European Agency for Special Needs and Inclusive Education.

## References

Barr, H., & Low, H. (2013). *Introducing interprofessional education*. Fareham, UK: CAIPE.
Barron, B., & Darling-Hammond, L. (2010). Prospects and challenges for inquiry-based approaches to learning. In H. Dumont, D. Istance, & R. Benavides (Eds.). *The nature of learning. Using research to inspire practice* (pp. 199–225). Paris, France: OECD.
Best, J., & Winslow, E. (2015). *Educational equity: Challenges for educator effectiveness. Policy Brief.* Denver, CO: McREL International. Retrieved from http://http://files.eric.ed.gov/fulltext/ED557602.pdf
Booth, T., & Ainscow, M. (2011). *Index for inclusion: Developing learning and participation in schools*. Bristol, UK: CSIE.
Burns, T., & Shadoian-Gersing, V. (2010). The importance of effective teacher education for diversity. In OECD (Ed.), *Educating teachers for diversity: Meeting the Challenge.* (pp. 19–40). Paris, France: OECD.
Caldwell, H., & Heaton, R. (2016). The interdisciplinary use of blogs and online communities in teacher education. *The International Journal of Information and Learning Technology*, 33(3), 142–158.
Cleland, G., & Smith, A. (2010). *Journey to work: Creating pathways for young disabled people in New Zealand*. Wellington, New Zealand: CCS Disability Action, Workbridge, Creative Solutions.
Cochran-Smith, M. (2015). Teacher communities for equity. *Kappa Delta Pi Record*, 51(3), 109–113, doi:10.1080/00228958.2015.1056659

Commission of the European Communities. (2007). *Communication from the Commission to the council and the European Parliament. Improving the quality of teaching education*. Retrieved from http://eur-lex.europa.eu/legal-content/ga/ALL/?uri=CELEX:52007DC0392

Donofrio, N., Sophrer, J., & Zadeh, H. S. (2010). Research-driven medical education and practice: a case for t-shaped professionals. *MJA Viewpoint*. Retrieved from www.ceri.msu.edu/wp-content/uploads/2010/06/A-Case-for-T-Shaped-Professionals-20090907-Hossein.pdf

Education Act (1989). Retrieved from www.legislation.govt.nz/act/public/1989/0080/latest/DLM175959.html

Education Counts. (2014). *Attendance in New Zealand schools 2014*. Retrieved from www.educationcounts.govt.nz/publications/series/2503/attendance-in-new-zealand-schools-2014

European Agency for Development in Special Needs Education. (2011). *Teacher education for inclusion across Europe: Challenges and opportunities*. Retrieved from www.european-agency.org/sites/default/files/te4i-challenges-and-opportunities_TE4I-Synthesis-Report-EN.pdf

European Agency for Development in Special Needs Education. (2012). *Teacher education for inclusion: Profile of inclusive teachers*. Retrieved from www.european-agency.org/sites/default/files/Profile-of-Inclusive-Teachers.pdf

Florian, L. (2009). Preparing teachers to work in 'schools for all'. *Teaching and Teacher Education: An International Journal of Research and Studies*, 25(4), 533–534.

Gilbert, J. H. V., Yan, J., & Hoffman, S. J. (2010). A WHO Report: Framework for action on interprofessional education and collaborative practice. *Journal of Allied Health*, 39(1), 196–197.

Hattie, J. (2009). *Visible learning: A synthesis of over 800 meta-analyses relating to achievement*. (1st ed.). London: Routledge.

Holck, L., Muhr, S. L., & Villeseche, F. (2016). Identity, diversity and diversity management: On theoretical connections, assumptions and implications for practice. *Equality, Diversity and Inclusion: An International Journal*, 35(1), 48–64.

Levy, P. (2009). Inquiry based learning: A conceptual framework. Sheffield: CILASS, University of Sheffield. Retrieved from www.shef.ac.uk/ibl

Luciak, K. (2010). On diversity in educational contexts. In OECD (Ed.), *Educating teachers for diversity: Meeting the challenge* (pp. 41–62). Paris, France: OECD.

Mentis, M., Kearney, A., & Bevan-Brown, J. (2012). Interprofessional learning and its contribution to inclusive education. In S. Carrington & J. MacArthur (Eds.), *Teaching in inclusive school communities* (pp. 295–311). Milton, QLD: John Wiley & Sons.

Mills, C., & Ballantyne, J. (2016). Social justice and teacher education: A systematic review of empirical work in the field. *Journal of Teacher Education*, 67(4), 263–276.

Ministry of Education (2007). *The New Zealand Curriculum*. Wellington, NZ: Author.

New Zealand Human Rights Commission (2010). *Human rights in New Zealand. Ngā Tika Tangata O Aotearoa*. Retrieved from www.hrc.co.nz/files/7014/2388/0544/Human_Rights_Review_2010_Full.pdf

Office for Disability Issues. (2008). *Disability and education in New Zealand in 2006*. Wellington, New Zealand: Author

Organisation for Economic Cooperation and Development (OECD). (2005). *Teachers matter: Attracting, developing and retaining effective teachers*. Paris: OECD Publications.

Organisation for Economic Cooperation and Development (OECD). (2008). *Policy brief*. January 2008. Retrieved from www.oecd.org/education/school/39989494.pdf

Organisation for Economic Cooperation and Development (OECD).(2010). *Educating teachers for diversity: Meeting the challenge*. Paris: OECD Publications.

Organisation for Economic Cooperation and Development (OECD). (2012). *Equity and quality in education: Supporting disadvantaged students and schools*. Paris: OECD Publications.

Organisation for Economic Cooperation and Development (OECD). (2015). *Education at a glance 2015*. Retrieved from www.keepeek.com/Digital-Asset-Management/oecd/education/education-at-a-glance-2015/new-zealand_eag-2015-72-en#page1

Pantic, N., & Florian, L. (2015). Developing teachers as agents of inclusion and social justice. *Education Inquiry*, 6(3), 333–351.

Spradlin, L., & Parsons, R. (2008). *Diversity matters: Understanding diversity in schools*. Belmont, CA: Thomson Wadsworth.

The Education Trust. (2012). *Building and sustaining talent: Creating conditions in high-poverty schools that support effective teaching and learning*. Retrieved from edtrust.org/sites/edtrust.org/files/Building_and_Sustaining_Talent.pdf

United Nations General Assembly. (1989). *Convention on the Rights of the Child*, 20 November 1989, United Nations, Treaty Series, vol. 1577, p. 3. Retrieved from www.refworld.org/docid/3ae6b38f0.html

Wenger, E. (1998). *Communities of practice: Learning, meaning, and identity*. Cambridge, UK: Cambridge University Press.

Wenger-Trayner, E., & Wenger-Trayner, B. (2015). Learning in landscapes of practice: A framework. In E. Wenger, M. Fenton-O'Creevy, S. Hutchinson, & C. Kubiak (Eds.), *Learning in landscapes of practice* (pp. 13–31). New York: Routledge.

Women in Science & Engineering Leadership Institute (WISELI). (2010). *Benefits and challenges of diversity in academic settings*. Retrieved from https://wiseli.engr.wisc.edu/docs/Benefits_Challenges.pdf

# 8

# TEACHER EDUCATION AND NOTIONS OF DIVERSITY IN MALAWI

*Myriam Hummel and Petra Engelbrecht*

### Introduction

This chapter looks at dimensions of diversity in schools in Malawi, as well as teachers' perceptions of diversity in this context. Its aim is to illustrate the interaction between pre-service teacher education programmes and educational and support practices with regard to the diversity of learners in mainstream schools. The contents of these teacher education programmes are linked in interactive ways to the resultant actions and beliefs of teachers who were trained in these programmes within their own classrooms. This chapter is based on an international research project on inclusive education in Guatemala and Malawi, which concluded in 2015. The initial data analysis has been followed up with an in-depth analysis of the interviews and focus group discussions which were conducted with stakeholders in the Malawian teacher education sector.

The conception of diversity which will underpin this chapter is that it refers to numerous forms of difference, including socio-economic differences, and to those pertaining to language, ethnic identity, gender, cultural identity, ability and age (Vertovec, 2015). The benefit of using this conception of diversity is that it acknowledges a wide range of minorities (Koenig, 2009 in Vertovec, 2015, p. 6). In the context of schools, such an understanding of diversity challenges previous methods of addressing it, such as categorising learners with disabilities or learners with Special Educational Needs. Teacher education of pre-service teachers plays a vital role in transmitting concepts and categories which teachers then apply in their professional work. It is, as stated earlier, therefore worthwhile to focus on the dynamic interaction between teacher education and notions of diversity.

It is also important to reflect briefly on the context of Malawi. As a background to this chapter, we need to establish an understanding of the country's history as well as the dimensions of diversity in Malawian schools. It is a relatively small country with a colonial history. Any scholarly engagement with education in a post-colonial country requires a recognition of the ongoing implications of what Tikly calls "the colonial encounter and the post-colonial conditions for education" (2011, p. 4). As in many African countries, formal education was introduced in Malawi by missionaries during the era of colonialism, and was modelled on the British education system (MacJessie-Mbewe, 2004). It is therefore not surprising that the adopted system is described as "alien, selective and elitist" (Hauya, 1991 in MacJessie-Mbewe, 2004, p. 309). Since the country's independence, many education policies have been introduced, with the introduction of free primary education in 1994 being the most pivotal (Inoue & Oketch, 2008). Malawi is among the world's least developed countries, and was ranked 173 out of 188 countries in the 2015 Human Development Index (United Nations Development Programme, 2015, p. 210). The economy is primarily based on commercial and subsistence farming, and 85 per cent of the population occupy rural areas (World Bank, 2016). As a result, the population faces economic inequalities and high levels of poverty, which result in resource constraints in the formal education system. Furthermore, the Malawian school population is highly diverse with regard to the socio-economic status of learners, as well as their home language, ethnic identity, age and gender (Matiki, 2003; Chimombo, 2009; Chisamya, DeJaeghere, Kendall, & Khan, 2012; Dickovick, 2014).

Despite the fact that increased access to primary education was established by introducing free primary education in 1994, the retention and completion rates of learners in primary education remain low in Malawi (Chimombo, 2009). For many Malawian children growing up in poverty-stricken communities, income-generating activities and household responsibilities compete with regular school attendance and lead to high drop-out numbers in primary schools (Sankhulani, 2007). Other than socio-economic status, a barrier that influences the completion of primary education is that school children in Malawi are very likely to have a home language that is different from the language of instruction. Various ethnic groups comprise the population of Malawi, and besides English and Chichewa, around eight other local languages are spoken (Dickovick, 2014). The last population census collecting data regarding language was conducted in 1966, and linguistic aspects have been omitted in the population census since then. The 1966 census revealed that 50.2 per cent of the Malawian population claimed Chichewa as their home language (Matiki, 2003). At present, the language of instruction in the first four years of primary school is Chichewa. Thereafter, the medium of instruction changes to English. Another factor which needs to be considered is that socio-cultural norms continue to privilege men over women with regard to access to resources and services. Therefore, gender still comprises one of the persistent inequalities affecting access to and completion of education (Chimombo, 2009; Chisamya et al., 2012). While initial primary school enrolment rates show more gender parity, girls still drop out of school earlier and more frequently than boys (Chimombo, 2009).

## Teacher education for primary school teachers in Malawi

Historically, primary school teachers have been trained at Teacher Training Colleges (TTCs) in Malawi. The subject Foundation Studies is obligatory for every pre-service teacher of primary school education, and contains a module on Special Educational Needs. This module is based on the conception of Special Needs Education which appears in the National Policy in Malawi, which characterises those in need of such education as:

> Learners who require special service provision and support in order to access education and maximise the learning process. Learners with special educational needs as defined in this document refer to those children who fall into any of the following categories: sensory impairment which covers vision, hearing, deaf-blind; cognitive difficulties which include intellectual, specific disabilities and gifted and talented; socio-emotional and behavioural difficulties which includes autism, hyperactivity and other vulnerable children; physical and health impairments which include spina bifida, hydrocephalus, asthma and epilepsy.
>
> *(Ministry of Education and Vocational Training, 2007, p. 6)*

The core element Special Educational Needs is subdivided in the Malawian primary teacher education curriculum into the topics Special Needs Education (SNE), Impairment Categories, Impairment Identification Process, Rehabilitation Services, Educational Placement and the process of designing an Individual Educational Plan (IEP) within the Foundation Studies syllabus (Foundation Studies TTC Syllabus, 2015). As is the case in most countries, Special Education Needs is presented as a separate element within a wider module or subject.

The original analysis of the Foundation Studies curriculum in Malawi which was conducted in the original project revealed that teachers in the pre-service training programme for primary education learn that certain learners have specific Special Educational Needs based on various categories of disabilities. This trend persists despite the high levels of diversity within primary schools as well as emerging education policies that support inclusive education. Those who design the programmes appear to assume that these needs can only be met through specially developed learning materials, specialised teacher skills, and learning support, preferably in segregated settings (Werning et al., 2016). This approach reflects a medical deficit model of disability, which assumes that disability is a deficit within the individual that needs to be cured, treated or fixed in order for them to conform with normative expectations. It does not reflect the international move towards inclusive education which emphasises that all students who have traditionally been marginalised from meaningful education, including those from varied multi-cultural and multi-diverse backgrounds, as well as students with disabilities, should be welcomed and supported in mainstream education (Engelbrecht & Ekins, 2017).

## Teacher education for Special Education teachers in Malawi

Primary school teachers in Malawi who have teaching experience can enrol for an additional diploma course in Special Needs Education within the following four disability-based specialisation areas: learning difficulties, hearing impairment, visual impairment and deaf-blind. This course qualifies them as Special Education teachers, which is in line with the traditional approach in which learners who are regarded as qualitatively different based on theories of deficit are considered to be in need of educational responses that are uniquely tailored to respond to those differences (Florian, 2009; O'Neill, Bourke, & Kearney, 2009). The result has been that, as in most countries around the world, including sub-Saharan countries, teacher education in Malawi has been compartmentalised. The barriers between special and mainstream education have been entrenched, and innovative alternative approaches have not been introduced (Engelbrecht, 2013).

## Teacher education for inclusion

As in other countries, including the United States, the United Kingdom, and most sub-Saharan countries, this additional approach to Special Education in Malawi is not extended to broaden the boundaries of understanding diverse educational needs by integrating or infusing its contents into the broader curriculum and pedagogical practices of mainstream classroom settings (Engelbrecht & Ekins, 2017). As pointed out by Loreman (2010), these self-contained units of study may not be the most effective, efficient or desirable option to address the realities of diverse educational needs in mainstream schools. In response to the increasing diversity of students in mainstream schools and the international acknowledgement that mainstream schools should provide for the educational needs of all students, more non-traditional, innovative approaches within teacher education for inclusion have emerged (Arthur-Kelly, Sutherland, Lyons, Macfarlane, & Foreman, 2013). These include both content-infused as well as hybrid approaches. In a content-infused approach, the attitudes, skills and knowledge normally taught in single units on Special Education or inclusive education are embedded in all modules in an initial teacher education programme (Loreman, 2010; Engelbrecht & Ekins, 2017). Other innovative approaches involve variations of the hybrid approach, which include both content-infused and stand-alone approaches. Walton and Rusznyak (2016) have reviewed an example of a hybrid approach in South Africa, in which inclusivity as an implicit part of a teacher's work is infused in the first year of study, and an explicit focus on student and context diversity follows in the final year of study.

## Research design and methodology

This chapter is derived from the international research project titled "Research for Inclusive Education in International Cooperation,"[1] which focused on identifying constructions of inclusive education and success factors and barriers to inclusive educational systems in Guatemala and Malawi (Werning et al., 2016). The research was conducted using a qualitative and multi-perspective research design that combined analyses at the macro (national), meso (district) and micro (school/community) levels and focused on primary education (Refie, 2015).

Data collection strategies in the overall research project included a preliminary document analysis (Wolff, 2008) which focused on existing country-specific research results regarding the implementation of inclusive education, policy papers and practice papers for each country examined, namely Guatemala and Malawi. At the macro level, six focus group discussions (Lamnek, 1998) with various stakeholders (including members of government and non-government institutions) were utilised as data collection strategies in Malawi. At the meso level, seventeen focus group discussions and problem-centred interviews with district officials from education, health and social sectors (Witzel & Reiter, 2012) were conducted. Additionally, data was gathered on a micro level through four instrumental case studies (Stake, 2005) at selected schools and their surrounding communities in both countries. Problem-centred interviews and focus group discussions were conducted with learners, teachers, parents, school principals, local authorities, and community members. Participatory observations were also carried out in classrooms and school grounds. Furthermore, interviews and focus group discussions were organised with stakeholders in teacher education, namely two professionals from the National Ministry of Education, Science and Technology (MoEST), four professionals (principal, lecturers) from a Teacher Training College, and three professionals from a Special Needs Education College, two pre-service teachers in primary education, and twelve pre-service teachers in Special Education.

For the purposes of the research project, data collection and analysis in both countries were performed by the national research teams in cooperation with international researchers between March 2014 and December 2014.[2] In composing the national research teams, diversity of the team members in terms of qualification, ethnicity, language and gender was considered to reflect the diversity of interview partners.

A deeper analysis that went beyond the initial research project and focused on teacher education and notions of diversity in Malawi is presented in this chapter. Data available from official Malawian sources were used and combined with the results of a deductive analysis of interviews and focus group discussions with teachers and head teachers from the four case study schools on a micro level. This was done to ascertain how the social dimensions of diversity, as described in the introduction to this chapter, manifested in Malawian primary schools. Furthermore, an inductive analysis of interviews and focus group discussions with stakeholders in teacher education looked at how dimensions of diversity are constructed by the respective stakeholders. An overview of the data collected in the overall research project and the particular data used for this analysis is displayed in Table 8.1.

**TABLE 8.1** Overview of data collection

| Level | Data collection | No. and function of participants | Used for this analysis |
|---|---|---|---|
| Macro level | 6 focus group discussions | 41 stakeholders from government, private sector, civil society, donor organisations | |
| Meso level | 17 interviews/ focus group discussions | 19 district officials (education, social welfare, health) | |
| Micro level | 4 case studies (8 interviews, 27 focus group discussions, 22 participatory observations) | 4 head teachers<br>24 teachers<br>54 parents<br>96 learners<br>16 SMC members<br>1 school nurse<br>1 chief<br>22 lesson observations | 4 head teachers<br>24 teachers |
| Teacher education | 10 interviews/ focus group discussions | 2 MoEST officials<br>4 professionals from TTC (principal, lecturer)<br>3 professionals from SNE College (principal, lecturer)<br>12 pre-service primary school teachers<br>2 pre-service teachers in SNE programmes | 2 MoEST officials<br>4 professionals from TTC (principal, lecturer)<br>3 professionals from SNE College (principal, lecturer)<br>12 pre-service primary school teachers<br>2 pre-service teachers in SNE programmes |
| *Total* | *68 interviews/ focus group discussions, 22 observations* | *279 persons, 22 observations* | *51 persons* |

Transcribed interviews and focus group discussions as well as observations and field notes were analysed according to Flick's thematic coding (1996, 2004) and Strauss's open coding (1994, pp. 95ff; Strauss & Corbin, 1996). Thus, constructions of diversity were analysed from different perspectives against the background of existing teacher education programmes in Malawi.

## Findings

In the following section, the findings of our data analysis are presented, and these are used to illustrate how different actors perceive dimensions of diversity, as well as how these dimensions are displayed in Malawi's official statistics. Furthermore, we identify specific notions of diversity which are incorporated in teacher education programmes. We then look at the perceptions regarding the placement of learners and the responsibilities of teachers and schools that these notions of diversity result in.

## Acknowledgement of dimensions of diversity

Acknowledgement of diversity in schools in Malawi and access to education for learners with diverse needs have both increased in recent years, mainly as a result of the increased involvement of international donor organisations working in the fields of HIV and Aids, gender-related issues, and disabilities (World Bank, 2016). A Malawian teacher confirms that classrooms are increasingly characterised by diversity as follows:

> Nowadays it is a high percentage because most of the learners we teach in class are orphans, street kids and some with disabilities. You should have come long time ago, those with disabilities were not there and orphans were not there. Now it is a high percentage because we can say these NGOs, some of the groups in the villages, they are the ones patrolling the villages and bring those kids to schools.
>
> *(Teacher from an urban school)*

However, official government documentation still tends to focus on learners with identifiable forms of disabilities. According to statistical data from the MoEST, around 2.4 per cent of all primary school learners have special learning needs due to impairments in one of the following categories: low vision, blind, hard of hearing, deaf, physical impairment, and learning difficulties (MoEST, 2015, p. 24). This is confirmed by the statements of teachers and head teachers, who stated that differences due to disabilities are usually present in most mainstream classrooms:

> There are some children who are physically challenged or impaired, any sort of impairment, hearing impairment, visual, deaf and so on, so, in most schools such children are not taught well because they need to have specialist teacher for them. For example, here we are having one but he is for hearing impairment only.
>
> *(Head teacher from a rural school)*

Given that around ten different languages are spoken in Malawi, it is remarkable that data on home languages of learners in primary or secondary school are not documented in the Educational Management Information System of MoEST. In the formal education system, the diversity of home languages is not acknowledged, and the language of instruction in Standard 1 to 4 (or Grade 1 to 4 in other countries) is invariably Chichewa. As noted previously, English is the language of instruction from Standard 5 onwards. This means that often the language of instruction does not correlate with the home languages of learners. This has consequences for their participation in learning.

A range of ages in a particular class occurs regularly, particularly in the rural areas, due to learners entering primary education at a later stage because of their family's financial circumstances. According to the MoEST, children of between 4 and 17 years of age were enrolled in Standard 1 in the school year 2012/2013 (MoEST, 2013, p. 36). In 2015, the Education Management Information System (EMIS) data documented that 2.7 per cent of new entrants to primary school were under aged (5 years or younger), and 35.5 per cent were over aged (7 years or older) (MoEST, 2015, p. 26). Age heterogeneity is also evident in secondary education, for example, in 2012/2013, learners aged between 11 and 26 were enrolled into Form 1 (the first year of secondary school) (MoEST, 2013, p. 72). The prevalent age differences in one learning group may lead to less participation in learning or even reduced attendance for over-aged learners:

> The older ones feel that they are too old for the class and are shy and they absent themselves most of the times.
>
> *(Head teacher from a rural school)*

In Malawi, which has a high level of poverty, the socio-economic status of learners varies significantly. Children living in poverty are often orphans, and due to their socio-economic situation, these learners lack the financial means to meet their basic physical needs or to obtain the necessary learning materials for school.

> The disadvantaged children include orphans who are living with their old grandparents and they fail to get basic necessities. Not only orphans, some children have their parents but are so poor. Their parents fail to provide even the basic necessities like clothes.
>
> *(Teacher from a rural school)*

Another consequence of poverty is absenteeism of learners as a result of their duty to generate income for their families, as is the case in child-headed households.

> They [child-headed households] meet a lot of problems. The biggest challenge is food. They are constantly trying to find means to find food for the younger ones. They leave school to get piece work to support their siblings.
>
> *(Teacher from a rural school)*

Numerous forms of difference therefore exist in Malawian primary school classrooms as confirmed both by the data provided by the MoEST, and by Malawian teachers and head teachers. Our analysis of the interviews and focus group discussions with education professionals, teachers and head teachers confirms that they are aware of these forms of difference, which result in the educational marginalisation of certain groups of learners.

## Specific notions of diversity and skills needed

The country's initial teacher education programme curricula employ the traditional expert/specialist model of meeting the needs of learners, which emphasises disabilities, and this therefore continues to be deeply entrenched in current educational systems in Malawi, both pedagogically and organisationally.

Our findings regarding the influence of pre-service teacher education programmes indicate that there is a dynamic interaction between pre-service teacher education programmes and notions of diversity. This emerged in the responses to questions during interviews regarding participants' own notions of diversity and inclusive education. As mentioned earlier, all pre-service teachers in primary school programmes study the subject Foundation Studies at the Teacher Training Colleges, and this includes a module on Special Education. The head of Foundation Studies at one Teacher Training College describes the curriculum content in the Special Education module as follows:

> We have topics like Special Needs as a topic where you differentiate Special Needs Education and Special Education Needs. We also have rehabilitation as a topic. We also have inclusive education as a topic. We have categories of impairments well described in the course outline.
> *(Head of Foundation Studies at TTC)*

The classification of learners in categories based on a medical deficit approach is viewed by participants (lecturers, pre-service and in-service teachers) as a necessary pre-requisite for learning and teaching:

> They are taught on how to handle learners depending on the categories of learners that are found in the primary schools.
> *(Dean at TTC)*

> We look at each category's characteristics so that they can easily identify, if the learners are there, the causes and how to deliver a lesson so that each and every learner can participate fully during teaching and learning.
> *(Special Needs Education lecturer at TTC)*

> Let me add on to that, they [lecturers at Teacher Training College] teach us the challenges that we teachers may face when handling learners with disadvantages, they were mainly emphasising on the meaning of disability and the

categories, who are impaired learners and their categories, so they were teaching us how to identify learners with disadvantages.

*(Pre-service teacher)*

Although the introduction of Special Needs Education in the curriculum of Foundation Studies is described by MoEST officials as a recent achievement, they also acknowledge that the competencies gained are insufficient if the realities teachers face in primary schools are taken into account.

> The regular primary school teacher training has got a module on Special Needs Education. That's in the foundation studies. So, it has been there, but I think its running short somewhere because of it's not so comprehensive and also implementation sometimes is not desirable. [...] So, there are a lot of shortfalls still in that module. So, we are trying to find a way to review it.
>
> *(MoEST Official)*

> But now, it's all the TTCs the teachers now have got a dose of some sort, although we are saying it's not adequate. But they have a dose of inclusive and Special Needs Education through Foundation Studies. So, that's the positive development and it has been deregulated in all the Teacher Training Colleges in this country.
>
> *(MoEST Official)*

The feeling of being unprepared is highly prevalent, not only in statements by in-service teachers, but also in comments by pre-service teachers, such as the following:

> We don't have the skills on how to teach these children, therefore when their teachers are not around and they ask us to get these learners in our classrooms we just keep them while the Special Needs teacher knows how to handle them. The Special Needs teachers were trained and we did not undergo that training. We just keep them in our classes to pass time.
>
> *(Teacher from an urban school)*

## Inclusive education as a matter of placement and responsibility

Although teachers acknowledge that there is a range of diversity in their classrooms, their responses in the interviews focused strongly on disabilities and the placement of learners with disabilities in their schools. Malawi has very few special schools, and these are not run by the government but by charity or religious organisations, and only learners with severe disabilities can be accommodated in these schools. This is confirmed by a MoEST official who said:

> Many people are now looking towards inclusive education whereby we need to educate our learners, our children, and young people in regular schools and

colleges other than in separate schools. Yah. We are actually encouraging inclusive education as a Ministry of Education by policy. But we do have other severe disabilities that we are still sending them to special schools like special school for the deaf-blind children or special school for the blind children. So, we think that there are other people that can learn better in special schools still.

*(MoEST Official)*

Most teachers expressed that these learners should be accommodated in mainstream schools, and made specific reference to resource centres within these schools. The main approach to providing additional support for learners who are regarded to have Special Educational Needs due to disabilities in mainstream schools is the use of resource centres. In Malawi, 2.5 per cent of public primary schools are equipped with a resource centre (MoEST, 2013, p. 15 and 51) and the Ministry's intention is that each school with a resource centre should have a trained Special Education Needs teacher permanently located at the school. However, different Special Education Needs teachers judge the placement requirements of learners with diverse educational needs within a school differently. Some argue for permanent placement of these learners in the resource centre:

Inclusive education is there but I would prefer if at all the government can still implement the system of resource centres because there the learners learn comfortably rather than being in the mainstream because in the mainstream there are a lot of happenings.

*(Special Needs teacher)*

Other professionals consider placement of learners in the resource centre to be only a temporary solution:

I also suggest that disadvantaged learners should not spend all their time in the resource room but they should be there for a short time and be taken to the mainstream, so I would have loved it if the resource centres just to be an entry point, just for us to find out the learner's problem and take him or her to the mainstream. I feel when they are kept here full time inclusive education will not be achieved. We need them be mixed with the regular learners, play together and specialist teachers help them while in the mainstream.

*(Special Needs teacher)*

Regarding who should have the primary responsibility of providing support to these learners, it is striking that the perceptions of both Special Needs teachers and mainstream teachers are that only specially qualified teachers, preferably in resource centres, can work with them. A common opinion is that the mainstream teachers are not adequately trained:

> The other thing we can say is about the shortage of teachers, in that I am talking about those who have been trained as specialist teachers because they are the only people who can handle better such type of learners but those in the mainstream haven't gone through such training so they find it difficult to handle such type of learners.
>
> *(Special Needs teacher)*

Only one teacher (out of a total of 24 in-service classroom teachers interviewed) stated that all teachers should take responsibility for all learners.

## Widening perceptions and acknowledgement of diversity

It is important to note that in many statements of both in-service and pre-service teachers, an increased awareness of diversity in learners which has consequences for their learning was identified. Despite the categories of impairment which are part of the Foundation Studies curriculum at Teacher Training Colleges, and which are referred to by participants when diversity within their own classrooms is discussed, teachers are increasingly acknowledging several forms of social differences in their classrooms. As mentioned earlier, these differences are related to the language of instruction and the home language of learners, the education of girls, as well as family-related socio-economic challenges. The family situation of learners is regarded as an important element that can influence the learning achievements of the children:

> There are some learners who do not perform well at school because of the activities in their respective homes, or the learners do not have peace of mind, or whether their fathers come home drunk and start beating them up. So with such kind of problems, learners may not perform.
>
> *(Pre-service teacher)*

Pre-service teachers recognise the need to be sensitive and to be informed about the learners' family situations:

> As a teacher, we need to study the children. By looking at their background like where they are coming from and their status. This will help in understanding their performance.
>
> *(Pre-service teacher)*

Teachers also indicate an increasing sense of acceptance of differences in their classrooms. One pre-service teacher says, "The learners are different in many ways, it could be in disabilities or other ways." An in-service teacher confirms this, saying "To say the truth, in my class you cannot say this one is an orphan, this one what, you take them all on board to improve them through the lessons."

## Preparing teachers for real-life conditions in pre-service training programmes

It appears that the main external contextual challenges of large classes and lack of resources are being partially addressed in pre-service teacher education programmes at present. Pre-service teachers report covering strategies for multi-grade teaching and dealing with large classes in their training. They also describe improvising by using found materials:

> Also, the resource you are supposed to buy and you don't have money, you can improvise by looking at locally found materials for the lesson. You can go into the hill and look for the materials to improvise due to lack of money.
>
> *(Pre-service teacher)*

## Discussion

As discussed in the introduction to this chapter, the primary school population in Malawi is not only characterised by differences caused by disabilities, but also by difference in terms of social dimensions such as home language, gender and socio-economic contexts, as well as a high age variety.

As has been pointed out by Kozleski and Siuty (2014), the standards which determine what teachers need to know and what they need to be able to do should incorporate an awareness of the contexts of the schools and local school districts they will teach at in the future. In Malawi, however, the Special Education Needs module in Foundation Studies, which all primary school pre-service teachers must complete, is based on a medical deficit approach and does not reflect the dimensions of diversity present in actual Malawian schools. The awareness of diversity that is taught in pre-service teacher education programmes is focused on disabilities and on the physical placement of learners with disabilities in need of special support. This approach merely incorporates a traditional understanding of Special Needs within mainstream education, and actually comprises 'Special Education' renamed as 'Education For All' (Göransson & Nilholm, 2014). A more nuanced approach to understanding and responding to dimensions of diversity, with an emphasis on the changing patterns of access and enrolment in Malawi, is therefore needed. This includes the following: understanding patterns of access to education including late entry to primary school, grade repetition and interrupted schooling due to household income as a main cause of barriers to entering as well as progressing in education, as well as the influence of cultural differences in specific rural areas in the country including gender inequality, especially during the later phases in primary education based on complex traditional notions of the role of women in rural areas (Croft, 2006; Little, 2006; Lewin, 2009). Furthermore, the realities of learning in a second or third language of instruction should be recognised and examined from a pedagogical and linguistic point of view, and support strategies in this regard should be developed (Cantoni, 2007).

Our findings indicate that most teachers, especially those who completed their training some time ago, find it difficult to grasp nuanced conceptions of diversity, and, as a result, fail to adapt their teaching strategies to accommodate and support diverse learning needs as well as learner heterogeneity in their classrooms. This remains the case even though they are increasingly recognising dimensions of diversity in their classrooms. In a further illustration of the way in which the content of pre-service teacher education programmes interacts with teachers' own confidence in teaching and supporting learners with diverse needs, most of them tend to conceptualise diversity not as difference in terms of social dimensions but as Special Needs caused by disabilities as conceptualised in teacher education programmes. They also have deep-seated assumptions regarding the special knowledge and skills needed to teach learners who may require additional support, and specific beliefs related to where the responsibility for improving the learning outcomes of all learners lies. In general, they prefer the specially trained teachers to take responsibility for learners with Special Educational Needs. As mentioned by Rouse and Florian (2012), this is a serious, if unintended, outcome of separate training programmes for mainstream teachers and Special Needs teachers. These authors point out that by only preparing certain teachers to deal with difference, a teaching culture is created in schools in which mainstream teachers can claim that teaching learners who may need additional or different instruction is not their responsibility. The way in which the contents of teachers' initial teacher education programmes continue to interact with their everyday activities in their classrooms can therefore not be underestimated.

Despite the fact that the medical deficit approach continues to shape teacher education programmes and teachers' subsequent actions in their classrooms, it needs to be noted that some head teachers and classroom teachers increasingly acknowledge the influence social factors have on the learning process. As mentioned before, they are becoming more aware of dimensions of difference which lead to marginalisation. A positive trend that was observed is that a more comprehensive view of learners who are labelled as having Special Educational Needs is emerging in school communities. This view differs substantially from the way in which it is conceptualised in teacher education programmes. If this view of difference within the Malawian context were to be included in teacher education programmes, pre-service teachers would be empowered to develop a deeper understanding of the individuality of learners' educational needs. As a result, the necessity for individual as well as collective approaches and responsibility in improving the learning outcomes of learners with diverse educational needs would be emphasised. Against this background, opportunities for pre-service as well as in-service teachers could be created to enable them to mediate and negotiate their own views of what diversity within the contexts of their classrooms is and to adapt their teaching and learning support activities accordingly.

Collaboration and consultation between teacher education institutions and policy-makers in education systems to address issues related to expanding the scope of pre-service teachers' knowledge also needs to be emphasised. For example,

Malawi recently developed and published a National Strategy on Inclusive Education, which goes beyond a focus on disabilities. In the document it is stated that:

> The concept of inclusive education in Malawi is linked to learners with SEN and disabilities. This is demonstrated by the fact that most inclusive education projects and activities in Malawi only focus on learners with disabilities. This is a worrying trend that needs to be addressed given that the term inclusive education has a deeper connotation, which includes all those who face some kind of barrier and exclusion to learning.
>
> *(MoEST, 2016, p. 10)*

The document designates teacher education as a Strategy Priority Area with activities conducted in order to "Develop inclusive education training manuals for ECD [Early Childhood Development], primary and secondary teacher education" and to "Conduct CPDs [Continuous Professional Development] for teacher educators on IE [Inclusive Education]" (MoEST, 2016, p. 18f). Preparing teachers to support diverse educational needs within their own classrooms therefore should be the collective responsibility of teacher education institutions, of teachers, as well as of policy-makers. Systematic collaboration between these partners in Malawi could lead to the development of innovative approaches to initial teacher education that are multi-layered and contextually relevant. Knowledge gained in innovative approaches (e.g. hybrid or content-infused teacher education approaches) could enable student teachers to gain the relevant knowledge and skills for the context in which they will teach (Forlin, 2010).

## Conclusion

A fundamental requirement for the provision of support for diverse educational needs in mainstream schools and classrooms is the recognition and valuing of human diversity within international education systems and the promise of quality education for all. If pre-service teacher education programmes were to include strategies to accommodate and support diverse educational needs in mainstreams classrooms, more could be done than merely placing learners with disabilities in mainstream education classrooms. Instead, opportunities could be provided to all learners to participate fully in classroom activities (Engelbrecht & Ekins, 2017). The need to do this within the Malawian context is clear, but the challenges in this regard include not only addressing the traditional medical deficit approach to what is regarded as differences in learning and development (Hummel, Engelbrecht, & Werning, 2016), but also the lack of sufficient resources and relevant policy development or of clear and supportive implementation guidelines.

Teacher education is an important and essential factor in any educational reform, but the responsibility of acceptance and participation of all learners cannot rest exclusively at the door of teachers. The dynamic interaction between the contents of pre-service teacher education programmes, developing new notions of diversity in Malawian schools, and contextual complexities at all system levels such as relevant policy development, learner-teacher-ratio and available learning and teaching resources need to be recognised if education is to be transformed to ensure access, acceptance and participation of learners with diverse educational needs and social backgrounds.

## Notes

1 The research project was implemented on behalf of the Federal Ministry for Economic Cooperation and Development (BMZ), and was mandated by Deutsche Gesellschaft für Internationale Zusammenarbeit (GIZ), by Leibniz Universität Hannover, Institute of Education for Special Needs and GOPA Consultants.
2 Members of the Malawi research team: Dr. Grace Mwinimudzi Chiuye, Anderson Chikumbutso Moyo, Evance Charlie, Dr. Elizabeth Tikondwe Kamchedzera, Lizzie Chiwaula. Members of the Guatemala research team: Marta Caballeros, Héctor Canto, Magaly Menéndez, Cristina Perdomo, Gerson Sontay. International researchers: Prof. Dr. Rolf Werning, Myriam Hummel, Prof. Petra Engelbrecht, Prof. Alfredo J. Artiles, Antje Rothe.

## References

Arthur-Kelly, M., Sutherland, D., Lyons, G., Macfarlane, S. & Foreman, P. (2013). Reflections on enhancing pre-service teacher education programmes to support inclusion: perspectives from New Zealand and Australia. *European Journal of Special Needs Education*, 28(2), 217–233.

Cantoni, M. (2007). *What role does the language of instruction play for a successful education? A case study of the impact of language choice in a Namibian school*. Vaxjo, Sweden: Vaxjo University, unpublished thesis.

Chimombo, J. (2009). Changing patterns of access to basic education in Malawi: A story of a mixed bag? *Comparative Education*, 45(2), 297–312.

Chisamya, G., DeJaeghere, J., Kendall, N., & Khan, M.A. (2012). Gender and education for all: Progress and problems in achieving gender equity. *International Journal of Educational Development*, 32, 743–755.

Croft, A. (2006). Prepared for diversity? Teacher education for lower primary classes in Malawi. In A.W. Little (Ed.), *Education for all and multigrade teaching: Challenges and opportunities* (pp. 103–126). Dordrecht: Springer.

Dickovick, J.T. (2014). *Africa. The World Today Series. 2014–2015*. 49th Edition. Lanham, MD: Rowman & Littlefield Publishers.

Engelbrecht, P. & Ekins, A. (2017). International perspectives on teacher education for inclusion. In E. Talbot & M. Hughes (Eds.), *The handbook of research on diversity in special education* (pp. 425–444). New York: John Wiley & Sons.

Engelbrecht, P. (2013). Teacher education for inclusion: International perspectives. Guest editorial as invited guest editor. *European Journal of Special Needs Education*, 28(2), 115–118.

Flick, U. (1996). *Psychologie des technisierten Alltags*. Opladen: Westdeutscher Verlag.

Flick, U. (2004). *Qualitative Sozialforschung*. (Vollständig überarbeitete und erweiterte Neuausgabe, 2. Aufl.). Reinbek bei Hamburg: Rowohlt.

Florian, L. (2009). Towards inclusive pedagogy. In P. Hick, R. Kershner, & P. Farrell (Eds.), *Psychology for inclusive education: New directions in theory and practice* (pp. 38–51). London: Routledge.

Forlin, C. (2010). Reframing teacher education for inclusion. In C. Forlin (Ed.), *Teacher education for inclusion: Changing paradigms and innovative approaches* (pp. 3–12). London: Routledge.

Foundation Studies TTC Syllabus (2015). Malawi Teacher training colleges.

Göransson, K. & Nilholm, C. (2014). Conceptual diversities and empirical shortcomings: A critical analysis of research on inclusive education. *European Journal of Special Needs Education*, 29(3), 265–280.

Hummel, M., Engelbrecht, P., & Werning, R. (2016). Developing an understanding of inclusive education in Malawi. In R. Werning, A.J. Artiles, P. Engelbrecht, M. Hummel, M. Caballeros, & A. Rothe (Eds.), *Keeping the promise? Contextualizing inclusive education in developing countries* (pp. 29–46). Bad Heilbrunn: Klinkhardt.

Inoue, K. & Oketch, M. (2008). Implementing free primary education policy in Malawi and Ghana: Equity and efficiency analysis. *Peabody Journal of Education*, 83(1), 41–70.

Kozleski, E.B. & Siuty, M.B. (2014). *From challenges to opportunities: Professional educator development systems that work for students with disabilities.* University of Kansas, USA: unpublished research report.

Lamnek, S. (1998). *Gruppendiskussion: Theorie und Praxis.* Weinheim: Beltz.

Lewin, K.M. (2009). Access to education in sub-Saharan Africa: Patterns, problems and possibilities. *Comparative Education*, 45(2), 151–174.

Little, A.W. (Ed.) (2006). *Education for All and multigrade teaching: Challenges and opportunities.* Dordrecht: Springer.

Loreman, T. (2010). A content-infused approach to pre-service teacher preparation for inclusive education. In C. Forlin (Ed.), *Teacher education for inclusion: Changing paradigms and innovative approaches* (pp. 56–64). London: Routledge.

MacJessie-Mbewe, S. (2004). Rural communities-education relationship in developing countries: The case of Malawi. *International Education Journal*, 5(3), 308–330.

Matiki, A.J. (2003). Linguistic exclusion and the opinions of Malawian legislators. *Language Policy*, 2(2), 153–177.

Ministry of Education and Vocational Training, Malawi. (2007). *National Policy on Special Needs Education.* Lilongwe: Ministry of Education and Vocational Training.

Ministry of Education, Science and Technology, Malawi (MoEST). (2016). *National Strategy on Inclusive Education. Towards an Inclusive Education System.* Lilongwe: Ministry of Education, Science and Technology.

Ministry of Education, Science and Technology, Malawi (MoEST). (2015). *Education Management Information System. Education Statistics 2015.* Lilongwe: Ministry of Education, Science and Technology.

Ministry of Education, Science and Technology, Malawi (MoEST). (2014). *Education Sector Implementation Plan II (2013/14–2017/18). Towards Quality Education: Empowering the School.* Lilongwe: Ministry of Education, Science and Technology.

Ministry of Education, Science and Technology Malawi (MoEST). (2013). *Education Management Information System. Education Statistics 2013.* Lilongwe: Ministry of Education, Science and Technology.

O'Neill, J., Bourke, R., & Kearney, A. (2009). Discourses of inclusion in initial teacher education: Unravelling a New Zealand 'number eight wire' knot. *Teaching and Teacher Education*, 25(2009), 588–593.

Refie (2015). *Final report.* Hanover. Retrieved from www.refie.org/fileadmin/user_upload/final-report/refie-finalreport-10032015.pdf

Rouse, M. & Florian, L. (2012). *Inclusive practice project: Final report.* Aberdeen: University of Aberdeen, unpublished research report.

Sankhulani, L. (2007). Responding to the needs of the community: Examining the educational opportunities for girls in rural Malawi. *International Education Journal*, 8(1), 100–107.

Stake, R.E. (2005). Qualitative case studies. In N.K. Denzin & Y.S. Lincoln (Eds.), *The Sage handbook of qualitative research* (pp. 443–466). Thousand Oaks, CA; London; New Delhi: Sage Publications.
Strauss, A.L. (1994). *Grundlagen qualitativer Sozialforschung*. München: Fink.
Strauss, A.L. & Corbin, J. (1996). *Grounded theory. Grundlagen qualitativer Sozialforschung*. Weinheim: Psychologie Verlags Union.
Tikly, L. (2011). Towards a framework for researching the quality of education in low-income countries. *Comparative Education*, 47(1), 1–23.
United Nations Development Programme (2015). *Human development report 2015. Work for human development*. New York. Retrieved from http://hdr.undp.org/sites/default/files/2015_human_development_report.pdf
Vertovec, S. (2015). Introduction: Formulating diversity studies. In S. Vertovec (Ed.), *Routledge international handbook of diversity studies* (pp. 1–20). New York: Routledge.
Walton, E. & Rusznyak, L. (2016). Choices in the design of inclusive education courses for pre-service teachers: The case of a South African university. *International Journal of Disability, Development and Education*. doi:10.1080/1034912x.2016.1195489.
Werning, R., Artiles, A.J., Engelbrecht, P., Hummel, M., Caballeros, M., & Rothe, A. (Eds.) (2016). *Keeping the promise? Contextualizing inclusive education in developing countries*. Klinkhardt: Bad Heilbrunn.
Witzel, A. & Reiter, H. (2012). *The problem-centred interview*. London; Thousand Oaks, CA; New Delhi: Sage Publications.
Wolff, S. (2008). Dokumenten- und Aktenanalyse. In U. Flick, E. von Kardorff, & I. Steinke (Eds.), *Qualitative Forschung. Ein Handbuch* (pp. 502–513). Reinbek bei Hamburg: Rowohlt.
World Bank. (2016). *Primary education in Malawi: Expenditures, service delivery and outcomes*. Washington, DC: The World Bank.

# 9

# TEACHER EDUCATION FOR DIVERSITY IN BRAZIL

Perspectives from the National Observatory on Special Education

*Enicéia Gonçalves Mendes and Leonardo Santos Amâncio Cabral*

## Introduction

This chapter aims to provide a discussion of teacher education in the field of Special Education in Brazil. Currently, teacher education is one of the main pillars of the Brazilian National Educational Plan (BNEP) 2014–2024. The preparation of student teachers in the country aims to yield professionals who are equipped to teach in a way that is inclusive of various identities pertaining to ethnicity, religion, socio-economic status, culture, gender and sexual diversity, among others. In line with this, the BNEP states that it aims to:

> promote the improvement of the quality of pedagogy and undergraduate courses, […] in order to enable graduates to acquire the necessary qualifications to conduct the pedagogical process of their future students, combining general and specific training with didactic practices, beyond the education for ethnic-racial relations, diversity and the needs of people with disabilities.
> *(Brazil, 2014, p. 76)*

The objective that teachers should be prepared to teach inclusively in mainstream classes is relatively new in Brazil. In recent years, more critical and scholarly attention has been paid to the inclusion of children and young people who are most likely to be excluded in mainstream schools. Specifically, children and young people who tend to have less access to formal education are those who live in rural areas, those who are incarcerated, those whose educational needs fall within the ambit of 'Special Education', Brazil's indigenous people, and immigrants such as Afro-Brazilians and Quilombolas (who are descendants of African slaves). However, there are no established teacher education programmes in Brazil that adequately prepare teachers to deal with this diversity within regular schools (Mendes, 2009;

Landini, 2010). One challenge that hinders the development of such a comprehensive programme is that current courses that aim to prepare teachers to teach inclusively vary widely, and the format of a comprehensive course would need to be more coherent and less fragmented (Oliveira, 2013; Mendes, Cia & Cabral, 2015). In short, teacher education curricula in Brazil have not yet responded to the level of diversity present in the country. The necessary legal changes to formalise a curriculum that would respond adequately to the diversity mentioned here are also difficult to formalise.

According to a report published in 2013 by the National Institute of Educational Studies Anísio Teixeira (INEP), which is a local agency that coordinates the census and educational evaluation processes in the Brazilian education system, Brazil had 2.1 million teachers in 2012, 22% of whom were not adequately prepared to teach for diversity. There are currently about 415,000 (20%) teachers who are in need of training to be able to include the diverse learners mentioned in the previous paragraph, and as a result of this shortage, there is a risk that several Brazilian schools may face difficulties in welcoming learners with these differences (Mazzotta, 1996; García, 1999; Soligo, 2004; Mendes, 2006; Michels, 2011). What can be seen, however, is that the concept of diversity has led to a shift in Brazilian educational policies. To begin to address repressive and exclusionary behaviour, diversity can be embraced by the implementation of new policy strategies (Rodrigues & Abramowicz, 2013). This chapter presents the results of nationwide research on teacher education in Brazil which aims to address the challenges linked with diversity, particularly those related to the needs of learners in Special Education. In Brazil, those who fall within the ambit of what is termed Special Education are those with disabilities, with developmental disorders, or indeed those who are gifted.[1]

## Special Education in Brazil: A national framework

According to the last census (Portal Brazil, 2015), it is estimated that learners with special educational needs comprise 6.2% of the Brazilian population. The Brazilian Federal Constitution (Brazil, 1988) has stipulated that there should be preferential enrolment for these learners in regular public schools. However, despite this political provision, there is evidence that some public schools are not allowing such students to enrol. Teachers in these schools tend to be overwhelmed with a huge range of special educational needs in their teaching-learning environment. Nevertheless, this policy has prompted school communities to rethink their practices, organisation, functioning and professionalisation of school staff and teacher education (Mazzotta, 1996; Jannuzzi, 2004; Mendes, 2006). In the 1990s, the mainstream school system in Brazil was obliged to be creative, and seek solutions to include all learners in the regular classroom and to enable them to obtain satisfactory results in their academic and social performance (Mazzotta, 1996). Today, a pedagogy of diversity has necessarily expanded within this context, encompassing the inclusion of support, service and resources in regular schools. It is also now understood that successful inclusion requires adequate funding (Mendes, 2006).

It can be observed that the enrolment of learners with disabilities in regular or mainstream schools has increased significantly in recent years. According to official data, between 2003 and 2014, the percentage of such learners enrolled in basic education increased from 29% to 79% (Portal Brazil, 2015). Consequently, several opportunities for teacher education and training in the field of Special Education have been implemented nationally. These opportunities took different forms in various Brazilian states. Some states prioritised initial teacher preparation, and others resorted to in-practice education for teachers. What has become apparent, however, is that there is a lack of clear policy guidelines for the preparation of specialised teachers. This is despite the fact that the Ministry of Education (MEC) has made state-level systematic investments to overcome challenges related to diversity. The effects of this lack of legislation are gradually spreading across the country (Mattos, 2004).

## Political scenario: national guidelines for teacher education and their reflections on the Brazilian educational framework

In Brazil, the 'Law of Guidelines and Bases of National Education', or *Lei de Diretrizes e Bases* (LDB) (Brazil, 1996), states that people with disabilities must have teachers with adequate specialisation, as well as mainstream teachers trained to include them in regular classes (Brazil, 1996, art. 59, item III). However, with regard to teacher education, there is no nationwide consensus on the form that specialisation and training should take, and this has caused serious difficulties. Some of what causes the lack of consensus, for example, are varied responses to the questions of whether a national policy could propose a teacher education model and determine the particularities of each work plan, how this should be organised, where these courses would be offered, and whether these would be sufficient. In addition, the role of teachers in Special Education needs to be more clearly defined, and this needs to be paired with an interrogation of what knowledge would be required in the curriculum for the initial and postgraduate education of specialised teachers.

As has been intimated, there are divergent perspectives with respect to these discussions. Some researchers advocate for a model of general education in which a teacher should be able to teach all learners, including those who require Special Education. Others support teacher education which is tailored to specific categories of disability. Despite these disagreements, some concrete proposals for higher education, training and expertise have been implemented in Brazil. Prior to 2000, however, the number of courses was insufficient to meet the national demand. According to Bueno (2002), there were only 31 pedagogy courses with a specialisation in Special Education throughout the country. There was only one degree-level course in Special Education, and it was offered at the Federal University of Santa Maria. In 2006, the Resolution CNE / CP No.1 reformed the pedagogy courses, determining that training to include learners with disabilities should be part of all teachers' preparation. This eliminated specialised qualifications, leaving the traditional teacher education model as the only model in the country. However, since 2009, two degree courses in Special Education have been offered in Brazil.

Nozu and Bruno (2013) have found that government training courses have prioritised a general approach to awareness and appreciation of diversity, and contend that this is at the expense of a more focused proposal, which might be enriched by the particularities of those in need of Special Education.

> Thus, in the context of neoliberal governance, teacher education courses have been characterized by superficiality and occurred on an industrial scale, in order to qualify the most teachers in the shortest possible time, and at the least expense. Moreover, such courses can be understood as a neoliberal device for producing teachers who will work for the government and serve its ends.
> (Nozu & Bruno, 2013, p. 1236)

Thus, shortcomings in the policy on the development and training of Special Education teachers, either with regard to their expectations or the definition of their functions, result in conflicting interpretations of the guidelines related to the training when applied to local contexts.

The National Special Education Policy from the Perspective of Inclusive Education (PNEE-EI) (Brazil, 2008) has very broad and ambiguous specifications as to what initial, in-practice, and postgraduate education should offer and how teachers engaged in Special Education should conduct their work. Moreover, the policy imposes the responsibility for acquiring multiple skills on these professionals. This results in professionals attaining the required credentials and skills belatedly, due to their other commitments. The policy clearly envisions a multi-faceted professional who can meet the needs of all, which is encompassed in the following statement:

> All types of learners with special educational needs (intellectual disability, physical impairment, hearing impairment, visual impairment, multiple disabilities, pervasive developmental disorders, and those who are gifted) at all levels and types of education (kindergarten, elementary school, high school, higher education, rural education, technical education, adult education) and all kinds of loci (special schools, resource classes, hospital classes, home education, except in special classes, choice is prohibited by the policy).
> (Mendes, 2010, p. 24)

Moreover, PNEE-EI holds that the initial education of the specialist teacher should take the same form as that of all other teachers, and that specialised training should be acquired subsequently through degrees, postgraduate degrees, or in-service training programmes. At the moment, these forms of training do not offer any coherent and standardised specialised preparation with respect to Special Education after the initial training process. Consequently, most teachers end up acquiring additional skills on a need-to-know basis, based on problems they encounter in practice. Landini (2010) indicates that one of the great challenges of teacher training is to:

> Reframe the role of the teacher as that of a mediator, not as merely instrumental, but as an active subject who identifies with the learners personally, and engages with the realities they face autonomously, so as to have the potential to transform those realities.
>
> *(Landini, 2010, p. 23)*

In this regard, the Decree No. 7611, promulgated under the 'Programme of Living Without Limits', is committed to providing technical and financial support to promote:

> [...] training managers, educators and other school professionals for education from the perspective of inclusive education, particularly in learning, participation and the creation of interpersonal bonds.
>
> *(Brazil, 2011, Article 5°, Paragraph 2°, section IV)*

This decree attempts to counter the opinion of teachers in regular classrooms that Special Education is a different mode of education altogether. However, it remains the case that teachers can send learners to specialised teachers, while simultaneously developing their own ability to intervene and monitor Special Education learners (Oliveira, 2013). In spite of these policy provisions, there remain severe hindrances to the implementation of Special Education policies from an inclusive perspective because there is a shortage of initial training opportunities in undergraduate courses.

The Ministry of Education (MEC) has been developing programmes and projects and implementing training courses such as the 'Inclusive Education Programme: Right to Diversity' or *Programa Educação Inclusiva: direito à Diversidade*, the 'Training in Inclusive Education' or *Formação em educação inclusive*, and the 'Support Program for Special Education', or *Programa de Apoio à Educação Especial*. Evidently, two of these programmes are directed at teachers already in service, and one of them is a postgraduate course in which teachers are trained in the production of knowledge (research, monographs, articles, etc.). The fact that there is only a course, and no undergraduate degree offering, for initial training indicates that specialised training at the undergraduate level has been dropped. This state of affairs goes against the policy provisions of LDB 1996, as well as those of Resolution No. 02/2001. The two training programmes for in-practice teachers are designed to meet an emergency demand, and do not address the gap in initial training. These programmes therefore have limited capacity to solve the problem of a general lack of specialised initial training. The practitioners of the Specialised Educational Services (known locally as *Atendimento Educacional Especializado*) will need to have knowledge of various types of learners, and skills appropriate to the instruction of each of them. The service will need to be offered at all levels and in all types of education, as well as in different environments. This raises the question of whether distance training, which only offers 40-, 180-, and 260-hour courses, will be enough to achieve the desired upskilling.

In the document 'National Policy on Special Education from the Inclusive Education Perspective', there are statistics which reflect the country's progress in the training of Special Education teachers. In 2006, there were 54,625 teachers in this role (0.62% of whom had only an elementary school qualification, 24% of whom had completed high school, and 75.2% of whom had tertiary qualifications). 77.8% of these teachers had completed a specialised course in their area of knowledge. This data is somewhat paradoxical, considering the gradual extinction of the initial training courses and the instability of in-service training and postgraduate courses.

Researchers at the National Observatory on Special Education (or *Observatório Nacional de Educação Especial* – ONEESP) have begun to conduct enquiries into teachers of Special Education in Brazil. These pertain to the model of training the specialised teachers have, to what the training requirements are, and to whether teachers are able to perform in an inclusive school, particularly in the Multi-functional Resource Classes. And finally, these researchers want to discover what perceptions and concerns teachers have about their work. These threads of enquiry will be elaborated on in the following section.

## National Observatory on Special Education: Notes from 17 Federal States in Brazil

The Brazilian Special Education policy seeks to provide access to a mainstream class in a full-time programme (i.e. for five hours every weekday) for learners with special educational needs. In addition, Specialised Educational Services should be offered at regular schools within Multifunctional Resource Classes (MRCs), and conducted by a specialist teacher. To this end, the ONEESP study has been conducted with the participation of more than 500 teachers and 36 educational managers from 58 municipalities in 17 states of the country. From 2010 to 2014, data were collected through surveys, interviews and focus groups. This data made it possible to identify several elements concerning the general implementation of additional Special Education policies in schools. In particular, the MRCs emerged as a useful means to address some of the obstacles to teach inclusively, and which need to feature prominently in teacher training (Mendes, Cia & Cabral, 2015).

In the past, training of Special Education teachers was limited because they were required to seek such training in addition to their work in regular classes and special schools. The MRCs, along with Specialised Educational Services, have brought even more training demands. Several changes are required as a result of the introduction of these initiatives. Firstly, learners that are to be included now span the entire spectrum of those in need of Special Education, and services can no longer only be administered to learners with certain categories of disability. Secondly, the Special Education curriculum, which was previously restricted to certain levels of education, and sometimes contained outdated curricular topics, should now include learners of all levels, from kindergarten to higher education. Lastly, Special Education should now target the whole school and community environment. What must now be ascertained is whether the teacher education policy is responding to these new demands of development in Brazil. What follows is a summary of some challenges observed in the survey data of the National Observatory on Special Education around teacher education in Brazil, which is linked to the implementation of MRCs.

## Lack of specialist teachers

The results of the ONEESP study revealed a lack of teachers who are adequately specialised to take on the work of MRCs in inclusive schools. There is also clearly a shortage of teacher education opportunities to prepare teachers to work in the Special Education sector. In attempts to address this deficiency, institutions have resorted to employing teachers without specific training. Consequently, 'emergency training' is becoming a permanent need. There is therefore consensus across related Brazilian studies that it is necessary to provide specialised training and to expand Special Education opportunities in teacher education in the country. The question, however, is precisely how this specialised training should be accomplished in the field of initial, in-service training and/or postgraduate education.

## Failure of initial education

Regarding specialist teacher initial education, the survey data indicate that teachers tend to value the form of training that they themselves have been exposed to. Those who have specialised initial training, such as those who have obtained a full degree in Special Education, or a degree in Education/Pedagogy with a specialisation in Special Education, are in favour of expertise in the field being developed right from the initial training. Those who have a general teacher training base are often in favour of increasing competence as much as possible through in-service training and/or postgraduate education. The data reflect that there is however consensus on the following:

i   there is generalist initial teacher training for teachers who work in MRCs;
ii  Special Education issues are treated peripherally; and
iii some subjects do not respond to current demands of teaching learners with disabilities or developmental disorders, nor teaching gifted learners, in inclusive schools.

Teachers with Special Education expertise also complain of insufficient training from their initial training. Upon graduating, they were prepared to work with learners with one or two categories of disability or learning difficulty. It is therefore unjust to expect them to deal with all the Special Education learners, as demanded by the current policy. On the issue of initial teacher training in Special Education, three aspects should be emphasised in relation to these results. Firstly, there is inadequate research on the experience of teachers in the MRCs. The reason for this is that MRC service is very new, as is the policy of inclusion in the country. Accordingly, the limited experience of these teachers in this area does not allow for a proper assessment of their training. Secondly, teachers with initial training and/or with postgraduate education in the area of Special Education have reported that the introduction of MRCs has required a change in their roles and functions. Given this, the old training model is no longer appropriate, and a new model is still to be defined. Finally, it must be taken into account that teachers with specialised initial training are in the minority in the country, since in most states there are no undergraduate courses in Special Education. Survey results indicate that postgraduate and in-service training models, rather than an initial education training model, have been prioritised by universities and school systems in the training of Special Education teachers. It is therefore of interest to the researchers how teachers evaluate the training they have received.

## *Failure of in-service training and postgraduate courses*

The range of instruction offered through in-service training and postgraduate education has been well diversified in Brazil. Teachers of MRCs have sought to improve their training, and municipal secretaries of education throughout the country have provided opportunities for all teachers to participate in-service training programmes, as well as specialisation or postgraduate courses. Many teachers also realise that it is necessary to seek other opportunities on their own by way of independent reading and distance education. Accordingly, in-service training and postgraduate education programmes have assumed two formats: specialisation courses offered by higher education institutions, and courses promoted by education systems. Because of the joint effort of universities and school systems, the specialist teacher has access to various courses. Consequently, there are reasonable opportunities for further education, either through contact or distance modes. Despite all this, these opportunities are still considered insufficient to meet the needs of professionals in relation to teaching practice in MRCs and common classrooms of the regular schools.

The reasons for this sense of available training being inadequate may include:

- An educational policy that invests in in-service training and postgraduate education based on the contested premise that one can work without specialised initial training;
- A lack of awareness that the need for continuous professional development is a permanent state, and should be considered as a norm rather than a problem;
- The complexity of the role of specialist teachers in the context of MRCs and the inclusion policy;
- The low quality of the courses offered for in-service training and/or postgraduate education related to Special Education.

These factors are not mutually exclusive, and therefore each is useful to an analysis of the current in-service training and postgraduate education offerings.

## Critics of the current process of teacher education for learner inclusion

Criticism of training, particularly that of in-service education, is expressed by teachers in terms of:

- The omission of relevant content (for example, that which is related to the educational processes of learners in Special Education and the assessment of specific needs in MRCs);
- Course offerings which are unsystematic and fragmented;
- Programmes which are planned without consideration of the different stages of professional development of the participants;
- The prioritisation of theoretical aspects and a lack of concern with how they might be put into practice. In this regard, teachers are expected to discern the practical applicability of theoretical content of courses independently;
- Inadequate course formats (lectures and courses with reduced hours which are mainly offered in distance mode);
- The persistence of the medical model of disability, i.e. giving priority to the deficit instead of the human rights approach to education and necessary environmental and curricular changes.

In addition to these criticisms, teachers were eloquent in offering suggestions about improving the teacher training policy for inclusion in schools.

## Definition of the roles of educators

The survey results indicate that in different circumstances teachers adopt the varied roles that are mentioned in the school inclusion policy. They insist that this flexibility is necessary, but this unpredictable behaviour can result in varied interpretations of the policy. Some teachers believe that the role they are required to play in inclusion is too extensive, while others believe that the role of teachers in ensuring inclusion should not be understated because the current trend is that MRC teachers in schools are afforded less respect and authority than healthcare professionals in the same setting. In the official documents of the Ministry of Education, the specialised teacher is characterised as the main articulator of the school inclusion policy. This means a specialised teacher is responsible for attending to the learners in Special Education and their families, as well as for initiating collaboration with the teacher of the regular class, school staff and community agencies. However, teachers of MRCs emphasise that the promotion of school-wide inclusion is the responsibility of everyone involved, including teaching staff, managers, family and school community. Accordingly, they ask for a clearer definition of the roles of each professional involved in the training of learners in Special Education.

In practice, policy considers the role of the MRC teacher to be that of a manager of specialised resources and customised service plans, who is guided by the completion of the teaching process of their learners. However, this conception of teachers' roles may be contributing to the isolation of the specialised services and to that of the teachers themselves within schools. It may also adversely affect the learning processes of their learners. Specialised teachers appear to believe that regular curriculum teaching affords those who teach in mainstream classes their own space, and that they are more valued by departments of education, educational systems and schools. They complain of feelings of isolation and devaluation.

## Working conditions of the specialist teacher

The challenging working conditions facing Brazilian education professionals in general are also seen in MRCs. However, teachers in MRCs have been observed to face additional challenges. In several of the municipalities surveyed, the MRC teachers are on temporary or part-time contracts. This, along with the mindset that they are not effective, generates employment instability. Teachers often take up positions in MRCs due to a lack of other options, which may result in disinterest in the work. It must be considered that in most cases, MRC teachers are regular education teachers who may or may not have specialised in Special Education. They may at any time choose to return to the regular classroom. Their precarious employment circumstances, as well as a lack of identification with the work in the MRC, increases teacher turnover in specialised services. This has been exacerbated by some government policies, which terminate services and instil changes in the employment structure of teachers in schools. The high turnover of teachers is not unique to Special Education. However, in the case of specialist teachers, the challenge is more dire because the system is not able to replace these professionals to counter high turnover rates. Moreover, this turnover amounts to a wasted investment in in-service training programmes to work in MRCs.

Many specialised teachers still complain about the inadequate infrastructure of schools and the facilities available in MRCs. They also bemoan the insufficient number of specialised teachers and the hours that available teachers are therefore expected to work. Although working hours can vary, specialised teachers find that they have limited time to liaise with regular teachers, and this is a problem because specialised services must connect with the regular classroom. In relation to the MRC teacher work, one of the teachers says that "*the room is multifunctional, but the teacher is not*". This expresses this teacher's sense that she is unable to manage the complexity of the MRC, as well as her sense of isolation. However, despite complaints of this kind, teachers and education systems find different ways to circumvent these difficulties. Some such measures include transferring learners with a specific disability to another teacher who feels more prepared to receive them, referring learners to specialised institutions, or creating specialised centres for a single category of learner. The study provided opportunities for teachers not only to analyse, but to participate in collaborative research. This combines the production of knowledge and training, and has opened up training possibilities to specialist teachers that they had not previously envisioned.

## *University and research*

During the survey, discussions around the training of teachers were important and linked with the ONEESP objectives. These are to provide opportunities for researchers and teachers to reflect on policy and practice, and to propose changes in this time of need. The meetings which focused on groups consolidated an awareness of the role of the university in developing research, which aims to understand local realities and highlight successful experiences. Such research should also endeavour to describe and analyse the demands of each school system so as to advise the government on the review and reorientation of educational policies. Those working in the field of Special Education are charged with the production of knowledge in terms of training proposals. To face this challenge, partnerships were developed between the universities and educational systems which participated in this study, to continue to seek new teacher education models and develop joint strategies to address issues. Thus, the responsibility of working in collaboration with the specialised teachers of MRCs was a methodological resource which strengthened relational links among the academic stakeholders.

## Conclusions

The results showed two main critiques of the current Special Education policy in terms of teacher training for diversity. There is a need to improve both the working conditions and the training programmes of specialised teachers. These aspects are crucial because financial investment in Special Education can be wasted if no action is taken to address them. It is useless to equip rooms with teaching resources if teachers do not know how to use them. Furthermore, the system does not provide decent working conditions for these professionals. Teacher education is multi-faceted. It reflects the complexity of society, in which public policies manifest in complex and context-specific ways in institutional spaces. It is defined by the teaching strategies which are emphasised, and it is also affected by the formative experiences that each teacher has had as a result of their initial, in-service training and/or postgraduate education. Therefore, teacher education is a constant learning path, and in the case of Special Education teachers, both initial and in-service training programmes have failed to equip teachers to develop an integrated practice between regular and Special Education. This makes it difficult to provide an inclusive education that promotes socialisation, participation, independence and learning of Special Education learners in regular schools.

Most teacher training courses in Brazil are offered by private universities, which do not always have an established research culture. These institutions are profit oriented, and contributing to improving teachers' qualifications is not necessarily a priority in these spaces. Another worrying trend is the increase in teacher training courses offered in the form of distance education. In addition, the country does not offer attractive working conditions for talented young people to join the teaching profession. The current educational policy provides a generalised training model, and teachers are nevertheless expected to be multi-faceted professionals who are able to meet the different needs of their learners, and to work in different areas, including public schools. Even those who have completed postgraduate courses do not feel equipped to respond to the breadth and complexity of the demands of diversity. Hence, the current development of an inclusive education system requires an urgent revision of the guidelines for initial, in-service training and/or postgraduate teacher education.

To propose new models of teacher education, some questions still need to be answered, because there is no consensus about the definition of the required professional. These questions include:

- Is it best to have a specialised teacher who is the primary champion of inclusion in school environments, or is it best to upskill all teachers to be responsible for promoting inclusion?
- Should the specialised teacher be trained at undergraduate or postgraduate level?
- Which kind of training should be offered – either general preparation to work with all Special Education learners, or specialised preparation, to work with specific categories of learners?
- Where should specialised teachers work – within specific environments prioritised by policy (MRCs), or in all existing service environments, such as itinerant education, special classes, special schools, hospital classes, and home schools?

These issues require rigorous debate and careful analysis. Some current teacher education programmes should be reworked due to their unrealistic requirements. Such programmes assume the following:

i MRCs offer services to all Special Education learners. This idea requires a multifunctional teacher who requires more preparation than what is offered by any existing initial courses, in-service training or postgraduate education programme.
ii The role of the specialised teacher includes all levels of education, from kindergarten to higher education. This assumption ignores the differences between the levels of education and the fact that each one has its own requirements which need different forms of training.
iii The current postgraduate training is the ideal model to meet the requirements. This assumption overlooks the fact that short training models do not provide a broad-enough education that integrates theory and practice. Instead, short training models prioritise the specific needs of Special Education learners without considering general teacher education.

What is required to revamp the system is a collaborative model, which employs research as a guide for developing area-specific knowledge. The established culture in the Brazilian educational system, however, favours isolated work, making collaborative work difficult. A model of cooperation should be built which promotes training and intentional collaborative practices between various projects. Although this study has analysed teacher education for Special Education in Brazil, it has revealed the need to promote inclusive education in initial and postgraduate teacher education programmes. Changes to policy in Special Education and teacher training are difficult to achieve because this would be a joint task of the education departments of the 26 states and federal departments of higher education institutions and the Ministry of Education.

In general, low-cost, lightweight models have been resorted to because other measures are expensive. In addition, many universities, including public ones, may charge fees for in-service training and postgraduate education programmes tailored to meet the needs we have outlined in this chapter. Moreover, if the education sector is absorbing unprepared professionals, there is less incentive to invest more resources for producing qualified teachers. We argue for an urgent change in the legislation, forcing the development of enhanced content of teacher training courses and the creation of initial courses for Special Education teachers. However, the teaching profession is not becoming more valued, and if working conditions are not improved, the problems of teacher education in Brazil will remain.

## Note

1 In Brazil, we call such learners *público-alvo da Educação Especial*, which loosely translates as "the target audience of Special Education".

## References

Brazil (1988). *Constituição da República Federativa do Brazil, de 05 de outubro de 1988.* Brasília, DF: Casa Civil.

Brazil (1996). *Lei No. 9.394, de 20 de dezembro de 1996.* Brasília, DF: Presidência da República.

Brazil (2008). *Política nacional de educação especial na perspectiva da educação inclusiva.* Brasília, DF: Ministério da Educação. Secretaria de Educação Especial.

Brazil (2011). *Decreto No. 7.611, de 17 de novembro de 2011.* Brasília, DF: Subchefia para Assuntos Jurídicos.

Brazil (2014). *Planejando a próxima década conhecendo as 20 metas do Plano Nacional de Educação.* Brasília, DF: Ministério da Educação.

Bueno, J. G. S. (2002). *A educação especial nas universidades Brazileiras.* Brasília, DF: MEC-Secretaria de Educação Especial.

García, C. M. (1999). *Formação de professores: Para uma mudança educativa.* Porto: Porto Editora. Coleção Ciências da Educação 2: Século XXI.

INEP (2013). *Censo da educação básica: 2012 – resumo técnico.* Brasília, DF: Instituto Nacional de Estudos e Pesquisas Educacionais Anísio Teixeira.

Jannuzzi, G. S. M. (2004). *A educação do deficiente no Brazil: dos primórdios ao início do século XXI.* Campinas, SP: Autores Associados.

Landini, S. (2010). As transferências no trabalho docente: o debate sobre a imaterialidade do trabalho e algumas reflexões sobre formação. *Revista de Educação – Instituto de Educação da Universidade de Lisboa,* 17(2), 29–41.

Mattos, N. D. (2004). *Cidadania, deficiência e política educacional no Estado de Sergipe: 1979–2001.* São Carlos, SP: Programa de Pós-Graduação em Educação Especial – Universidade Federal de São Carlos.

Mazzotta, M. J. S. (1996). *Educação especial no Brazil: história e políticas públicas* (5th ed.) São Paulo: Cortez Editora.

Mendes, E. G. (2006). A radicalização do debate sobre inclusão escolar no Brazil. *Revista Brasileira de Educação,* 11(33), 387–405.

Mendes, E. G. (2009) A formação do professor e a política nacional de Educação Especial. In: *Proceedings of the V Seminário Nacional de Pesquisa em Educação Especial.* São Paulo: V Seminário Nacional de Pesquisa em Educação Especial, vol. 1, pp. 1–15.

Mendes, E. G. (2010). Breve histórico da Educação Especial no Brasil. *Revista Educación y Pedagogía,* 22, 93–110.

Mendes, E. G., Cia, F., & Cabral, L. S. A. (2015). *Inclusão escolar e os desafios para a formação de professores em educação especial.* São Carlos, SP: Marquezine & Manzini – ABPEE.

Michels, M. H. (2011). O que há de novo na formação de professores para a Educação Especial? *Revista de Educação Especial,* 24(40), 219–232.

Nozu, W. C. S., & Bruno, M. M. G. (2013). Política de (con)formação de professores para o atendimento educacional especializado: estratégias de governamentalidade neoliberal. In: *Act of VIII Encontro da Associação Brasileira de Pesquisadores em Educação Especial,* pp. 1229–1240.

Oliveira, G. R. (2013). *Efeitos da formação – O caso de uma ação de formação inserida no Programa de Formação Contínua de Professores em Atendimento Educacional Especializado.* Lisboa, PT: Instituto de Educação – Universidade de Lisboa.

Portal Brazil (2015). *Número de pessoas com deficiência nas escolas cresce 381% em 12 anos.* Available at: www.brasil.gov.br/educacao/2015/09/numero-de-pessoas-com-deficiencia-nas-escolas-cresce-381-em-12-anos

Rodrigues, T. C., & Abramowicz, A. (2013). O debate contemporâneo sobre a diversidade e a diferença nas políticas e pesquisas em educação. *Educação e Pesquisa,* 39(1), 15–30.

Soligo, R. (2004). A formação de professores. In: *Prefeitura Municipal de São Luís (MA). Formação de educadores: uma ação estratégica e transversal às políticas públicas para educação.* São Luís: Prefeitura Municipal de São Luis. Secretaria de Educação. SEMED.

# 10

# DIFFERENCE IN CURRENT POSTAPARTHEID EDUCATION

*Nazir Carrim*

## Introduction

The importance of recognising 'difference' in contemporary postcolonial and postmodern schools and classrooms is the focus of this chapter. The argument advanced is that the notion of 'difference' is one that speaks to current global postmodern and postcolonial contexts, and is therefore likely to be more useful and generative than notions such as 'diversity' and/or 'inclusivity'. Part of the reason for this argument is a recognition that the notions of 'diversity' and 'inclusivity' both have their genesis, frames of reference, and discursive points of emphases under conditions of modernity, and not postmodernity or postcoloniality. To ensure that the important insights and gains that have been made through approaches of 'diversity' and 'inclusivity' are taken forward in contemporary postcolonial and postmodern times, it is suggested that the notion of 'difference' may prove to be more useful. 'Difference' is not used in this chapter to convey a simplistic sense of 'all things are different' or 'all people are different'. Rather, it is viewed ontologically, epistemologically and methodologically. It is also viewed herein as a phenomenologically convergent feature of postmodernity.

This chapter views 'modernity' in two senses. Firstly, modernity is viewed in relation to time. It is considered herein to have been ushered in by the industrial revolution at the turn of the twentieth century, and the 'fracturing' of modernity is viewed as having accelerated from the late 1960s onwards (see Hall, Held & McGrew, 1992 for more on this). Secondly, modernity is also viewed in this chapter in relation to the ways in which human identities are conceptualised. Under modernity, human identities are generated in relation to social categories and across these categories. Part of the fracturing of modernist views is the recognition of the ways in which such identities intersect with each other, and noting that people belong to more than just a single category. Modernist views are also considered to have been impacted by reductionist tendencies where singular 'essences' or causes are determinant, and where polarising logic prevails. In this regard, 'difference' is shown to provide a way of going beyond modernist social categories and allowing for non-reductionist explanations.

This chapter covers the notions of 'diversity', 'inclusivity', 'postmodernity' and 'difference'. In its conclusion, the impact of postmodernity on education is considered, as well as how 'difference' may take forward the discourses of 'diversity' and 'inclusivity' into the twenty-first century. The chapter is written from a South African perspective, and while this South African experience and perspective relates to experiences elsewhere in the world, there are specific aspects that may not be shared by people in other contexts. Where such differences may exist, an attempt is made to point them out.

## Diversity

'Diversity' has a specific meaning in South Africa, and this is due to the experiences of apartheid. To oppose the blatantly racist segregationism of apartheid, the notion of 'diversity' is supposed to indicate recognition of different cultures and 'races',[1] and this recognition is supposed to extend to the languages, belief systems, traditions, customs and rituals of all South Africans. It is for these reasons that the 'new'[2] South Africa's coat of arms bears the phrase 'unity in our diversity', which recognises the 'diversity' among South Africans as a resource and strength of the country based on equality (see www.sahistory.org.za/article/national-coat-arms). This understanding of 'diversity' in the South African context indicates that it has largely been about diversity of racial, cultural and ethnic groups. This is not coincidental because racial segregation, a hallmark of apartheid, was justified historically and used cultural and ethnic differences among South Africans to segregate them on racial grounds (see also Carrim, 1995). This idea of inequality of people based on their assumed culture was used to justify the racist architecture and demographic landscape of apartheid in terms of 'group areas', which divided South Africans racially, and 'bantustans' or 'homelands', which further divided the African population along tribal and ethnic lines.

The idea of 'unity in our diversity' is thus meant to indicate a 'unity' as opposed to the inequality and separation instituted by apartheid. 'Diversity', too, is meant to indicate a positive approach to the differences among South Africans, in which these differences are considered to be a resource and strength of the country rather than a basis of dominance, subordination and inequality. 'Diversity' within the South African context, has therefore been linked to 'race' relations, and this continues to be the most dominant of its uses. In this regard, South Africa is no different from other countries in which a particular conception of 'diversity' has emerged largely in response to race relations.

Following World War II, the United Kingdom, for example, began to deal with issues of 'race' relations in a concerted way to address what it then expressed as a coloured immigration problem (see for example, Rex & Mason, 1986). The discourse that was constructed at the time about 'race' relations took on the language and ideological focus of 'culture', and went through many permutations of the notion. Culture, in relation to 'race', was spoken about in terms of 'assimilationism', 'integration', 'multiculturalism', and 'anti-racism'. Except for the anti-racist approach, all the others used the notion of culture as their discursive pivot, with recognition of diversity of cultures, as implied in 'integrationist' and 'multicultural approaches', which developed in turn from 'assimilationist' approaches. For the anti-racists, though, such discursive constructions around notions of culture and diversity were viewed as a displacement of 'race' into culture, and did not in fact address serious experiences of racism and racial inequality. In this regard, too, the anti-racists pointed out that 'diversity' functioned ideologically to reproduce patterns of 'white' superiority and perpetuate 'white' privilege (see Braham, Rattansi & Skellington, 1992). South African anti-apartheid struggles made the same point about the ways in which culture, and its attendant use of the notion of diversity, were not only mechanisms to justify apartheid, but also to allow it to persist (see Carrim, 1995). Nonetheless, what this illustrates is that even in the United Kingdom, the notion of 'diversity' had its point of emergence in relation to issues related to 'race'.

In the wake of such developments, and significantly bolstered by anti-racist, anti-colonial and anti-apartheid struggles, the discourse of 'race' and 'diversity' was problematised, critiqued and contested on two grounds. Firstly, 'diversity' was contested because the extent to which it actually assists in the eradication of forms of racism is debatable. Secondly, it was contested on the grounds of what the privileging of culture and 'race' silenced as diversity constructed itself. Other variables and social categories such as class, gender, ability, and sexual orientation, among others, were rendered marginal due to the privileging of notions of 'race' and culture. 'Diversity' was seen to only refer to differences among 'races' and cultures. It is this second response that allowed the notion of 'diversity' to develop to include more in its meaning and to increase its reach.

Vertovec (2015) remarks:

> Why is there so much interest in 'diversity' now? There are many reasons offered. Perhaps the foremost reason is the success, increasingly and cumulatively since the 1960s, of the key identity-based public/political campaigns among women, African American, lesbian and gay, age- and disability-based movements.
>
> *(Vertovec, 2015, p. 1)*

As can be seen from this quotation, 'diversity' has now (since the 1960s) come to refer to issues related to class, gender, sexual orientation, ability and other identities which go beyond 'race'.

There are two important points in this regard. The first is to do with what Hall et al. (1992, pp. 279–291) refer to as the "de-essentialization of the subject" and the second is about "intersectionality". The recognition that people are more than just 'raced' means that 'race' is not regarded as the 'essence' or 'core' or only significant characteristic of being human. Human beings are more than only being 'raced' subjects. They are gendered, classed, with different sexual orientations, different religions, levels of ability, and so on. The claim that only one 'essence' can be assumed to be the all-defining feature of any individual is, therefore, fundamentally counterfactual. An individual can be 'black', female, working class, lesbian and disabled, and this is what they in fact are – more than just one thing at any given point in time.

The second point to emerge from this recognition of the 'de-centring' of the self or individual is that if an individual is constituted by many identities, it then follows that such identities intersect with each other. Such intersections also vary from one person to another. For example, 'black' women may be raced and gendered, but 'black' women will also differ from each other in that some 'black' women may be middle class and lesbian, while others may be working class and heterosexual, and so on. These women differ significantly from each other, and the varied intersections of 'race' with class, gender, sexual orientation and ability matter. Such intersections result in people differing across social categories as well as within these categories.

The notions of 'de-centred' identities and 'intersectionality' have impacted 'diversity'. They have shifted its meaning from signalling differences across groups or social categories, to recognising differences within groups or social categories. As Vertovec (2015, p. 1) indicates, it is due to such developments that 'diversity' has been impacted by "identity politics since the 1960s". Given that these experiences and developments were constructed by modernity, it is fair to suggest that the notion of 'diversity' has its genesis and has been framed by modernity and the constitutive forces within it.

However, in 'new' South African schools, 'diversity' continues to be more about 'race', ethnicity and culture. In order for the 'new' South Africa's schooling system to be based structurally on equality, apartheid laws needed to be undone and replaced by a single, non-racial and democratic system for all South Africans. This is what the *National Education Policy Act of 1996* (DoE, 1996b) does. Ensuring that the schools of the 'new' South Africa are not used as mechanisms to re/produce 'race' and racism, and monitoring that the 'new' South Africa's schools are racism free is an ongoing and prioritised objective of the educational system. Nonetheless, the assertions of identities other than 'race'-based identities are also present in 'new' South African schools, and these include identities linked to gender, class, religion, ability and sexual orientation. Nevertheless, the dominant meaning of 'diversity' in 'new' South African schools continues to be linked to 'race' and issues related to racism (see Carrim, 1998, 2009; Soudien, 2012).

## Inclusivity

Unlike the origins of 'diversity', the origins of the notion of 'inclusivity' have been more linked to schooling and to education more generally (see Walton, 2016, for example). This has also been the case in South Africa. In this country, the notion of 'inclusivity' was first spoken about as a policy-framing idea in the postapartheid situation, and used in conjunction with the notion of 'human rights'. For example, in the *National Education Policy Act of 1996* (DoE, 1996b) and *Curriculum 2005* (DoE, 1996a) – the curriculum that was put into place after 1994 in postapartheid South Africa – the notion of 'inclusivity' is consistently used in relation to the idea of 'human rights'. *Curriculum 2005*, for example, enshrines "Social Justice, a Healthy Environment, Human Rights and Inclusivity" (DoE, 1996a, p. 5) as foundational principles. The linking of 'inclusivity' with 'human rights' in post-1994, post-apartheid South Africa was informed mainly by the *Bill of Rights* of the 'new' South African *Constitution*. This document states that 'inclusivity' needs to include within its reach all the identities that are recognised in the *Bill of Rights*, and that the recognition of such identities is a matter of 'human rights'. Being 'inclusive', then, means that all people, no matter who they are, are part of the 'new' South Africa, and all are recognised as equal. It is on this basis that *White Paper Six: Special Needs Education* (DoE, 2001) framed 'inclusivity' as conjoined with human rights, which keeps within the provisions of the *Bill of Rights of the Constitution* of the 'new' South Africa.

*White Paper Six: Special Needs Education* also highlighted the notion of 'barriers to learning'. This idea served two important functions. Firstly, it recognised that the challenges or barriers people experience in terms of learning are due to various factors, which may include and may also go beyond learning 'disabilities'. Poverty, for example, can be just as constricting to access and achievement in education as a cognitive and/or physical disability. 'Barriers to learning' thereby served the function of placing learning disability issues in the mainstream and enabled them to be viewed as similar to the 'barriers' to learning people may experience due to 'race', class, gender, sexual orientation, etc. It is in this light that Walton (2016, p. 51) notes "inclusive education is positioned simultaneously as an issue of disability and special need, but also more broadly as concerned with all barriers to learning that learners may experience".

However, in 2008, the National Department of Education released the *National Strategy on Screening, Identification, Assessment and Support* (DoE, 2008). This document tends to narrow the meaning of 'inclusivity' and 'inclusive education' to the schooling of people with disabilities and special needs. The "screening, identification, assessment and support" that are referred to in this *National Strategy* refer mainly to the identification and assessment of disabilities and special needs rather than the many ways in which people may experience 'barriers to learning', as indicated in the earlier *White Paper Six* of 2001. It is in this regard that the genesis of 'inclusivity' and 'inclusive education' in South Africa is somewhat curious. While the notion of 'inclusivity' is progressively broadening in its scope and meaning (see Walton, 2016), in South Africa the opposite seems to be true. Postapartheid South Africa began by viewing 'inclusivity' in broad terms, but by the time the *National Strategy on Screening, Identification, Assessment and Support* (DoE, 2008) was released in 2008, the meaning of 'inclusivity' and 'inclusive education' began to become narrower and reduced in scope.

The above discussion demonstrates that 'inclusivity' in South Africa had its genesis mainly in postapartheid South Africa. Its links with 'diversity' can be seen by the emphasis these notions have on consolidating a democracy based on the human rights and equality of all the country's citizens, not only in terms of disability or special needs but in the broader sense and in keeping with the *Bill of Rights* of the 'new' South African *Constitution*. In this regard, the frame of 'inclusivity', like 'diversity', suggests that it is modernist in its construction. 'Inclusivity', in its postapartheid South African formulation, is framed in the 'identity-based' politics of modernity. The reach of 'inclusivity' is about recognising multiple forms of identity which have emerged and have been constructed within modernity. Identities and identity-based politics then characterise the modernist ways in which the notions of 'diversity' and 'inclusivity' have been framed in postapartheid South Africa.

## Postmodernity

The notion of 'difference' is increasingly viewed as one of the more significant characteristics of the postmodern condition. How and why this is the case is explored in relation to the economic, political and socio-cultural aspects of postmodernity.

### *Postmodernity economically*

Postmodernity is characterised by a global economy that has "ICTs as its engine" (Castells, 2001, p. 3). ICTs (Information Communications Technologies) have revolutionised the way in which the economy functions by allowing for more rapid money exchanges to take place through electronic money transfers than was possible before the ushering in of this "information age". Castells (2001, p. 3) also notes that this information age, through its use of ICTs, enables the world to become more "networked", which some consider to have enabled the world to become a "global village". Trade exchanges have consequently become more diversified and customised, allowing for products to be produced to meet specific individual needs, tastes and preferences, and on a global scale. The postmodern global economy, with "ICTs as its engine" is also characterised by high skills and high knowledge and a highly complex and differentiated system, albeit 'networked'. It rests on diversification and pluralisation, while simultaneously enabling multinational corporations and international monetary agencies to rise in ascendency (see Castells, 2001).

### *Postmodernity politically*

Due to the increase in global exchanges within the global economy, political systems too have undergone notable changes. It should be noted, however, that these are all contested, and while examples of these will be provided in what follows, political systems under postmodernity have become more global or international in their enunciated dominant forms. Melluci (1989, p. 165), for example, has described the political changes under postmodernity as a shift from the importance of nation states to "supra-national" states or organisations, which is why organisations such as the European Union, African Union, BRICS (Brazil, Russia, India, China and South Africa) and the United Nations are increasing in their dominance (and importance). Indeed, the decline of nation states and the rise of supra-national states are contested. 'Brexit' is one example that captures such contestations. Brexit refers to the decision by the United Kingdom (UK) to 'exit' the European Union and not be part of its supra-national state. Instead, the UK has reasserted its nationalism as opposed to the European Union. What impact this will have on both the UK and Europe, and how the UK will be able to 'go it alone' in the networked global economy of postmodernity remains to be seen (see www.independent.co.uk/topic/brexit for news on developments about Brexit).

Politically, the postmodern condition is also characterised by a "shift from the politics of identity to a politics of difference" (Hall et al., 1992, p. 280). Hall et al. (1992, p. 280) describe this shift as "arising, especially, from the erosion of the 'master identity' of class and the emerging identities belonging to the new political ground defined by the new social movements". Later, Hall et al. remark that "This gives rise to the postmodern subject, conceptualised as having no fixed, essential or permanent identity. Identity becomes a 'moveable feast'" (p. 277). This means that people's identities, which include those of learners in classrooms, are not fixed or permanent. Learners too need to be viewed as having identities which are complex – which intersect within an individual – which shift, change and develop.

## *Postmodernity socio-culturally*

The clearly visible and widely shared socio-cultural effect of postmodernity on people's lives and on socio-cultural levels is undoubtedly related to the impact of ICTs. Cell phones, smart phones, tablets, etc. are now part of people's 'survival kit'. ICTs, in this sense, are the staple diet of postmodern living. The possession and use of ICTs has also impacted how social relations and social communications happen. The increase in social networking through Facebook and Twitter, for example, reconfigures the way in which people communicate with each other. Face-to-face communication in real space and time is being replaced/displaced by virtual space communications. Such virtual space communications through social networks, and online, are also used in important ways for political mobilisation. In addition, social relations are being re/defined and occur more in virtual space than in person-to-person contact. As a result, people have started to develop virtual personae, and these virtual identities further fracture, de-centre and pluralise people's selves. In socio-cultural terms, then, postmodernity has profound implications for social relations, social communication, virtual and dispersed identities of selves. Multiplicity, plurality and assertions of 'difference' increase.

This discussion shows that in economic, political and socio-cultural terms, the postmodern condition is one that has a profound impact and implications. At all levels, 'difference' is not only being foregrounded, but is a phenomenologically congruent emergence. This means that whether one is looking at an economic, political or socio-cultural level of postmodernity, multiplicity, plurality and 'difference' emerge consistently as key features. It is important to note here that the emergent politics of 'difference', and its constitutive effects in the construction of postmodernity, is much more than what both the notions of 'diversity' and 'inclusivity' could and did entail. 'Difference' within postmodernity is more than just about difference between social categories of people such as 'race', gender and class. It also refers to more than the differences within social categories such as those between a working-class, heterosexual 'black' woman and a middle-class, lesbian 'black' woman. 'Difference' within postmodernity is also about the interface between people and ICTs, between people and virtual space, and about the complex, contradictory and pluralised selves people are being, becoming and inhabiting in a networked global village.

## Difference

This chapter has argued that both 'diversity' and 'inclusivity' are modernist constructions. They speak to a world and a time that is located within the twentieth century. 'Diversity' and 'inclusivity' use the social categories of modernity as their discursive points of emphases. As such, modernist social categories such as 'race', class, gender, age, disability, sexual orientation *inter alia* have been crucial to constructions of both the discourses of 'diversity' and 'inclusivity'. To clarify, such social categories, and the differences across them and within them, provided the discursive points of references and emphasis for 'diversity' and 'inclusivity'. 'Diversity' and 'inclusivity' have also been significant in contesting and redefining modernist constructions and patterns of dominance and subordination. 'Diversity' and 'inclusivity' have aided in struggles for greater equality and justice for all. Notwithstanding the ways in which both 'diversity' and 'inclusivity' have been contested and critiqued, they have contributed to raising awareness about difference among people and the need to treat all people equally in socially just ways.

But, we are now well into the second decade of the twenty-first century. Not only have conditions of modernity shifted to postmodern conditions, the social categories upon which 'diversity' and 'inclusivity' depend are also undergoing significant fracturing, dispersion and dislocation. The question, then, is whether 'diversity' and 'inclusivity' can be sustained into the twenty-first century. I would argue that continuing to speak of 'diversity' and 'inclusivity' in terms of social categories is not currently viable because they continue to speak to the conditions and formation of selves under modernity. The notion of 'difference', if it is to take forward the gains accrued by 'diversity' and 'inclusivity' into postmodernity, needs to go beyond the politics of identity and work beyond the social categories of modernity. The question is how this may be done.

It is argued here that a way in which this may be done is to view 'difference' ontologically, epistemologically and methodologically. While shifts from modernity to postmodernity are discernible, this does not mean that old forms of identities, or modernist conditions or previous forms of politics do not persist in the present.

Forms of the old are always in the present. What makes the present different is that in addition to the old it produces something new. Thus, while modernity persists in many of its forms, postmodern conditions are new and they characterise the present.

## *Difference ontologically*

One of the problems bedevilling 'diversity' and 'inclusivity' is that to oppose the constraints of marginalisation, inferiorisation and oppression of people, proponents of these constructs tended to speak of the need for equality of all, and could only demonstrate this by employing the language of social categories. Thus, one would speak of the diversity of all 'races', of equality in terms of gender, or of the need to include all people, irrespective of ability. In so doing, 'diversity' and 'inclusivity' approaches not only demonstrated who is excluded and how, but who is constructed as hegemonic and dominant and how. As necessary and important as these contributions have been, they reinforce social categories to the point where people are fixed within them; the categories are reified and rest on a polarising logic (black/white, male/female, included/excluded, dominant/subordinate, etc.).

The conditions of postmodernity, as discussed previously, fracture, de-centre and pluralise such social categories. Under modernity, 'diversity' and 'inclusivity' approaches have led to the notion of 'intersectionality'. Under postmodernity, people's multiple identities shift and change and constantly redefine the social categories in which they are re/presented and re/imagined. These identities are "de-centred", and do not have a "fixed core" (see Hall et al., 1992, pp. 279–291), and there are many ways in which different identities intersect with each other, across and within categories. Given this, it seems reasonable to suggest that in postmodern conditions one needs to view human beings and being human in ways that transcend such social categories.

One way to do this would be to view human beings in terms of an ontology of becoming. This means that human beings need to be viewed as constantly being in a state of becoming, evolving, changing and developing (see Nietzsche, 1968). Human beings in this light are always different, and their ontological condition is marked by an ontology of difference. Their "centres", "cores" or senses of self (Hall et al., 1992, pp. 279–291) constantly shift, and various identities which pertain to 'race', class, gender, ability, and so on, intersect with each other in shifting, dynamic and complex ways. An ontology of difference, as constantly being in a state of becoming, will be able to hold within it the fluidity, multiplicity and explosion of difference within postmodernity. It will, thus, also provide a way to speak beyond social categories.

It is important to note that while theories of modernity, and even those prior to it, also emphasised change and development, in postmodernity such development and change are not reductionist. For example, theories of Marxism (see Hall et al., 1992) reduce things to the economy. Another example of this reductionism is when development is viewed as progressions in a somewhat linear order which allude to a totalising grand narrative. Postmodern theories avoid such polarising logic. Instead, the ontology of difference under postmodernity is multi-layered, plural, dispersed, contradictory and specific, as much as it is with macro-sociological impact and implication.

## Difference epistemologically

Viewing difference epistemologically would entail recognising that there are many perspectives to things. It would also require a recognition that there are many causes to events and phenomena, and mono-causal explanations simplify reality to 'essences' and singularities. Such mono-causal explanations therefore fail to recognise the complexity, multi-dimensionality and dynamism of human life and the world(s) we occupy.

The increasing complexity, multiplicity and pluralisation materially embedded within postmodernity require an epistemological approach that can view phenomena in multiple ways and from different perspectives. Because of the interface between human beings and ICTs, and given the explosion of information in this postmodern 'information age', singular views on anything will be difficult to justify, let alone sustain. An epistemology of difference which recognises multi-causality, and that works with dynamism and complexity in virtual and real space and time is crucial. It should be noted too that an epistemology of difference is not in itself a singular view but is an epistemology which recognises multiple views.

An epistemology of difference need not lapse into epistemological relativism of 'anything goes'. The problems of epistemological relativism are well debated and such debates point to the resultant difficulties of making judgements about anything, which in turn lead to a lack of action. To reiterate, if all things are relative and no judgements can be made, on what basis will one then be able to act? (see Sayer, 2000). The epistemology of difference suggested here maintains that the need for logic and argument as pointed out by Nietzsche remain important (see Nietzsche, 1968). In addition, utilising judgemental rationality, which has been put forward by Sayer (2000) and Potter and Lopez (2001), provides ways in which epistemological relativism may be avoided while maintaining an epistemology of difference. Furthermore, notions of postmodernity, postmodernism and difference are themselves 'decentred', with varied meanings. 'De-essentialisation' and multiplicity under postmodernity permeate all levels and the notions mentioned here are also points of contestation with multiple meanings (see Kumar, 1995 for a useful coverage of such debates).

## Difference methodologically

The ontology of difference and the epistemology of difference comprise distinct methodological considerations. If one accepts an ontology of difference and an epistemology of difference, then methodologically, one needs to be open to various and varying approaches, from quantitative to qualitative approaches. One may also need to approach issues and phenomena from different perspectives and disciplines. Methodologically, if one were to work with difference in these ways, it would entail capturing phenomena and issues in their complexity and multi-causal dimensions as opposed to attempting to view reality in mono-causal ways and generating singular explanations.

Difference methodologically, then, would entail mixed-method, multi-, cross- or inter-disciplinary approaches. The complexity and fluidity of the postmodern condition will require such a methodology of difference so that the multi-dimensional aspects and dynamism of things may be explored and not reduced into singular 'essences', paradigmatically or otherwise.

This discussion on difference, which approached the matter ontologically, epistemologically and methodologically, albeit in brief, demonstrates how the notion, if viewed in these ways, may provide a way in which issues and concerns of 'diversity' and 'inclusivity' may be taken into postmodernity.

## *Difference educationally*

The main concern in this chapter is to address the educational challenges under postmodernity and postcoloniality. The discussion thus far has been presented to lay the basis for an exploration of how difference may help in these contemporary classrooms, and what follows builds on this foundation.

Current South African classrooms are filled with learners who are glued to their cell phones, smart phones, and tablets. While there are various types of device that they have access to, almost all learners, even in the most rural and disadvantaged schools, at least have a cell phone (see Carrim & Taruvinga, 2015). The current presence of technology in the classroom is unprecedented. South Africa is no different to some contexts in terms of the extent to which ICTs have become predominant in contemporary classrooms (see Collins & Halverson, 2009). Instructions given by teachers now include statements like 'all cell phones need to be switched off', or teachers put up posters in their classroom which say 'this is a cell phone free zone'. Such posters and statements of instruction would have been unheard of in previous times. These are indeed postmodern classrooms.

Emerging evidence indicates that most learners are engaged with social networks while on their phones/devices in the classrooms. They also 'surf the net', and what they access is as broad as the internet itself (see Carrim & Taruvinga, 2015). What the presence of ICTs in the classroom indicates is that learners in contemporary classrooms are aware of, engaging with and immersed in virtual reality. They are remarkably adept at using ICTs (see Collins & Halverson, 2009), and their immersion within cyberspace has also led to them having a presence on the internet and constructing virtual identities. It is not being suggested here that the use of ICTs necessarily leads to learning or that they are used for effective teaching. While this is occasionally the case, what is being emphasised here is that the presence of ICTs in classrooms points to material conditions that did not exist before.

Learners' immersion in cyberspace has significantly aided in releasing their voices and popularising and mobilising support for their struggles. Two recent examples in South Africa demonstrate this. The first is the #FeesMustFall campaign, and the second is the #RhodesMustFall campaign.

The #FeesMustFall campaign began in 2015, and is still underway. It pivots around the demand of students at universities in South Africa that university education should be accessible and free to all South Africans (see ewn.co.za/Topic/Fees-Must-Fall). The #RhodesMustFall campaign was initiated by University of Cape Town students in 2015, who demanded that the statue of Cecil John Rhodes be removed from the campus because it was a symbol of colonialism, of the subjugation of colonised 'black' people, and of inequality, (see https://en.wikipedia.org/wiki/Rhodes_Must_Fall). While there are many dimensions to these campaigns (see related comments by Reygan, Walton and Osman [this volume]), both campaigns firmly reflect South Africa in its postapartheid, postcolonial moment. These campaigns by students at universities were launched as hashtag campaigns. This means that these students used the internet and social networking in virtual space to muster support for their struggles, to popularise their struggles and have their voices heard throughout the world. And, they could do so within minutes! As such, these campaigns reflect the postcolonial moment in which these campaigns are situated, and their postmodern character. The movement is postcolonial because it calls for the removal of a colonial symbol (the Rhodes statue) and postmodern because of the extent and kind of technology used (ICTs and social media). No educational system has ever had students who asserted themselves in these ways. This is a phenomenon that is only possible within current postmodern conditions. As much as such phenomena come from postmodern, ICT-saturated classrooms, these are also about the postmodern students of contemporary classrooms.

The notions of 'diversity' and 'inclusivity' do not have within their repertoire the language or conceptual tools to deal comprehensively with these postmodern classrooms and students. This is because, as discussed earlier, the genesis of both 'diversity' and 'inclusivity' were situated in times without ICT-saturated classrooms, social media or cyberspace. But the notion of difference may very well be able to engage productively with these new conditions. Postmodern classrooms and students can be viewed as shifting and changing through an ontological view of difference. Postmodern students can also be viewed through this lens as having multiple, pluralised identities, which include virtual identities, and this would allow for such students to be viewed as constantly being shaped and reshaped as they develop and grow. Students may be viewed with 'difference' as occupying intersecting social categories and piercing them in virtual space.

In schools, though, one consequence of ICTs is the ways in which they have been used, rather viciously, by learners to bully each other in cyberspace. Posting videos, texts and images of people on social media, and using these to intimidate, harass, undermine, defame, debase and humiliate learners, is also a phenomenon that was unheard of in previous times. While previous iterations of bullying used pictures, texts, etc., in postmodern schools cyberbullying can go 'viral' within seconds. Cyberbullying then increases the reach and pace of such acts of bullying and is becoming more prevalent (see Popovac & Leoschut, 2012), and South African schools are no exception in this regard (see www.cyberbullying.org, for example). Cyberbullying also manipulates and re/defines images, modes of signification and representation, and meanings, in ways that are not possible in real time and space. 'Photoshopping', and other means of manipulating images, are examples of ways in which such images are currently re/shaped and manipulated. In this regard, cyberbullying re/shapes modernist imaginations into new and postmodern forms. This is made possible by the dextrous use of ICTs by postmodern learners.

An ontology of difference would be able to engage with cyberbullying by recognising that it is a new and shifting phenomena. This approach would have to acknowledge that there are many types and forms of bullying, and cyberbullying is but a part of the picture. An epistemology of difference would be able to acknowledge and work with the understanding that there are many views to things. There are no fixed ways in which images and significations acquire their meanings and in which they are re/presented or projected. An epistemology of difference would be able to work with the multiple meanings of cyberbullying, what informs them, and how such views are constructed. Neither the notions of 'diversity' nor 'inclusivity' would be able to do the same.

The #FeesMustFall and #RhodesMustFall campaigns and cyberbullying are used here as illustrative examples of how in postapartheid South Africa, virtual students are present in virtual spaces. South African education is already being interpenetrated by postmodernity, in which ICTs and their use are prevalent. The notions of 'diversity' and 'inclusivity' would not be able to adequately deal with such phenomena, but the notion of difference might. It follows that the #FeesMustFall and #RhodesMustFall campaigns, as well as cyberbullying, could also be investigated by using difference methodologically. Methodologically, difference would allow such events to be researched in quantitative and qualitative ways. It would be able to view such events in multidimensional ways, as complex phenomena with many layers for which explanations are needed, as opposed to mono-causal explanations that would attempt to squash the multi-dimensionality of these events to singular essences, or causes. #FeesMustFall is about more than fees, as much as #RhodesMustFall is about more than a statue. Methodologically, 'difference' would allow such events to be viewed as movements of people as they become who they are while they constitute their worlds in complex ways.

## Conclusion

The purpose of this chapter has been two-fold: Firstly, to indicate that 'diversity' and 'inclusivity' have their genesis, frames of reference and discursive foci within conditions of modernity and are thus modernist constructs. Secondly, this chapter has indicated that the notion of 'difference' may prove to be a notion that may assist in taking forward the insights and gains of 'diversity' and 'inclusivity' approaches into postmodernity. 'Difference' is a notion that is argued to resonate more profoundly with current postmodern and postcolonial times. Such postmodern and postcolonial times have also been shown in this chapter to be present in postapartheid South Africa by using the examples of the #FeesMustFall and #RhodesMustFall campaigns. Cyberbullying was also used to illustrate the presence of virtual learner identities in cyberspace. The importance of recognising all people based on equality, which was central to the 'diversity' and 'inclusivity' approaches, both in postapartheid South Africa and the rest of the world, can be taken forward. It has been argued that this can be done by employing the notion of 'difference', if that notion is viewed ontologically, epistemologically and methodologically.

## Notes

1 The use of 'race' and racial descriptions of people such as 'black' and 'white' people are used in scare quotes throughout this chapter. This is to indicate that this chapter distances itself from apartheid racist constructions and it views such racial descriptions of people as false.
2 The 'new' in the 'new' South Africa is put in scare quotes throughout this chapter for two reasons. Firstly, after twenty-two years of being in a post-apartheid situation it is odd to still describe the democratic South Africa as 'new'. Secondly, many have also argued that a lot of apartheid is still very much intact currently, and thus how 'new' the democratic South Africa in fact is, is debatable.

## References

Braham, P., Rattansi, A. & Skellington, R. (Eds) (1992). *Racism and Antiracism: Inequalities, Opportunities and Policies*. London: Sage.
Castells, M. (2001). The new global economy. In J. Muller, N. Cloete & S. Badat (Eds), *Challenges of Globalisation: South African Debates with Manuel Castells* (pp. 2–22). Cape Town: Maskew Miller Longman.
Carrim, N. (1995). From "race" to ethnicity: Shifts in the educational discourses of South Africa and Britain in the 1990s. *Compare* 25(1), 17–33.
Carrim, N. (1998). Anti-racism and the "new" South African educational order. *Cambridge Journal of Education* 28(3), 301–320.
Carrim, N. (2009) Hair, markings on the body and the logic of discrimination. *Perspectives in Education*, 27(4), 375–384.
Carrim, N. & Taruvinga, M. (2015) Using ICTs (educationally) for development in an African context: Possibilities and limitations. *Perspectives in Education* 33(1), 100–116.
Collins, A. & Halverson, R. (2009). *Rethinking Education in the Age of Technology: The Digital Revolution and Schooling in America*. New York: Teachers College Press.
Department of Education (DoE) (1996a). *Curriculum 2005*. Pretoria: Government Press.
Department of Education (DoE) (1996b). *National Education Policy Act*. Pretoria: Government Press.
Department of Education (DoE) (2001). *White Paper Six: Special Needs Education*. Pretoria: Government Press.
Department of Education (DoE) (2008). *National Strategy on Screening, Identification, Assessment and Support*. Pretoria: Government Press.
Hall, S., Held, D. & McGrew, T. (Eds) (1992). *Modernity and Its Futures*. Cambridge: Polity Press.
Kumar, K. (1995) *From Post-Industrial to Post-Modern Society*. Oxford: Blackwell.

Melluci, A. (1989). The democratisation of everyday life. In J. Keane & P. Meier (Eds), *Nomads of the Present* (pp. 160–181). London: Hutchinson.
Nietzsche, F. (1968). *Will to Power*. Translated by Walter Kaufman. New York: Vintage.
Popovac, M. & Leoschut, L. (2012). *Cyberbullying in South Africa: Impact and Responses*. CJCP Issue Paper No. 13, June. Claremont: Centre for Justice and Crime Prevention.
Potter, G. & Lopez, J. (Eds) (2001). *After Postmodernism: The New Millennium*. London: Athlone.
Republic of South Africa (1996). *The Constitution of the Republic of South Africa*. Pretoria: Government Press.
Rex, J. & Mason, D. (Eds) (1986). *Theories of Race and Ethnic Relations*. Cambridge: Cambridge University Press.
Sayer, A. (2000). *Realism and Social Science*. London: Sage.
Soudien, C. (2012). *Realising the Dream: Unlearning the Logic of Race in the South African School*. Cape Town: HSRC Press.
Vertovec, S. (2015). Introduction: Formulating diversity studies. In S. Vertovec (Ed.), *Routledge International Handbook of Diversity Studies* (pp. 1–20). London: Routledge.
Walton, E. (2016). *The Language of Inclusive Education: Exploring Speaking, Listening, Reading and Writing*. Abingdon: Routledge.

## Websites

www.gov.za (accessed 05 September 2016)
www.independent.co.uk/topic/brexit (accessed 05 September 2016)
https://en.wikipedia.org/wiki/Rhodes_Must_Fall (accessed 05 September 2016)
ewn.co.za/Topic/Fees-Must-Fall (accessed 05 September 2016)
www.cyberbullying.org (accessed 05 September 2016)

# ABOUT THE CONTRIBUTORS

*Nazir Carrim* is Associate Professor at the Wits School of Education at the University of the Witwatersrand in Johannesburg, South Africa. He is currently the Head of Division of the Division of Studies in Education and his area of specialisation is sociology of education.

*Doria Daniels* is Professor of Educational Psychology at Stellenbosch University in South Africa, where she teaches Qualitative Research Methodology and Adult Learning and Support modules in postgraduate Honours programmes. She holds a PhD in International and Intercultural Education, which cemented her passion for understanding marginalised populations' experiences of educational access and inclusion. She is an NRF-rated researcher whose publications stem from her empirical research on empowerment and basic education for illiterate women, indigenous knowledge and the role of gender in the depiction of women in community history, and the potentialities of adult education and training for active citizenship. Her most recent research is with immigrant parents on their roles in the educational support of their schoolchildren.

*Petra Engelbrecht* is a Professor and Senior Research Fellow in the Faculty of Education Sciences, North-West University, Potchefstroom campus and Emeritus Professor of Education, Canterbury Christ Church University, England. Previous positions include Executive Dean, Faculty of Education Sciences, North-West University, Potchefstroom campus, South Africa and Senior Director, Research, Stellenbosch University. She was awarded an Honorary Doctorate in Education by the University of Eastern Finland, Finland in August 2014. Her research focuses on equity in education with specific reference to the implementation of inclusive education in diverse cultural-historical contexts and she has published extensively in this regard.

***Enicéia Gonçalves Mendes*** is Full Professor at the Federal University of São Carlos, Brazil, in the postgraduate Special Education programme and the graduate Special Education course. She has a PhD in Psychology from the University of São Paulo, and a Master in Special Education from the UFSCar. She graduated in Psychology from the University of São Paulo. She developed her postdoctoral studies at the University of Paris V Sorbonne in France and from internships in the United States, France, Mexico and Peru. Currently she is the coordinator of the National Observatory of Special Education, President of the Brazilian Association of Special Education Researchers (ABPEE) and Member of the Advisory Committee of the CNPq (Research Productivity Scholarship of the CNPq – 1C Level).

***Navan N. Govender*** is currently a lecturer at the Wits School of Education at the University of the Witwatersrand, Johannesburg, South Africa. He lectures and conducts research within the field of (English) language and literacy education at both undergraduate and postgraduate levels, specifically focusing on the theory and practice of critical literacy, the teaching of controversial topics, language, gender and sexuality, as well as visual literacies and multimodal text design. His research and teaching interests stem from his doctoral thesis, *Negotiating the Gendered Representations of Sexualities through Critical Literacy*.

***Myriam Hummel*** is a researcher at Leibniz Universität Hannover, Institute of Education for Special Needs in Germany. A special education teacher by training, she has professional experience teaching students with and without special educational needs. In the past, she has implemented numerous technical assistance projects in the education sector on behalf of bi- and multilateral donors in teacher education and school development in Asia, Africa and Central America. Her main research interests lie in the field of inclusive education in so-called developing countries, with a focus on the interrelation of international, national and regional levels in the discourses and practices of inclusive education.

***Alison Kearney*** is an Associate Professor in the Institute of Education at Massey University, New Zealand, where she coordinates the Masters of Education (Learning & Teaching) Programme. She is co-director of the Equity through Education Research Centre and editor of the New Zealand educational journal, *Kairaranga*. Prior to taking up her position at Massey University, Alison was a primary school teacher. Her teaching and research interests include education for equity and inclusive education.

***Peace Kiguwa*** (PhD) is Senior Lecturer in the School of Human and Community Development in Psychology at the University of the Witwatersrand, South Africa. Her research interests include gender and sexuality, critical race theory, critical social psychology and teaching and learning. Her current research projects include a focus on young women's leadership in higher education and a destabilising heteronormativity project with the African Gender Institute (AGI) and Action Aids

International (AAI). She has co-edited three books (UCT and ZED press releases) and has published in both local and internationally accredited journals. She is currently co-editor of the accredited journal *Psychology in Society* (PINS) and recently *African Studies*. She is also co-editor on three Special Issue journals.

**Ora Kwo** has taught in the Faculty of Education, HKU for three decades. Much of her work focused on the dynamics of teachers' learning and the power of community discourses. In 1997, she was awarded a University Teaching Fellowship for her excellence in teaching. During 2007–2009 she took sabbatical leave in Paris, where she participated in global conferences by UNESCO and undertook consultancy assignments. Her current interest in studying the relation between mainstream schooling and private tutoring is driven by her vision of education in providing human resources for sustainable development.

**Alfred Masinire** is a lecturer and researcher at Wits School of Education at the University of the Witwatersrand in South Africa. He teaches modules on curriculum at undergraduate and postgraduate levels, specialising in theories knowledge. His research interests focus on gender and schooling in rural schools and teacher education for rural schools. He keeps a social justice and rurality thrust at the centre of his work.

**Mandia Mentis** is an Associate Professor in the Institute of Education at Massey University, New Zealand, where she coordinates the postgraduate Inclusive Education programme. She is co-director of the Equity through Education Research Centre and coordinator of the national inter-professional programme for Specialist Resource Teachers. She has practised as a teacher and educational psychologist in primary, secondary, and tertiary settings. Her teaching and research interests include dynamic assessment, teaching for diversity, and inquiring into the affordances of digital technologies to support life-long and life-wide learning.

**Ruksana Osman** is Dean of the Faculty of Humanities and Professor of Education at the University of the Witwatersrand. Prior to her appointment as Dean, she was the Head of the Wits School of Education. She convenes the UNESCO Chair in Teacher Education for Diversity and Development. She has extensive teaching and research experience in the field of teacher education and higher education and is an elected member of the Academy of Sciences of South Africa (ASSAF). Her particular expertise is higher education policy, pedagogy and students' lived experiences of equity and access to higher education. She has published her work in a variety of journals and books. She is also co-editor of *Research-led Teacher Education: Case Studies of Possibilities* (2012); *Large Class Pedagogy: Interdisciplinary Perspectives for Quality Higher Education* (2013); *Service Learning in South Africa* (2013); and *Transforming Teaching and Learning in Higher Education: Towards a Socially Just Pedagogy in a Global Context* (2017).

***Finn Reygan*** (PhD) focuses on issues of sexual and gender diversity in transnational contexts and particularly in South Africa. While his work is lifespan oriented, he concentrates on issues of diversity in education and on interventions at the national and regional levels to create more inclusive school spaces. He works across sectors, including civil society and government, and is currently based at the Human Sciences Research Council (HSRC) in Pretoria, and is a Visiting Senior Research Fellow at the Wits Centre for Diversity Studies (WICDS) at the University of the Witwatersrand in Johannesburg.

***Lee Rusznyak*** (PhD) is an Associate Professor at the Wits School of Education. She is currently the Academic Head of Teaching and Learning. Her research focuses on the recognition and development of professional teaching practices of new and experienced educators. In particular, she explores the contributions of teacher knowledge, pedagogical reasoning and reflection on experience in effective teaching. As a C-rated researcher, she is concerned with making research-led contributions that seek to improve the quality of teaching and learning in the South African context. She is a forum member of the UNESCO Chair in Teacher Education for Diversity and Development and has contributed to several national research projects on teaching and teacher education.

***Leonardo Santos Amâncio Cabral*** is Adjunct Professor II in Special Education at the Federal University of São Carlos, with Master, Doctorate and Post-Doctorate qualifications in Special Education from the Federal University of São Carlos. He also developed his Full Doctorate in *Culture, disabilità, inclusione: educazione e formazione* at the Università degli Studi di Roma 'Foro Italico', Italy, with the attached title of 'Doctor Europeaus' by the European Commission. With internships abroad developed in France, England, Denmark and Ireland, his main fields of study focus on Special and Inclusive Education: policies and practices and Inclusion in Higher Education.

***Elizabeth Walton*** is an Associate Professor in Inclusive Education at the Wits School of Education where she teaches undergraduate and postgraduate courses in inclusive education, as well as supervising postgraduate students' research on aspects of inclusive education. She is an NRF-rated researcher and a member of the forum of the UNESCO Chair for Teacher Education for Diversity and Development. Her current research projects are investigating teacher education for inclusive education in South Africa, and exclusionary schooling practices.

***Jing Xiao*** is a lecturer in the Department of Capital Basic Education Development and Research at Capital Normal University in Beijing, China. In 2015, she was awarded a doctoral degree in the Faculty of Education at the University of Hong Kong. Since then, she has been actively involved in training of both pre-service and in-service English teachers in the project 'University Partnership with Suburban Schools'. With a pedagogical shift from transmissive teaching to inquisitive learning, she centres her research on construction of a safe learning community space through narrative inquiry to accommodate teachers' diverse learning needs.

# INDEX

Note: 'n' after a page number indicates a note; 'f' indicates a figure; 't' indicates a table.

age heterogeneity 128
agency xiii, 32. *See also* autonomy
Allan, J. xi
Amin, N. 56, 65, 66
Anderson, I. 23
apartheid 154–5. *See also* racism
'artefacts'. *See* pedagogical 'artefacts'
assimilation: defined 88; and disabilities 4; as discourse of diversity 2–4; and politics of hair 15; and race 155
autonomy xii, 70–85. *See also* agency

Baglieri, S. 18n2
Banks, J. 2
Barron, B. 110
Bejoian, L. M. 18n2
Bernstein, B. 94
Bevan-Brown, J. 107
Bhana, D. 37
Boler, M. 26
Bourdieu, P. 89, 94, 98
Bozalek, V. 26
Brantlinger, E. 8
Brazil xii; inclusion in 139, 140–1; special education in 140–51; working conditions for teachers in 148–9
Brexit 159
Broderick, A. 8
Broderick, A. A. 18n2
Bruno, M. M. G. 142
Bueno, J. G. S. 141

bullying 17, 164–5. *See also* cyberbullying
Butler, J. 46–7
Byrne, B. 3

Cabral, Leonardo Santos Amâncio xii
Carolissen, R. 26
Carrim, N. 15, 18n2
Castells, M. 158
CDL. *See* Critical Diversity Literacy (CDL)
celebration: as discourse of diversity 4–5, 6–7t, 8; and politics of hair 15
Chataika, T. xiv
China xii; education reform in 69–70; learner autonomy in 70–1; teacher autonomy in 71–85
Cochran-Smith, M. 2
communication 111–13
Confucius 84
Connor, D. J. 18n2
contextually responsive teaching: approaches to 53–6; in South Africa 56–66; study of 58–66
Critical Diversity Literacy (CDL) xi; analytical criteria of 11, 13t; as challenge to dominant discourse 9–12, 14; and curriculum design 25–7; defined 24–5; and pedagogy of discomfort 26–7; and politics of hair 15–16; and politics of hair in South Africa 14–17; as "reading practice" 25; and self-reflection 27–34; as

# Index

social justice pedagogy 22–4; in teacher education 9–12, 13t, 14
critical literacy: goals of 37; and materials design 38–50, 41f, 43f, 45f, 46f, 47f, 49t
critical reflection 37–9. *See also* self-reflection
critical thinking 23
cultural capital 94, 98, 99
curriculum design: and Critical Diversity Literacy (CDL) 25–7; and materials design for critical literacy 38–50, 41f, 43f, 45f, 46f, 47f, 49t
cyberbullying 164–5

Daniels, Doria xii
Darling-Hammond, L. 55, 110
Dass, M. 3
Delgado-Gaitan, C. 99
Dell, P. 23
difference xiii; vs. diversity 153; epistemology of 162; and methodology 162–3; ontology of 161–2; pathologisation of, in diversity discourses 4–5; and postmodernity 159–65; recognition of 27–9; use of term 18n2. *See also* diversity; the Other
disability: deficit model of 123, 129, 135; and inclusive education 157–8
disabled learners: in Brazil 139–41; and discourse of assimilation 4; and discourse of celebration 5; and "dysconscious ableism" 8; in Malawi 123–4, 127, 129–36; in New Zealand 104. *See also* special needs
discomfort, pedagogy of 26–7
discourse, defined 8–9
discourses of diversity: assimilation 2–4; celebration 4–5, 6–7t, 8; current approaches to, in teacher education 1–2; overview xi; pathologisation of difference in 4–5; and politics of hair 15–16; and privilege 2–5, 8; and racism 5. *See also* Critical Diversity Literacy (CDL)
diversity: benefits of 103–4; as concept in South Africa 154–6; defined 103, 121; vs. difference 153; and inequity 104; multi-dimensionality of x, xiii, xiv; and race 155; study of, in Malawian educational system 124–36; in teacher education x, xi–xii; use of term 18n2. *See also* difference
Donaldson, N. 3
Du Bois, W. E. B. 31–2
'dysconscious ableism' 8

Economic Freedom Fighters (EFF) 14
economics, and postmodernity 158
education: as intergenerational project 94–5; parental support of xii, 88–90; religious 95–6; Somali parents' views of 96
education reform, in China 69–70
Elbaz, F. 50
Elliston, D. 37, 38
emotionality 32–4
Engelbrecht, P. 4
Engelbrecht, Petra xii
epistemology 162
Epstein, J. L. 97
equity 104–6. *See also* inequity
ethnicity 104
European Union 159

Fairclough, N. 48
fairness 104–5
fatalistic thinking 23
#FeesMustFall movement 4, 164, 165
Florian, L. 134
'forced introspection'. *See* self-reflection
Foucault, M. 46–7
Francis, D. 10
Frank, G. 18n4
Freire, P. 23, 37, 38, 39

Gee, J. P. 8–9
gender: and biological sex 46, 46f; and educational inequity 122; views of, in South Africa 36–7. *See also* heteronormativity
gender diversity 36
gender violence 36
global economy 158
Gopal, N. 3–4
Govender, Navan xi
Grant, C. A. 1
Greene, M. 85
Gu, H. 84

habitus 89
Hackman, H. W. 22, 24
hair, politics of 14–17
Hall, S. 155, 159, 161
Held, D. 155
Hemson, C. 10
heteronormativity: and materials design for critical literacy 36–50, 41f, 43f, 45f, 46f, 47f, 49t. *See also* gender
Holck, L. 103
homophobia 36
Horn, I. S. 58
hospitality 2–4

Huberman, A. M. 72
Hummel, Myriam xii

ICTs. *See* Information Communications Technologies (ICTs)
identity: multi-dimensionality of 156, 161; professional 115–16; and race 28
'identity gem' 47, 47f
immigrants xii, 90–100
inclusive education 88, 105; in Brazil 139, 140–1; and modernity 153; in South Africa 156–8
inequity: consequences of 105; and diversity 104; educational, in New Zealand 104; and gender 122. *See also* equity
Information Communications Technologies (ICTs) 158, 163–5
inquiry-based learning 110–11
integration 88
intersectionality 155–6, 161

Janks, H. xiii, 9

Kearney, A. 107
Kearney, Alison xii
Keet, A. 56
Kiguwa, Peace xi, 11, 12
'knowledgeability' 113–15
knowledge curation 113–15
Kozleski, E.B. 133
Kumashiro, K. 40
Kwo, Ora xii, 69, 70

Lalvani, P. 8
Landini, S. 143
language: and immigrant parents 93–4, 98; instructional, in Malawi 122, 127–8; and materials design for critical literacy 40; as signifier of belonging 28–9
learners. *See* students
Leibowitz, B. 26
LePage, P. 2
Lesufi, Panyaza 14
Little, D. 71
Lopez, J. 162
Loreman, T. 124
Lucas, T. 53

MacJessie-Mbewe, S. 122
Maharaj, B. 3–4
Malawi xii; age heterogeneity of students in 128; educational context of 121–2; education of disabled learners in 123–4, 127; language diversity in 122, 127–8; student poverty in 128; study of diversity in education 124–36; teacher education in 123–4
Masinire, Alfred xi
materials design: for critical literacy 38–50, 41f, 43f, 45f, 46f, 47f, 49t; identifying theoretical concepts for 44–7
McDonald, M. 2
McGrew, T. 155
McLaren, P. 48
McRuer, R. 5, 8
Melluci, A. 158–9
Mendes, E. G. 142
Mendes, Enicéia Gonçalves xii
Mentis, M. 107
Mentis, Mandia xii
Merriam, S. B. 72
methodology 162–3
Miles, M. B. 72
modernity 153–4. *See also* postmodernity
Moll, L. 2
Mthethwa, Nathi 14
Muhr, S. L. 103
multi-dimensionality: of diversity, as construct x, xiii, xiv; of identity 156, 161
Multifunctional Resource Rooms xii

narration 115–16
National Disability Rights Awareness Month 5
Ndlovu-Gatsheni, S. xiii, xiv
networked mentoring 113
New Zealand: disabled learners in 104; educational inequity in 104; Resource Teacher programme 106–18
Nicholls, L. 26
Njovane, T. 3
Nozu, W. C. S. 142

ontology 161–2
Osman, Ruksana xi
the Other 29–31. *See also* difference

parental support of education xii; and English language 93–4, 98; research on 88–90; study of 91–100
parent-teacher relationship 97–8
Patton, M. Q. 72
pedagogical 'artefacts' xiii–xiv
pedagogic reasoning 57–8, 60, 65, 66
pedagogy. *See* social justice pedagogy; teaching
Peters, L. 89, 95, 98
politics 158–9
postcolonialism xivn1

postmodernity: and difference 159–65; and economics 158; and politics 158–9; socio-cultural effects 159–60. *See also* modernity
Potter, G. 162
poverty 128
Pretoria High School for Girls 14–17, 18n5
privilege: and discourses of diversity 2–5, 8; and social justice pedagogy 23. *See also* racism

race: and diversity as concept 155; and identity 28
racism: and assimilation 155; and discourse of celebration 5; and politics of hair 15. *See also* apartheid; privilege
Ramrathan, P. 56, 65, 66
*The Randburg Sun* newspaper 5, 6–7t
Rankin, S. 88
Resource Teacher programme: challenges of 116; and communication 111–13; effectiveness of 116–17; and identity narrative 115–16; and inquiry-based learning 110–11; and knowledge curation 113–15; overview 106–9; as 'T-shaped professional' 108–10, 109f
Reygan, Finn xi, 10, 12
#RhodesMustFall campaign 164, 165
Rich, A. 40
Richert, A. 2
Robinson, M. 55, 56
Rohleder, P. 26
Rouse, M. 134
Rusznyak, Lee xi, 12, 124

Sayer, A. 162
school culture 17
'second sight' 31–2
self-reflection xi; Elbaz on 50; and emotionality 32–4; and 'forced introspection' 21–2; and pedagogy of discomfort 26–7; and social justice pedagogy 23–4; of students, and CDL 27–34. *See also* critical reflection
Shulman, L. 58
Siuty, M.B. 133
Slee, R. 3
social capital 89, 95, 99
social class xiv, 90
social impact, of critical literacy pedagogy 41–2
social justice pedagogy: Critical Diversity Literacy (CDL) as 22–4; and critical thinking 23; and materials design for critical literacy 48, 49t, 50; and self-reflection 21, 23–4
social media 113–15, 159, 164–5
Somali parents 90–100
Sookraj, R. 3–4
South Africa xi, xii, xiii; Casual Day 5; discourse of assimilation in 3–4; diversity as concept in 154–6; #FeesMustFall movement 4, 164, 165; 'Heritage Day' 5, 6–7t; inclusive education in 156–8; politics of hair in 14–17; #RhodesMustFall campaign 164, 165; teacher education and contextual diversity in 56–66; and technology in education 163–5; University of Cape Town protests 4; views of gender in 36–7
South African Schools Act (SASA) 90
special education: in Brazil 140–51; in Malawi 129–36
special needs xii. *See also* disability
Steyn, M. 10, 12, 15; and CDL as "reading practice" 25; and defining CDL 24
students: age heterogeneity of, in Malawi 128; autonomy of xii, 70–1; poverty of, in Malawi 128; with special needs xii; teachers' knowledge about home lives 87–8, 97, 99–100, 132
Swartz, L. 26

teacher education: in Brazil 140–51; Critical Diversity Literacy (CDL) in 9–12, 13t, 14; diversity in x, xi–xii; and "dysconscious ableism" 8; in Malawi 123–4, 129–36; role of, in creating educational equity 105–6; urban bias in 54–6. *See also* Resource Teacher programme
teachers: relationship with parents 97–8; and students' home lives 87–8, 97, 99–100, 132; working conditions for, in Brazil 148–9
teaching: place-conscious 54. *See also* contextually responsive teaching; social justice pedagogy
technology 158, 159, 163–5
Tikly, L. 122
transphobia 36
'T-shaped professional' 108–10, 109f

UNESCO 69–70
United Kingdom 154–5, 159
'universal man' concept 45, 45f
urban bias 54–6

Valle, J. 18n2
Vandeyar, S. 2

the veil, as metaphor 31–2
Vertovec, S. 155, 156
Villegas, A. M. 53
Villeseche, F. 103

Walton, Elizabeth xi, 12, 124, 157
Wenger-Trayner, B. 113
Wenger-Trayner, E. 113

Xiao, Jing xii

Yosso, T. 89, 98

Zeichner, K. 2
Zembylas, M. 26
Zinn, D. 55, 56
Zwier, E. 1